GW00578126

DEATH AT DAWN

DEATH AT DAWN

CAPTAIN WARBURTON-LEE VC AND THE BATTLE OF NARVIK, APRIL 1940

ALF R. JACOBSEN

Translated from the Norwegian by J. Basil Cowlishaw

The publication of this translation has been made possible through the financial support of NORLA, Norwegian Literature Abroad.

Original Norwegian language edition titled *Angrep ved daggry*, first published by Vega Forlag in 2011

First published in English 2016

The History Press
The Mill, Brimscombe Port
Stroud, Gloucestershire, GL5 2QG
www.thehistorypress.co.uk

Translated from the Norwegian by J. Basil Cowlishaw

British Library Cataloguing in Publication Data.
A catalogue record for this book is available from the British Library.

ISBN 978 0 7509 6537 8

Typesetting and origination by The History Press
Printed in Malta

CONTENTS

FOREWORD

On Tuesday 12 December 1939, Adolf Hitler appended his signature to a draconian *Führerbefehl* demanding that ammunition production be increased by several hundred per cent in the course of the next few months.

'Ammunition was voracious in its appetite for raw materials,' wrote Adam Tooze in his book *The Wages of Destruction: The Making and Breaking of the Nazi Economy*. 'After aircraft production, supplying the enormous volumes of ammunition demanded by modern warfare was by far the largest industrial challenge facing the German economy in World War II.'[1]

A bolt from the blue, the dictator's order was greeted with dismay by the bureaucrats responsible for the smooth running of Germany's armaments industry. The Wehrmacht was already consuming the lion's share, 850,000 tonnes, of the nation's monthly steel output of 1.6 million tonnes. An increase in line with the Führer's demand would make deep and unforeseen inroads into precious stocks of iron and steel – at the expense of the civilian sector's burgeoning need for new investments in housing, electricity supplies, roads, railways and other essential facilities. The problem was exacerbated by the fact that Germany was already starting to feel the effects of the Allies' ever-tightening blockade. 'At the outset of World War II, thanks to French and British economic warfare, transport problems and its limited ability to pay, Germany found itself largely cut off from its overseas supplies of raw materials,' wrote Tooze. 'The significance of Germany's

1 See Adam Tooze, pp. 326ff.

sudden exclusion from world markets cannot be overestimated. It overshadowed every aspect of German military strategy and economic policy in the first decisive months of the war.'

Hitler, who had a better grasp of the situation than most of his minions, was well aware that he was living on borrowed time. He needed a quick victory – preferably by the end of 1940, before the Allies' stranglehold was complete and his ability to wage aggressive war became drastically reduced:

> In pursuit of a swift and decisive victory in the West, Hitler was willing to risk everything. He followed the same line in relation to the war economy. Through his closest confidants, Hitler repeatedly stressed his desire for an all-out production drive, regardless of the consequences either for the civilian population or the long-run viability of the German war effort.

On Thursday 14 December, two days after issuing his uncompromising order, Hitler received Vidkun Quisling, leader of Norway's dwindling National Union Party, at the Reich Chancellery. The dispute over industrial priorities was bitter, and it must have influenced his thinking when he heard Quisling voice his fears of an imminent British invasion of Norway.

'If England threatens to set up bases on the coast, Germany will be forced to intervene,' Hitler retorted, his voice rising in intensity. 'To prevent that happening, Germany will send in 6, 10, 16 divisions, as many as are needed!'

If Britain commanded the Scandinavian north flank, Germany's strategic position would be considerably weakened. But there was an additional factor, one which rendered the prospect still more acute. The steady flow of iron ore from northern Sweden via the Norwegian port of Narvik was vital for maintenance of the Nazi war machine; if that were cut off, it would be impossible to fulfil the terms of Hitler's order.

More than half of the iron ore required to sustain Germany's overall annual steel production of some 19 million tonnes came from imports, close on 85 per cent of which derived from the extremely rich Swedish deposits. If these supplies were cut off, some 6 to 8 million tonnes of steel would be lost to Germany, with fatal results to the nation's production of armaments and ammunition. As Tooze put it, 'If the British seized control of Narvik, they could strangle the Ruhr before the real war had even started.'

Quisling's news must have added to Hitler's worries over Germany's precarious raw materials situation, which most probably explains why the Nazi leader ordered preparations for an attack on Norway – a mere ten minutes after his Norwegian visitor had left the building.

On the Allied side, it was Winston Churchill who most clearly understood the parlous state of Germany's economy and who, in his capacity as First Lord of the Admiralty, advocated as early as September 1939 action against the enemy's iron ore sources; first by mining Norway's inshore channels, followed by occupation of Narvik and the Ofot railway line linking the port with the Swedish mines and, finally, seizure of the ore fields themselves.

There is little doubt that the German and Franco-British invasion plans developed as a reflection of each other in the later stages, especially from March 1940, when rumours and speculations of a Narvik clash began to appear in the international press with increasing frequency and information from various intelligence sources pointed to imminent Allied intervention.

However, to talk about 'a race for Narvik' is misguided, as the aims of the warring parties were diametrically opposed. The Allies wanted to save democracy and freedom from Nazi tyranny. Hitler, on the other hand, aimed to bring Norway under Germany's iron heel, to ensure an uninterrupted flow of raw materials for his armaments industry and enable him to continue his war of conquest. He brought violence and barbarism to the High North.

Death at Dawn is the third book in my series relating to the events preceding, during and following the German attack on Norway on 9 April 1940. Since the autumn of 1939, Narvik and iron ore shipments from this small Norwegian port had occupied a central place in the warring powers' strategic thinking. That is why I have found it necessary to outline the background to the events that followed, including how they were perceived in London, Paris,

Berlin and Narvik itself, as well as in the military units that were gradually drawn into the battle. As the reader will see, I have sought out authentic eyewitness accounts from a wide range of sources and also, in large measure, drawn upon contemporary letters and diary entries, to put together a picture that goes beyond and deeper than the official accounts.

I am especially grateful for having been allowed access to the private papers in Wales and Scotland of two of the principal protagonists in the battle for Narvik, Captain Bernard Warburton-Lee, commander of the 2nd Destroyer Flotilla on board HMS *Hardy*, and Major General Pierse Mackesy, who from February 1940 commanded the British forces earmarked for the Narvik landing. I am grateful to John Warburton-Lee and the late Piers Mackesy for enabling me to peruse and copy from these highly important sources of information.

Of particular value for an understanding of all that occurred in Narvik are the unpublished accounts and diaries of the commander of the Ofoten Squadron, Captain Per Askim, and his wife Signe, together with the papers of the wartime mayor of Narvik, the late Theodor Broch. My thanks are due to Dr Ole Børmer and Supreme Court Judge Lars Oftedal Broch for giving me access to this material.

In Germany, as always, my researcher Axel Wittenberg has afforded unstinting assistance, as has the curator of the War Memorial Museum in Narvik, Ulf Eirik Torgersen, who made available to me the museum's wealth of relevant documents. Of especial value were the unpublished memoirs of two central eyewitnesses, Lieutenant, later General, Albert Bach, who helped draw up the German plan for the capture of Narvik, and Lieutenant, later Colonel, Hans Rohr, who accompanied General Dietl ashore in the early hours of 9 April 1940.

I also wish to thank the staff of Norway's National Archives, the National Library and the University Library of Oslo, the National Archives in London, the Liddel Hart Centre at King's College, London, the Churchill Archives in Cambridge and, finally, the Bundesarchiv/ Militärarchiv in Freiburg, Germany, all of whom have afforded me valuable support and assistance. A complete list of sources is provided in the Notes and Bibliography at the end of the book.

Death at Dawn is structured around two fateful voyages – the 2nd Destroyer Flotilla's storm-racked crossing from Scapa Flow to the Vestfjord in the days immediately preceding 9 April 1940, and the 139th Mountain Regiment's concurrent expedition from Wilhelmshaven to Narvik. Both were highly dramatic forays, and I sincerely hope readers will find accompanying them as absorbing as I did.

Alf R. Jacobsen
Oslo, Norway, 2016

PROLOGUE

'INTEND ATTACKING AT DAWN HIGH WATER'

Vestfjord, Tuesday 9 April 1940

When, in the morning of 9 April, he received the Admiralty's order to press on to Narvik, Captain Warburton-Lee was put in a tight corner. Clearly, someone at Admiralty House had read the morning edition of the *Daily Express* and taken one of its news items for a good deal more than it was worth.

'About six this evening, a large grey Nazi ship, of similar appearance to the Altmark, the first to come in here today seeking shelter, went into an inconspicuous corner of the harbour,' the paper's correspondent, Giles Romilly, had written in a despatch from the Royal Hotel in Narvik, Norway, late on Monday 8 April. 'She was the Jan Wellem, a Nazi whaling ship. A large number of Nazi seamen crowded the deck staring curiously as she came into harbour. She was carrying no flag. German ships have been putting into harbours all down the Norwegian coast.'

It was a soberly worded report by the paper's 23-year-old reporter, who, in keeping with the idealism of the time, had rebelled against his privileged background and abandoned his studies at Oxford to take up the fight against fascism and capitalism in Britain's deeply rooted class conflict. However, Giles and his brother Desmond, two years his junior, had not been totally ostracised on account of their revolutionary escapades and beliefs. Their mother's sister Clementine was married to Winston Churchill, who, in the autumn of 1939, had for the second time been appointed First Lord of the Admiralty and made a member of the War Cabinet; and who, in the winter of 1939–40, emerged as the great war leader he was destined to become.

Churchill was inclined to follow the doings of his 'Red' nephews with close interest. It was in all probability he who had read the Narvik story and taken it as his cue when the Admiralty framed the following order to Warburton-Lee:

> Press report states one German ship has arrived Narvik and landed a small force. Proceed Narvik and sink or harass enemy ships. It is at your discretion to land force and capture Narvik from enemy presence. Try to get possession of battery if not already in enemy hands.

For the ambitious young captain, the order came as a tempting invitation to carry out a raid in keeping with the audacity and daring that were the hallmark of the Royal Navy – always assuming that the Admiralty's information relating to the strength of the German forces was correct.

Press reports were notoriously unreliable, however. Only that morning, off Lofoten Point, Warburton-Lee's destroyers had had a brush with two German battlecruisers. Moreover, barely a day earlier, some ten German destroyers had been sighted heading north – presumably making for the same strategically important iron ore port deep within the Vestfjord. Did Churchill and the Admiralty really know what they were about? Was there only one German ship in Narvik harbour, or were they pitting Warburton-Lee's destroyer flotilla against a far more formidable adversary?

There was only one way to find out. Charts showed that there was a pilot station on Tranøy Island, whose picturesque southern part was the favourite haunt of the Norwegian author and Nobel laureate Knut Hamsun. From this vantage point, day and night, pilots kept a watchful eye on ships entering and leaving Narvik, in the hope of securing lucrative assignments before the advent of spring and the break-up of the ice blocking the Gulf of Bothnia put a seasonal stop to exports of Swedish iron ore via Norway.

'The pilots operated in keen competition with one another, as well as with kindred stations elsewhere along the coast,' wrote Hjalmar Varde, a seasoned pilot who had spent countless days and nights in the watch hut at Loshaugen, with its breathtaking views of the serried peaks of the Lofoten Wall, the rugged cliffs of Tilthornet and the 28m-high, red-painted Tranøy lighthouse on the island of Stangholmen, some distance away to the west. 'Competition wasn't based on price alone, it was also a matter of taking turns. It wasn't uncommon to hear someone complain that so-and-so "stole my steamer".'

Alarmed by broadcast reports of German landings elsewhere that same morning, members of the local population flocked to the quayside when Warburton-Lee's destroyers hove to off Buøyneset Point at about 16.00 on the afternoon of 9 April. Pilots Sigurd Lund Jensen, Wilhelm Winther and Giæver Jensen turned out in full uniform, together with a local shopkeeper, Olav Elsbak, and his 11-year-old son Olav Jr.

'We parleyed partly in German and partly in English,' said Lieutenant Geoffrey Stanning, who came ashore from the flagship HMS *Hardy* along with a signalman and the destroyer's torpedo officer, Lieutenant George Heppel. 'To make things clearer, they drew diagrams in the snow with a stick, but we still couldn't understand all they were trying to tell us.'

Early that morning the duty lighthouse keeper, Erling Andreassen, and his son Harald had seen a number of German destroyers slip by, dark shadows in the driving snow. The pilot station was part of the Third Naval Defence District's warning system and had without doubt been informed that at least five German destroyers and two U-boats were moored in Narvik harbour, that some 800 men had been landed there and that Tjeldsund Sound might have been mined.

'It was Lund Jensen who did the talking,' says Olav Elsbak Jr, who to this day well remembers these dramatic events. 'It was the layout of Narvik harbour that he outlined in the snow when he was trying to explain the situation to the two officers.'

But the pilots' command of English left much to be desired and Stanning and Heppel had difficulty in grasping exactly what they meant:

> It seemed to us that the pilots didn't agree among themselves how many German destroyers had entered the fjord that night. A little boy said there were six, not five, as an older man maintained. They asked us if we intended to attack. We gave them a non-committal answer, at which one of them burst out: 'If you do, you'll need more ships!'

Captain Warburton-Lee was in two minds about his next move when Stanning and Heppel reported to him on the wind-swept bridge of the destroyer half an hour or so later. Born to succeed at all he set his hand to, the sandy-haired young flotilla commander loved a challenge, be it on the polo field or tennis court, and his cabin was full of sporting trophies. The second-eldest son of an old Welsh family, at the tender age of 13 he had entered the Royal Navy as a cadet in 1908, when the British Empire was at its zenith, and had grown up on tales of daring raids against heavily fortified harbours, among them Sir Francis Drake's audacious foray in 1587 against the Spanish Armada assembling in Cadiz and Admiral Edward Hawke's destruction of a French squadron in a storm in Quiberon Bay some 170 years later. As a young lieutenant on board the destroyer HMS *Wrestler*, in April 1918 he had served under Sir Roger Keyes when the admiral planned and carried out his assault on the German anchorage at Zeebrugge. It was an operation that has gone down in history and immortalised the admiral's name; it also precipitated a host of decorations for the men taking part, including eight Victoria Crosses.

On that occasion Warburton-Lee had been on the sidelines, a spectator, but now things were very different. After eight months of propaganda warfare, the British public, the War Cabinet and, not least, the First Lord needed a victory that would put the Allies on the offensive and restore hope of destroying the Nazi menace forever. Only 50 nautical miles to the east of Tranøy lay the Norwegian port of Narvik which, since Christmas 1939, had topped the list of the Allies' most pressing objectives. A raid directed against this important source of Germany's iron ore was the dream of many a destroyer captain, among them Warburton-Lee.

'Suddenly he had been presented with the opportunity,' said Lieutenant Stanning, the captain's secretary and confidant. 'The Admiralty had given him the chance, and he intended to take it.' Warburton-Lee was a man of action; but he was more than that. His instinct was to attack, but common sense held him back; it also put him in a quandary. On board the ships in the flotilla which, with the arrival of HMS *Hostile* that same afternoon, now totalled five destroyers, there were some 800 men, most of them youngsters in their early twenties. One and all admired and respected the flotilla commander, but that didn't entitle him to jeopardise their lives, as he was likely to do if the enemy's strength turned out to be vastly superior. The pilots had spoken of five or six German destroyers, all larger and more heavily armed than Captain Warburton-Lee's little force. What is more, at least one German U-boat had been sighted and there was a good chance that the harbour was protected by coastal batteries and minefields.

'It was a nasty situation,' Stanning said. 'He had been ordered to attack Narvik and had to do it – unless there were pressing reasons to refrain. It was clear that the Admiralty had no idea of how strong the enemy forces were, and it was doubtful whether they would judge the risk acceptable.'

That fateful spring day an icy wind was blowing from the Lofoten Islands to the north-west. Etched against the snowclad mountains on the horizon could be seen the fore and aft sails of hundreds of fishing boats. Although it was after Easter, the spring fishery was still in progress and, despite the bloody engagement that had taken place nearby the previous night, more than 23,000 fishermen had nets out that needed hauling in. While the destroyers slowly went astern off Tranøy Island and the lookouts scanned the horizon through powerful binoculars, Warburton-Lee summoned the other members of his staff to a meeting in the cramped confines of the *Hardy*'s sparsely furnished chart room. Handpicked one and all, and with promising careers in the Royal Navy before them, they comprised Geoffrey Stanning, a clergyman's son and gifted linguist; his friend George Heppel; ruddy-cheeked Lieutenant Russel 'Rusty' Gordon-Smith, the navigator; Signals Officer Lieutenant Charles Cross; and the flotilla's gunnery officer, Lieutenant Edward Clark, who had passed out from the Royal Navy's gunnery school on Whale Island top of his cohort.

'It was a quiet discussion,' Heppel recalled some months later:

> We were all gathered in front of the chart table, weighing up the pros and cons. We looked up to Warburton-Lee and were close to him. He was considered to be the best and most talented of the destroyer captains and many thought he would end up as the youngest admiral of the war.

Gordon-Smith plotted the course on the chart and assured his fellow officers that although recurring snow showers frequently reduced visibility to nil, navigation would pose no problem. But, as Stanning said:

> The dilemma was still real. If Warburton-Lee decided to attack and was unsuccessful, perhaps losing several ships, he would be told by the Admiralty that he had been mad to attack vastly superior forces. If, on the other hand, he chose to withdraw, he would be asked why he did so based on the unreliable assertions of young men, when the Admiralty had given him very specific intelligence which he had no reason to doubt.

There were other courses of action open to the young commander as well. That same morning, the 2nd Destroyer Flotilla had taken leave of HMS *Renown* off Lofoten Point, and there were a good many other cruisers further south in the Norwegian Sea. Warburton-Lee could have signalled for assistance, but that would have been contrary to his nature; moreover, it would have ruled out the all-important element of surprise. Neither Stanning nor Heppel were later willing to concede that that would have been a realistic alternative:

> If he had shown any sign of hesitance and asked for reinforcements, the operation would have had to be postponed by twenty-four hours. We had no idea how far away the rest of the fleet was and we feared that a postponement would have negative effects on other operations along the coast. The whole essence was to strike with surprise, before the enemy had time to gather their thoughts.

Stanning agreed: 'Wash was a lone wolf by nature. He enjoyed every opportunity to act alone without his superiors breathing down his neck. I don't think anything could have stopped him now.'

It was getting on for 17.00 on the afternoon of 9 April when Warburton-Lee retired to his cabin. He had heard the views of his fellow officers, but the final decision was his and his alone. 'There was nothing more we could contribute. We waited in silence for his decision.' Stanning, a religious man, added: 'He stayed alone in his cabin. For him it must have been an absolute Gethsemane.'

When, half an hour later, Warburton-Lee returned to the bridge, his mental anguish was over. He had made up his mind and was determined to fight. No matter how superior the German forces might be, the invaders were to be routed and Narvik retaken by his flotilla alone, without waiting for support from heavier vessels. Destined to become a legend in the annals of the Royal Navy, the signal Warburton-Lee dictated to Stanning in wind and swirling snow off Tranøy Island reached the Admiralty in London at 18.20. Brief and to the point, it read: 'Norwegians report Germans holding Narvik in force. Six destroyers and one submarine. Channel possibly mined. Intend attacking at dawn high water.'

It was a signal worthy of Nelson himself.

PART I

SOME DAYS EARLIER …

1

NARVIK THE FOCAL POINT – FOR THE THIRD TIME RUNNING

London, Wednesday 27 March to Thursday 28 March 1940

Although inwardly seething, when he bade his French counterpart Paul Reynaud welcome at Heston airport, Prime Minister Neville Chamberlain was, as always, the perfect gentleman. Seven months earlier, on Sunday 3 September 1939, Britain and France had declared war on Nazi Germany. Both countries scrambled to mobilise, but the alliance, shaky from the start, was led by badly compromised men. Most of them had profoundly misinterpreted the true nature of Nazism and had bent over backwards to placate Hitler. They had overlooked numerous violations of other countries' sovereignty, condoned the dismemberment and occupation of Czechoslovakia and signally failed to rearm. The two nations' lack of military preparedness had forced them onto the defensive in the face of an increasingly aggressive and contemptuous enemy who pursued the propaganda war to its limits.

Public support of their actions, already threadbare, had been dealt a severe blow just before Easter. Chamberlain's strongest supporter, Édouard Daladier, had been relieved of his post as Prime Minister of France and his successor, Paul Reynaud, had made it clear in speech and in writing that the so-called Phoney War was now at an end. If the British were once again planning on fighting to the last Frenchman, he said, they were making a bad mistake. The war was to be widened in scope and sharply stepped up everywhere – except on the Western Front. Reynaud had summed up his ideas and strategy in a rambling document which contained severe, if indirect, criticism of his predecessors. This document was the cause of Chamberlain's ire, and to the War Cabinet the prime minister gave vent to his feelings in no uncertain manner.

'The Cabinet brought forth a tirade from the P.M. about Reynaud,' recorded General Edmund Ironside, Chief of the Imperial General Staff (CIGS), in his diary. 'He was horrified when he saw the paper. It gave him the impression of a man who was rattled and who wished to make a splash to justify his position. He thought the projects put forward by him were of the crudest kind.'

It was a bad start to the first meeting of the Anglo-French Supreme War Council after the transfer of power in Paris, but Chamberlain was a master at concealing his true feelings behind a cool exterior. As a member of Britain's most influential political dynasty in the early twentieth century, he had taught himself to appear hard and unyielding, and to many people he came across as conceited, arrogant and petty-minded. 'I never saw any emotional reaction whatever except an annoying twitch of the moustache,' wrote one of his political opponents, Herbert Morrison. Others put it more crudely: 'He seemed to have a heart like a stone. If he was cut in half neither part would bleed.'

Only eighteen months earlier, in September 1938, the prime minister had been welcomed by thousands of jubilant Londoners at the same airport and acclaimed a political genius after signing the Munich Agreement with Hitler. Brandishing his rolled umbrella and the scrap of paper bearing the Nazi dictator's signature, he had uttered the words that were to haunt him to the end of his days: 'This means peace for our time.'

Hitler had proved to be a treacherous partner and it soon became apparent that peace was the last thing he had on his mind. When, a year later, he sent his panzers rolling across the frontier into Poland, the last shred of hope was gone. Britain and France, most reluctantly, declared war and despatched hundreds of thousands of their young men to man France's much-vaunted Maginot Line and hastily dug trenches in Flanders – only twenty years after the end of the last bloody conflict with German militarism. It was a bitter blow for Chamberlain, who had done his utmost to appease the Nazi leader with one concession after another, as he confessed in his speech to the House: 'Everything that I have worked for, everything that I have hoped for, everything that I believed in during my public life, has crashed into ruins.'

Chamberlain's policy of appeasement had not been prompted by naivety alone, however. It was also an attempt to buy time. In the years following the First World War, both Britain and France had rapidly disarmed, with the result that their military resources were at a minimum. Britain was still the world's strongest naval power because of its need to protect its colonies and the Empire's overseas trade routes, but its army and air force were badly lacking in personnel, weapons and equipment. A despondent General Ironside wrote in his diary:

> The Germans have 48 divisions, including 5 armoured, 3 mountain and 2 light divisions. They then have 20 reserve divisions and 36 Landwehr divisions. When one thinks that we have not got even 2 divisions it shows what a puny Army contribution we can make to any European war. I feel very desperate about it all. That I should possibly have to go on active service with such an Army at the end of my long service seems almost tragic to me. What a mess we are in. We are in no state to go to war. I can see the Field Army receding more and more into the far distance. There are no men and there is no money for their equipment and there is no will amongst the Cabinet Ministers to want an Army. And this is the state of our Army after two years' warning. No foreign nation would believe it if they were told it.

Appropriations were gradually increased, but when war came Britain was still far from ready – not only in terms of military strength but also mentally. 'Our unmilitary leaders would not believe that preparations were necessary,' the general wrote as New Year dawned at the end of 1939, four months after his appointment as CIGS. 'They even called it warmongering to do anything that might excite Germany. I am frightened of their complete complacency. They were frightened to tell the people the true state of affairs. The people were kept in ignorance.'

As the winter of 1940 gave way to spring, the critical voices grew louder. It would take time to build up an offensive capacity, which meant that, owing to shortages of ammunition, armour, aircraft and modern weapons, the Allies were forced to adopt a passive approach to the war. The French Army and the British Expeditionary Force had dug in behind the Maginot Line, seemingly unable – or unwilling – to mount offensive operations. Even a proposal to initiate bombing of military targets in Germany was turned down for fear of reprisals. By March 1940, what had become known as the Phoney War had been in progress for six months. More and more people were blaming Britain's inaction on Chamberlain and his government for having given in to Hitler at Munich in the belief that they could make him see reason. As Duff Cooper wrote: 'For [Chamberlain] the Dictators of Germany and of

Italy were like the Lord Mayors of Liverpool and Manchester, who might belong to different political parties and have different interests, but who must desire the welfare of humanity, and be fundamentally reasonable, decent men like himself.'

As a consequence, there were no cheering crowds to welcome the French premier when he landed at Heston at six in the evening on Wednesday 27 March 1940. All over Europe the winter had been the most severe in living memory and morale was dangerously low. It was still bitterly cold and a biting north wind swept across the runway. Paul Reynaud and his party were swiftly ushered into the waiting cars which discreetly transported them to the Hyde Park Hotel.

'The manager greeted the guests from Paris, and asked them to sign the book,' wrote *Daily Express* reporter Hilde Marchant:

> He realised that he was housing half the French inner war cabinet when he read the signatures. The hotel began to fill with Scotland Yard-detectives. They hung around the lounge and the cocktail bar, and tried to look like natives. So far as the hotel was concerned, the visit was completely informal. No special suites had been reserved, just room and bath for friends of the Embassy – ordinary dove grey rooms, furnished in semi-Louis style. Waiters and porters had instructions that they were not to use the names of the guests, even in orders.

Trim and athletic, Paul Reynaud, a lawyer by profession, kept in shape by boxing, cycling and other sporting activities. Sixty-one years old and heir to a fortune made in textiles, he was possessed of an exceptionally quick mind. His slanting eyes, thick eyebrows and slicked-back hair gave him an oriental appearance; pugnacious by nature and something of a maverick, he was often referred to as the 'Gamecock' by those who knew him well. Accompanying him to London were his principal military advisers: César Campinchini, Minister of Marine; Admiral François Darlan, Naval Commander-in-Chief; Laurent Eynac, Minister for Air; and General Joseph Vuillemin, Chief of Air Staff, together with General Maurice Gamelin, Commander-in-Chief of the army and a hero of the First World War. The only person missing was the Minister of National Defence and War, Édouard Daladier, who, until 20 March, had been prime minister and hated his successor with all his heart. Daladier's absence was a signal expression of the brittle state of French politics – and a threat to Reynaud's authority and Allied cooperation.

'Although Prime Minister, Reynaud was at the moment only a passenger in his own Government,' wrote General Edward Spears in his book *Assignment to Catastrophe*. 'The two men detested each other, and Daladier was determined to exert his utmost power to humiliate Reynaud in every possible way.'

By this time, the most critical period in the Third Republic's history, French politics had deteriorated to a new low, better suited to a tragicomic soap opera. The situation was not helped by the intrigues of Reynaud and Daladier's scheming mistresses, Countess Hélène de Portes and Marchioness Jeanne Crussol, who, consumed with jealousy, were conducting their own private catfight. 'The Marquise backing the one and the Comptesse backing the other were having a grand time,' General Spears wrote. 'All claws out and no holds barred. That France should develop such weakness at the top in these critical circumstances was indeed disquieting.'

The struggle for power between Reynaud, Daladier and the two Furies was a reflection of the deep schism in French society, which still harboured bitter memories of the First World War, an open wound that refused to heal.

'In the streets of Paris and the other cities and towns of France there was no shouting when war came,' wrote William Shirer in *The Rise and Fall of the Third Republic*:

> There was none of the enthusiasm, passion and ringing belief in the righteousness of the country's case which Frenchmen of all classes had felt and manifested when the soldiers marched off to war in 1914, just twenty-five years before. The millions of men called up responded to mobilisation stoically but most of them did not have their heart in a war whose coming had surprised them and whose causes they did not understand.

General Spears had encountered much the same attitude when he made a tour of northern France with Winston Churchill in August 1939. More than 1.7 million young Frenchmen had lost their lives in the trenches of the last war and more than 4 million had been wounded. Few had the desire or the stomach for a repetition, regardless of what they thought of Hitler's brutal conduct and mendacity.

The general was responsible for liaising between the British and French governments and looked upon France as his second home. He observed:

> I found the atmosphere heavy with apprehension. The fear of war was casting its gloom over uncomprehending people. Why, they asked, had the world gone mad? Our own generation had been cut down as with a scythe, the land must die if the present generation was also to be decimated. What was the matter with that clamorous lunatic house-painter, Hitler? Was there not some foundation for his claims? The Peace Treaty had not been wise, that was a fact. Could not a settlement be found that would avoid war? They were resentful that we as allies had so little to contribute to the common cause. If war did come it was France again that would be bled white. They did not think Britain was manoeuvring so as to bring about a war, with France as her shield, but they did think, reasonably, that if we had made up our minds to challenge Hitler, we should have provided ourselves with the means of doing so.

Daladier's fall from office a few days prior to the meeting of the Supreme War Council provided new evidence of the split at the top. For months the French government had been promising to intervene on the Finnish side in the Winter War against the Soviet Union, which had entered into a non-aggression pact with Nazi Germany. But no expeditionary force was ever despatched, and on 13 March Finland was forced to accept a humiliating peace settlement. In the highly charged reckoning that followed, Daladier was accused of lacking in vigour and, after a vote of no confidence, ousted from the premiership.

'Reynaud had a reputation for great energy, for decisiveness and for innovation,' wrote Shirer of Daladier's successor. 'He was an obvious choice for a parliament which had been demanding a more vigorous prosecution of the war.'

It was thus in hope of revitalising Allied politics and safeguarding his position as France's prime minister that Reynaud had flown to London with the new strategic plan in his briefcase. He was determined to present it, no matter the cost. The few who had read the document were far from impressed. One of them was General Ironside, who wrote:

> Monsieur Reynaud has issued the most extraordinary paper stating how he proposes to win the war. He says that so far nobody has done anything and he proposes to do it. The leading sentence of the paper from the Prime Minister is typical of the whole: The sudden outcome of the Finnish struggle has faced the Allies with a new and perhaps decisive situation. In order

> to seize again the initiative which they have lost, it is important that the two Governments, having learnt a lesson from recent events, should apply themselves without delay to draw from present circumstances all the possibilities of which an energetic and daring conduct of the war still allow them to take advantage.

Despite its convoluted phrasing, it was obvious that the paper was an indirect criticism of Reynaud's French and Allied predecessors. Chamberlain was incensed. 'This last sentence made the Prime Minister very angry,' Ironside continued. 'I understand that when the P.M. read the paper he went through the ceiling. For it includes him amongst them who have so far failed.'

The night before the Planning Committee's meeting, the general had woken up at 05.00 after only four hours' rest. With so many thoughts going round in his head, he found it impossible to get back to sleep.

> What a mess our weakness has got us into. Here we are fighting for our lives and, though Ireland is presumably in the Empire, we cannot use her western harbours for our destroyers. The new French direction of the war is to put an end to all this. Perhaps Reynaud is right. The moment has arrived for us to be as brutal as the Germans. I shall be most interested to see the reaction of the various members. I can see that we are not likely to have such a cordial meeting as we had with Daladier. The P.M. is already annoyed that he should be labelled as one of the men who failed in the last combination.

There was no doubt in the minds of those present when the War Cabinet convened at 10 Downing Street at 10.00 on Thursday 28 March, that the meeting would be a difficult one.

The main source of discord was Reynaud's proposal for a spectacular new strategy involving a massive air assault on Baku, Batum, Grozny and other Soviet oilfields in the Caucasus combined with a follow-up incursion by a Franco-British naval force into the Black Sea. The Baku region alone produced some 170 million barrels of oil annually, much of which was exported to Nazi Germany under the terms of the non-aggression pact between the two countries and also helped to meet the Soviet Union's own needs.

'The dependence on oil supplies from the Caucasus is the fundamental weakness of the Russian economy,' wrote General Gamelin in a highly confidential preliminary study of the operation, which was code-named Pike:

> The Soviet Armed Forces are totally dependent on this source as is their motorised agriculture. More than 90% of oil extraction and 80% of refinement is located in the Caucasus, primarily Baku. Therefore interruption of oil supplies on any large scale would have far-reaching consequences and could even result in the collapse of all the military, industrial and agricultural systems of Russia. An important source of raw materials would also be denied to Nazi Germany with the destruction of the oil fields.

Gamelin and a handful of like-minded military dreamers envisaged the establishment of bases in Iran, Turkey and Syria with provision for 120 bombers which, it was thought, would in the course of three months reduce the Soviet oil installations to ashes. They found an enthusiastic supporter in Reynaud, whose controversial paper included a request for Britain's assent to the operation 'to paralyze the whole economy of the USSR' before the country fell completely under the domination of Hitler's Third Reich: 'The French government is ready to examine immediately with the British cabinet the best justification to putting an end to our diplomatic relations with a government whose latest act of brigandage we condemn and whose collusion with the German government we denounce.'

Operation Pike would undoubtedly have shifted the fighting far away from French soil, but it suffered from a drawback that was painfully obvious to anyone possessing a modicum of political realism. It would inevitably result in full-scale war with the Soviet Union – in addition to the one in which the Allies were already engaged with Nazi Germany. William Shirer wrote:

> Later some Frenchmen would look back and shudder. France and Britain would have found themselves at war with Russia as well as with Germany – at war, that is, with the two greatest military and industrial powers in Europe. Events outside their control saved them in the end from such folly.

Chamberlain was under just as much political pressure as Reynaud. He recognised the need to do something 'spectacular' in order to strengthen his people's morale and support for the war, but he adamantly refused to countenance a military venture that would only exacerbate the Allies' difficult position. He had brought his anger under control and in the next few hours provided clear proof that his cold and overbearing exterior concealed a shrewd and calculating mind.

'These old rusty politicians like Chamberlain have a strategy of their own and he certainly had a good one this time,' Ironside wrote. 'He started off with a ninety minutes' [*sic*] monologue upon the general situation, apologizing every now and then for taking so long.' Step by step, with courteous, irrefutable logic, the prime minister proceeded to demolish the French paper until there was virtually nothing left. 'He took all the thunder out of Reynaud's mouth and left him gasping with no electric power left. All the "projects" that Reynaud had to bring forward, Chamberlain took away. It was most masterly and very well done.'

At this point the War Council adjourned for a long liquid lunch at the Carlton Hotel. Ironside had this to say of its aftermath:

> Little Reynaud sat there with his head nodding in a sort of 'tik', understanding it all, for he speaks English very well, and having to have it translated all over again for the benefit of the others. He was for all the world like a little marmoset. The new Air Minister, Laurent d'Eynac, was a little, short, immensely fat man with a beaky nose and dark hair. He had an enormous double chin, which seemed more marked when we came back in the afternoon after a lunch at the Carlton. He looked very like Stalin in a somnolent way. At the end, both he and Vuillemin, his Service Chief, were asleep. Vuillemin was what the French call an 'as' [ace] of the last war. Not very intelligent. Darlan, the French admiral, smoked his pipe all the time and drew pictures on his bit of paper.

Chamberlain had prevented the Allies from embarking upon what would have been a catastrophic conflict with the Soviet Union. He had also persuaded the French prime minister to agree to two other projects to intensify the Allies' economic warfare. One, designated Royal Marine, involved sowing floating mines in the Rhine and other German rivers and canals to disrupt the nation's inland waterborne traffic, which relied on riverboats and barges. The other project, code-named Wilfred, was more important, and also more controversial. The shipping channel along Norway's coastline was to be mined *inside* Norwegian territorial waters, in an endeavour to provoke German retaliation and thus, as Chamberlain's private secretary, John Colville, put it in his diary, 'extend the war to Scandinavia'.

The main object was to put a stop to the vital shipments of iron ore from the mines in northern Sweden to Nazi Germany. The small Norwegian port of Narvik had once again become a prime target.

2

'IRON AND WAR ARE INEXTRICABLY LINKED'

Norway, Sweden and Germany, at the Same Time

In 1940, a person viewing northern Sweden from the air would have been struck by a particularly stark feature of what was in other respects a trackless, snow-covered waste: the 160km railway line winding its way across the largely uninhabited mountains from the mining town of Kiruna in Sweden to the small port of Narvik on the north-west coast of Norway. Writing in 1938, British intelligence agent Alfred Rickman was awed by the sight:

> Rails of the heaviest calibre were used from the frontier on this 25-mile run where splinters are frequently ground out of the curves after the passage of heavy trains. From the border between Sweden and Norway, at 520 metres above sea-level, the ore trains descend into Narvik through twenty-one tunnels in wild and mountainous country protected by sheds from avalanches that sweep from the mountains. Rotary snow-ploughs ply up and down the line in winter and such is their efficiency that not a single day has been lost in the running of this Polar railway since 1903.

It was for purely geological reasons that the electrified line had been built across an arctic wasteland which was too inaccessible and infertile to sustain normal human activities. At some far-distant time in the past, molten magma had burst forth from the earth's crust near Lake Luossajärvi to transform the landscape into a blazing inferno of smoke and fire. When, millions of years later, the eruptions had come to an end and the crust had cooled, extreme temperatures and pressures had left their mark. Beneath the towering peaks of Luossavaara and Kirunavaara, the earth had been transformed to apatite-rich magnetite. When Swedish geologists and engineers made a detailed study of the area in the nineteenth century, they found that Mother Nature had been extremely generous with her bounty. Beneath the surface of the forbidding stretch of land surrounding Lake Luossajärvi lay deposits of iron ore on a par with the largest and richest in the world. Between 2 and 3,000 million tonnes, there was enough to keep the mines working for 200 years or more.

In a book entitled *Swedish Iron Ore* published in London in 1939, Rickman made no attempt to disguise his enthusiasm:

> The Kiirunavaara range of hills carries the largest single deposit of rich iron ore in Sweden and is one of the greatest in the world, holding moreover a unique position among all such deposits hitherto known, by virtue not only of its quantity but its chemical composition. Extensive bore-hole surveys, to a depth of 800 metres below the lake level, indicate that the ore continues to still greater depths and further, that the dimensions of the ore-body do not diminish at the depth reached by the drills. The iron content is unusually high and varies from 58 to 70 percent.

Around the turn of the twentieth century, the Swedish government acquired a majority holding in the mining company Luossavaara-Kiirunavaara Aktiebolag (LKAB) and, little by little, the small community of Kiruna was converted into an animated mining town, with the aid of German capital and Swedish and British know-how. The tumbling waters of the River Lule were harnessed to provide electricity to drive the mining machinery, ore crushers and conveyor belts, and a railway line was built from the ore fields to Luleå, high up on Sweden's north-east coast. But Luleå had one great disadvantage: when the Gulf of Bothnia froze over, as it did every year, the terminal from which the ore was exported was hemmed in by an impenetrable barrier of ice for some six months. It was not until completion of the Ofot railway in January 1903 and the first ore trains trundled off in the opposite direction – across the mountains into Norway and on to the ice-free port of Narvik – that the ore field's financial success was assured. To quote Rickman:

> With a population of 15,000, Kiruna is today the largest town north of the Arctic Circle.[2] Attractive in lay-out and quite free from smoke, this populous

2 The intrepid British agent had forgotten the ice-free Soviet port of Murmansk, which had more than 100,000 inhabitants.

> centre has excellent shops, fine public buildings, baths, gymnasiums, theatres and concert-halls. Up-to-date houses are provided by the company for its staff and about half of the workers. For the year ending September 1937 the gross profit shown was 91 million Swedish crowns, and royalties paid to the state reached 14.6 million crowns ... a considerable source of the national income.

By 1939 the depression of the interwar years had released its grip and burgeoning rearmament had led to an enormous rise in the demand for iron ore, with the result that some 12 million tonnes of the Kiruna mines' output went to export, 7 million tonnes via Narvik, the rest from Luleå and the southerly port of Oxelösund. Nearly 80 per cent (10 million tonnes) finished up in Hitler's munitions factories. Smelting and refining operations yielded some 6.5 million tonnes of pure metal, most of which went into armoured turrets, plating, gun barrels and other weaponry that required hard steel alloys; this was sufficient to cover a vital part of Nazi Germany's annual requirements.

An agreement had been reached for delivery of an additional 11 million tonnes to the German war machine in the course of 1940, with the consequence that the Kiruna mines found themselves working full out, day and night.

'The thunderous noises one can hear in the mining town of Kiruna are similar to the sounds emanating from a modern field of battle,' wrote *New York Times* reporter Harold Callender, who, as March gave way to April, made the long journey from Stockholm to Narvik. What he heard was blasting, which was carried out three times a day, deep below ground, and the monotonous drone of the crushers as they broke up the greyish-black stone into smaller chunks. These were discharged into 35-tonne railway wagons lined up in rows beneath a battery of floodlights. Everything proceeded at a rapid pace to a clamour of rumbles and crashes, punctuated by piercing blasts from a steam whistle. Every hour, a powerful locomotive would pull out of the terminal towing forty heavy wagonloads of ore.

Rickman, who had a technical background and was out to glean as much detailed information as he could for Britain's Secret Service, reported, 'With a total shipment of 35 000 tons, 25 trains a day make the 102-mile trip to Narvik. Running at a speed of 30 miles an hour, few stops are made and the journey is completed in a little more than 3 hours.'

The LKAB's mining operation ranked among the most efficient and impressive in Europe, and the Narvik terminal was quite on a par with its Swedish counterpart. 'On arrival from Kiruna, the ore trains run either to the waterside for unloading direct into the steamers, or are diverted to one of two stock-piles, each with the enormous capacity of 2,500,000 tons.'

The double-track railway ran across a steel platform above a 400m-long granite wharf equipped with thirty-two chutes; with the aid of heavy hawsers and electrically powered winches, these could be raised and lowered to avoid the tide as it rose and fell. Three ships at a time could berth beneath the chutes, reducing turnaround time to a minimum. A standard 5,000-tonner could load and cast off after a mere eight hours alongside the wharf.

'A record was achieved when, for the year ending October 1937, 848 ships were loaded with 6,350,000 tons,' Rickman reported. 'Most of the shipments are destined for consumers in Germany and are either directed through German ports or transshipped at Rotterdam and Amsterdam to 3,000-tonne steel barges for transport up the Rhine.' Demand seemed insatiable. A new record was set in 1939, despite a few dips following the outbreak of war, but throughout the stormy winter of 1940, when snowfalls were extremely heavy, the thunderous roar emanating from the chutes could be heard all over Narvik.

'Shipments continued to increase, and the company worked three shifts all through the winter,' wrote the ore town's mayor, Theodor Broch, in *Fjellene venter.* Published in London during the war as *The Mountains Wait*, his book was part reminiscences and part propaganda. 'Wharves and buildings lay bathed in the glare of floodlights. The place was humming. The world was again hungry for iron. There was an air of renewed prosperity among people. But most of the ships in the harbour flew flags emblazoned with a swastika.'

Dedicated and dark-complexioned, Theodor Broch came from a long line of academics. He had moved to Narvik at the age of 26 on completion of his legal training. His father was a colonel in the army and commander of the local regiment, but Theodor, like many young middle-class people at that time, was an ardent Marxist, inspired by dreams of a revolutionary utopia. Both a pacifist and a member of a Young Communists organisation, in 1924 he was given a suspended sentence for calling for a strike among the military – among his fellow firebrands, Einar Gerhardsen was destined to become Norway's prime minister.

Broch wrote of his journey to Narvik by the Ofot line in the summer of 1930:

> We came up from Oslo, from comradeship and convivial gatherings in restaurants, from meetings and discussions on Marx and Freud where we railed against injustice and dreamed of a better world. For the last few kilometres, we sat in silence, gazing down into the wild, uninhabited valley. The fjord was as blue and green as a glacial lake. Because of the many tunnels, it was like a film, scene after scene in ever-larger format. One last tunnel and there ahead of us was Narvik in sharp focus, as if it lay under a magnifying glass, though it looked smaller than we had imagined.

Over many leisurely dinners of 'roast beef and tinned pineapple' in a variety of grand houses, Broch got to know the distinguishing features of the town:

> Narvik was by no means a typical northern town. Not even in its origins was it typically Norwegian – there was a big-city atmosphere about it. In its brief, hectic history it had always been hostage to the world outside. From the outset there had been dissent over this crescent-shaped harbour at the head of the Ofot fjord and the small, sheltered valley tucked in between the Fagernes Mountains and Framnes Hills. In Stockholm and London and other big cities, money barons and politicians had pored over maps of Norway and decided the fate of the town.

Like many of his erstwhile revolutionary friends, Theodor Broch had mellowed and become a social-democrat, so much so that in 1934 he was elected mayor of Narvik on the Labour platform. Thanks to rapidly increasing exports of iron ore, the town's finances gradually improved. But there was a darker side to this new-found prosperity: heightened focus on the important role played by iron ore in Nazi Germany's rearmament programme.

Fear of war continued to grow, but the mayor had not entirely relinquished his pacifist leanings:

> We didn't really believe it and it never occurred to us that a war might affect us. We had long ago revised our views on defence and accepted its justification with a shrug, no more. We had also accepted the need to pay bigger insurance premiums in accordance with a reasonable scale of charges, but that didn't

> mean that we thought the house might burn down. After all, our country wasn't even in a flammable area. Mountains, granite rocks and boulders are hard to set alight.

It was a remarkably superficial analysis of the situation considering that it came from a politically trained man, a man who had once acknowledged that Narvik was 'a small metropolis'.

Broch's views were in sharp contrast to those of other observers. As Harold Callender wrote in the *New York Times*: 'Iron and war are inextricably linked, and since Narvik lives by the one it can hardly expect to be immune from the effects of the other.'

3

'EQUAL TO A FIRST-CLASS VICTORY IN THE FIELD ...'

London and Berlin, Autumn 1939 to Winter 1940

Callender's summing-up went to the heart of the matter, and in London Winston Churchill, in his capacity as First Lord of the Admiralty, had for months been pressing with all the passion and power he could muster for a blockade of iron ore exports from Narvik to Nazi Germany.

'It must be understood that an adequate supply of Swedish iron ore is vital to Germany and the interception or prevention of these Narvik supplies during the winter months, i.e. from October to the end of April, will greatly reduce her power of resistance,' he wrote to the War Cabinet – a bare three weeks after the outbreak of war.

Because of the unpreparedness of the army and air force, a frontal attack in the west would be out of the question for a long time to come; but Churchill, bold and restless as he was, hungered after an opportunity to take the offensive. To start with, he wanted to mine the north–south shipping channel inside the Norwegian 3-mile limit and thus force the German ore carriers out into international waters, where they would be at the mercy of the Royal Navy, which dominated both the Norwegian Sea and the North Sea. This would entail violating Norway's neutrality, but it would also contribute to the 'crippling of the enemy's war industry'.

Chamberlain, like his anything but bellicose cabinet, was unwilling to breach international law, and saw no reason for haste. Angry and frustrated, Churchill continued to urge action, but in vain – until war broke out between Finland and the Soviet Union and opened up new opportunities. In early December, Heinrich Liebe, the ruthless captain of *U-38*, sank one Greek and two British ore ships sailing south from Narvik, inside Norwegian territorial waters, and forty-seven seamen and two Norwegian pilots lost their lives.

The First Lord was determined that they should be avenged. 'These sinkings, Churchill felt, gave Britain the strongest possible case for retaliatory action,' wrote Martin Gilbert, his biographer. 'This action on the part of the enemy, he said, made it necessary that we should, in our own interest, claim and make use of a similar latitude, without delay.'

In a broad-based memorandum dated 16 December, Churchill summed up his views:

> The stoppage of the iron ore traffic would rank as a major offensive operation of the war. No other method is open to Britain for many months to come which would give so good a chance of abridging the waste and destruction of the conflict or of perhaps preventing the vast slaughters which will attend the grapple of the main armies.

The First Lord had correctly drawn attention to Nazi Germany's Achilles heel, a critical lack of vital raw materials, and expressed his faith in the success of the action he proposed:

> If it were possible to cut Germany off from all Swedish iron ore supplies until the end of 1940, a blow will have been struck at her war-making capacity equal to a first-class victory in the field or from the air, and without any serious sacrifice of lives. It might, indeed, be immediately decisive.

Mining Norway's territorial waters would, it is true, be a breach of international law but, as Churchill pointed out, this had to be viewed in a wider context. In the long run it was a matter of safeguarding democracy for all and providing *for* the rule of international law.

In arguments he would use again in various forms many times in the future, Churchill declared:

> The final tribunal [is] our own conscience. We are fighting to re-establish the reign of law and to protect the liberties of small countries. Our defeat would mean an age of barbarity and violence, and would be fatal not only to ourselves, but to the independent life of every small country in Europe. Small nations must not tie our hands when we are fighting for their rights and freedom. The letter of the law must not in supreme emergency obstruct those who are charged with its protection and enforcement. It would not be right or rational that the Aggressor Power should gain one set of advantages by tearing up all

laws, and another set by sheltering behind the innate respect for law of their opponents. Humanity, rather than legality, must be our guide.

At the same time as Churchill was working on his impassioned and powerfully worded memorandum in the Admiralty in London, in the Reich Chancellery in Berlin, Hitler issued an order to prepare to attack the very same target. He had been prompted to do so by Grand Admiral Erich Raeder and Norway's leader of the fascist National Union Party, Vidkun Quisling, who took the first fatal steps towards betrayal of his country on a visit to the German capital from 11 to 18 December. For reasons that still remain obscure, the Norwegian Nazi sympathiser had convinced himself that the British were planning to make Norway part of their empire – the result of a supposed conspiracy entered into by the charismatic chairman of the Norwegian Foreign Affairs Committee, C.J. Hambro, and Britain's Secretary of State for War, Leslie Hore-Belisha, both of whom happened to be Jewish. 'There is a very real danger that Norway may be occupied by Britain, possibly soon,' Raeder told Hitler after his first meeting with Quisling.

To forestall any such action, Quisling, whose name has become a synonym of treachery, tried hard to obtain German support for a *coup d'état*. He did all he could to substantiate his claim that the National Union Party enjoyed considerable support among Norwegian officers. 'He showed me the original of a letter he had recently received from the commanding officer in Narvik, Colonel Sundlo,' wrote Hitler's hateful and violently anti-Semitic ideologist Alfred Rosenberg, in a note that found its way into the Grand Admiral's war diary:

> In this letter Sundlo openly stresses the following: if present conditions continue, Norway will be destroyed. He only hopes that enough will be left of the nation to form a people which can rebuild Norway on a sound basis. The present generation is doomed, and rightly so. I will do nothing for that old soak Madsen, Minister of Commerce, or for that pacifist Monsen, Minister of War, it can be good and useful to risk your bones for the national uprising.

There is no record of what Hitler thought of these wild utterings of Quisling and his disciple. Whatever it was, it matters little for only a few minutes after Quisling left the Chancellery on 14 December, the Führer issued the following order to the Chief of the Operations Staff, General Alfred

Jodl: '1715 hours: The Führer orders that with the least possible staff a study be undertaken to determine how an occupation of Norway can be carried out.'

From 18 December on, Winston Churchill continued to urge for military action against the ore traffic with all the rhetorical power he possessed, but the War Cabinet was unable to reach a decision. In the ensuing weeks discussions became increasingly acrimonious and heated – especially when the Chiefs of Staff suggested going a big step further and quite simply occupying Narvik and the Swedish ore fields.

'The offensive through Narvik to Luleå gives us a chance of getting a big return for very little expenditure,' observed General Ironside, who, along with the Chief of Air Staff, Air Chief Marshal Sir Cyril Newall, and the First Sea Lord, Admiral Sir Dudley Pound, supported the proposal. 'It gives us the chance to take the initiative and to throw a little confusion into the German councils. At the moment it is too easy for the Germans. We only parry each devilment Hitler produces.'

From the military planners' point of view, it was essential that a landing in Narvik, followed by a thrust through to Luleå, be undertaken with the consent of Norway and Sweden; otherwise, they thought, the expedition would be doomed to failure. 'It would be a simple matter for the Norwegians and Swedes to render the railway running inland from Narvik useless to us, either by removal of rolling stock or the cutting off of electric power. There is no road linking Narvik with Gällivare.'

The chances of success were slim. When, early in January 1940, the Norwegian and Swedish governments both angrily and forcefully rejected the British approach, in reality there was no more to be done. Chamberlain and a majority of the War Cabinet vetoed any action that would turn Scandinavia into a theatre of war against the will of the countries concerned.

In the meantime, the Winter War was growing bloodier by the day. The Finns fought bravely but their resources were limited. As the new year advanced, it became increasingly apparent that they would not be able to withstand the might of the Soviet Union for much longer. A wave of sympathy swept across the world, and this in turn again raised the question of Allied military action in Scandinavia. Intervention would have a dual purpose: aid to Finland and occupation of the Swedish ore fields.

'It is now decided that we shall carry out our iron ore plan on the pretext of sending help to Finland through Norway,' wrote John Colville, Chamberlain's private secretary, in his diary on 7 February 1940:

> The Finns will publicly appeal to the Norwegians and Swedes to allow foreign volunteers through their country, and we shall then demand permission to land our 'volunteers' [in the approved 'non-intervention' manner] at Narvik and Trondheim, at the same time offering further troops to defend Norway and Sweden against any German invasion from the south.

If the Norwegians and Swedes assented, a force of some 20,000 men would be set ashore in Narvik and make their way into Sweden along the Ofot railway. Code-named Avonmouth, the plan was scheduled to be set in motion immediately before Easter, on Saturday 16 March. 'It will be under British command, and of course its primary objective will be, on its march to Finland, to seize the Gällivare iron ore fields and occupy or incapacitate them.'

It was a cynical plan, riddled with uncertainties, and the politicians' vacillations did nothing to improve matters. When, early that month, the Norwegian and Swedish governments again refused to open their borders, the whole scheme threatened to collapse.

'To try to get up the Narvik railway without help from Swedish and Norwegian railway personnel is madness. We simply cannot do it,' a despairing Ironside wrote in his diary on Friday 8 March. 'We are now threatened with a defeat. Germany has subdued Czechoslovakia, Austria and Poland completely and is keeping them in order with very few troops. She will perhaps get another victory without striking a blow.'

In Berlin, Hitler was well acquainted with the Allies' plans – partly thanks to leaks and speculation in the press, partly through intercepted wireless traffic, aerial reconnaissance and other sources of intelligence. He kept a close eye on the progress of his own projected invasion of Norway but work proceeded at a snail's pace. General Nikolaus von Falkenhorst had attempted to speed things up when, towards the end of February, he was put in charge of the operation, which was code-named Weserübung, but many senior officers thought the whole thing madness and declined to help. On Sunday 3 March, unable to stand the planning staff's procrastination any longer, Hitler flew into a rage and demanded immediate action. Rumours of an imminent Allied invasion in support of Finland were rife, and his nerves were on edge.

'In no uncertain terms the Führer expressed the need for immediate and vigorous action in Norway,' General Jodl wrote in his diary: 'He would tolerate no obstruction from any arm of the military. Work was to be accelerated.' Hitler wanted his forces ready for an attack on northern Norway as early as Palm Sunday, 17 March, but there was little chance of that. The severe winter weather showed no sign of relaxing its grip and many of the Baltic ports were still blocked by ice.

The day after the Führer's outburst, as a stop-gap measure, the 3rd Mountain Division, under the command of Generalmajor Eduard Dietl, was hastily moved to encampments near Berlin with instructions to prepare for immediate departure – for an unknown destination. But when, on 8 March, 29-year-old Lieutenant Albert Bach knocked on the unmarked door of the Planning Staff's office in Bendlerstrasse, most of the planning had yet to be done.

'You are here to assist me with the rest of the work,' Divisional Operations Officer Lieutenant Colonel Robert Bader told Bach, handing him a copy of the newly drawn-up plans for Weserübung. 'I was amazed by what I read,' Bach wrote in his unpublished memoirs. 'The task ahead of us had never been part of the curriculum at any military academy.' What so astounded the young lieutenant was the intention to occupy Norway and Denmark simultaneously in a lightning strike by land, sea and air. No such combined operation had ever been attempted before, and the risk involved was enormous.

Bach's own 139th Regiment was to form the core of Group Narvik, which, with a force of 2,000 men and ten destroyers, would take the ore port and the railway leading to northern Sweden:

> Hitler wanted to get the operation going as quickly as possible, which is why the move to Berlin was so precipitate. Everything had to be ready by the middle of the month, but the task was well-nigh hopeless. The need for secrecy meant that only a very few officers were privy to the planning process. The remainder would receive their detailed orders in sealed envelopes, which were not to be opened until the invasion fleet had left harbour. We worked at top speed and fell exhausted into bed, usually late at night.

In London, the situation was rapidly becoming critical. The expeditionary force was already embarking in Scottish ports, but the War Cabinet had still not made up its mind. In the end, it was decided that the ships should sail for Narvik and on arrival *demand* free passage for the troops on board, in defiance of protests from Oslo and Stockholm.

'We had a dreadful Cabinet,' General Ironside wrote on Tuesday 12 March after Chamberlain had promised full military support to Finland in a much-publicised statement in the Commons:

> Everybody had a different idea upon how much force we would have to use at Narvik. A more unmilitary show I have never seen. The Cabinet presented the picture of a bewildered flock of sheep faced by a problem they have consistently refused to consider. I came away disgusted with them all.

Major General Pierse Mackesy, who was to lead the landing force, was similarly aghast. 'It is hard to believe that a British Cabinet has ever issued more curious orders to a British Commander,' he wrote, 'or that more curious operations orders than those I had to issue to troops under my command in consequence have ever been written or issued.'

At the heart of the commander's discomfort was the question of what he was expected to do on reaching Narvik and the woolliness of the government's instructions, which read, in part:

> It is the intention of His Majesty's Government that your force should land provided it can do so without serious fighting. If the Norwegians or Swedes open fire on your troops a certain number of casualties must be accepted. Fire is only to be opened as a last resort. It is not the intention of His Majesty's Government that the force should attempt to fight its way through. Nonetheless, should you find your way barred by Swedish forces you should demand passage from the Swedish commander with the utmost energy.

It was impossible to understand what the government really meant, and Mackesy's attempt to explain things to the men under his command did little to help matters:

> Hostility, if it is shown, may prove to be neither widespread nor serious. It is to be hoped that it would disappear in the face of a good-humoured but determined attitude on the part of all ranks of the force and that our object will be achieved by moral persuasion and without warlike action. Our counter-actions should, within limits, rest upon the use of weight, discipline, the rifle-butt and the fist.

Finland capitulated to the Soviet Union on 13 March, a few hours before the Allied expeditionary force was due to sail. In consequence, the ships were held back, and not a few of those on board heaved a sigh of relief when, the next day, the whole project was cancelled.

But in the Admiralty, Churchill's disappointment knew no bounds. He wrote a letter to the Foreign Minister, Lord Halifax, who had been the most recalcitrant opponent of a violation of Norwegian and Swedish neutrality:

> I feel I ought to let you know that I am very deeply concerned about the way the war is going. It is not less deadly because it is silent. There never was any chance of giving effective help to Finland, but this hope – or rather illusion – might have been the means of enabling us to get to [the ore fields at] Gällivare. All has now fallen to the ground; because so cumbrous are our processes that we were too late.

Churchill had visions of Hitler rubbing his hands in satisfaction. He was sure he would strike when spring came and the ice in the Baltic melted:

> Can we suppose they have not been thinking about what to do? Surely they have a plan. We have none. There is no sort of action in view except to wait on events. In spite of all their brutality the Germans are making more headway with the neutrals than we with all our scruples. The Air Force is not catching up. The Army causes me much anxiety. The money-drain is grievous. There is no effective intimacy with the French. Public opinion is far from trustful of the Government. We have never done anything but follow the line of least resistance. That leads only to perdition.

He rounded off with a gloomy forecast:

> I am bound to tell you that we have sustained a major disaster in the North & that this has put the Germans more at ease than they have ever been. Whether they have some positive plan of their own which will open to us, I cannot tell. It would seem to me astonishing if they have not.

4

HITLER'S FATEFUL DECISION

London and Berlin, Spring 1940

Churchill had no idea how prescient he was to prove. Pursuant to Hitler's order, Lieutenant Colonel Bader, Lieutenant Bach and their fellow staff officers had hastily set about improvising plans for a lightning strike against Norway in mid-March; but the Finns' capitulation had caused the Führer to hesitate.

'The peace treaty signed in Moscow deprived both the British and us of every political reason for occupying Norway,' wrote General Alfred Jodl in his diary. 'Preparations have proceeded so far that 20 March can be designated Weser Day, but the state of the ice in the Baltic necessitates a couple of days' postponement.' When the ceasefire between Finland and the Soviet Union came into force on 13 March, the general noted: 'The Führer is not yet prepared to take a final decision on Weserübung. He is still looking for an acceptable justification.'

To the relief of the Planning Staff in the Bendlerstrasse, the days passed and still no order was forthcoming. 'We have to admit that the delay was a godsend,' wrote Albert Bach. 'Had the operation gone ahead, it would have been impossible to complete the necessary preparations in time. Many of the ports were still icebound and we needed time to identify and solve the problems facing us.'

Hitler had given his staff orders to continue their work 'without undue haste' before setting out to meet Mussolini in the Brenner Pass, after which he intended to take an Easter break at the Eagle's Nest, his lofty retreat on the Obersalzberg. On Tuesday 26 March, on his return to Berlin, the Führer was suntanned, rested and in high spirits. It was not until the situation conference that same evening at the Chancellery, attended by generals Wilhelm Keitel and Alfred Jodl and the Naval Commander-in-Chief, Erich Raeder, that the subject of Norway was again raised. Having carefully studied the situation both before and after 13 March, the Grand Admiral's staff had arrived at a unanimous conclusion.

'The occupation of Norway by Franco-British forces was imminent when peace in Finland came,' Raeder said, before going on to sum up the information available to him:

> U-boats were ready and waiting in the Skagerrak on 13 March. An intercepted signal had given 14 March as the deadline for bringing the British troopships to a state of readiness, and quite a lot of French officers had already arrived in Bergen. All in all, this affords sound indications that an attack was being prepared before peace was signed between Finland and the Soviet Union.

Analysis of the pattern of wireless traffic and information from other intelligence sources suggested that the British had stood down their attack force but stepped up operations at sea. At Easter, a mixed fleet of cruisers and destroyers had harassed German merchant ships in Norwegian territorial waters, opening fire on them and forcing them to seek refuge in neighbouring fjords.

Raeder's assessment of the situation left no room for doubt:

> The object of the Allies is and has always been to cut off Germany's imports of iron ore from Narvik. The question of what will happen in the North may be answered as follows: the British will make further attempts to disrupt Germany's trade with neutral countries and provoke situations which may then be used as a pretext to invade Norway.

Although the risk of another British probe appeared less acute, the Grand Admiral was in no doubt as to what should be done. 'Sooner or later Germany will have to face up to the need to mount Operation Weserübung. My advice is to do this as soon as possible, and by 15 April at the latest. After that, the nights will be too light.'

The overall plan for a combined attack on Norway had by then been complete for about two weeks and all the Kriegsmarine's available ships were still being held in readiness. They made up an armada of between fifty and 100 warships of varying sizes plus a number of merchant vessels which, it was planned, would in the initial phase land some 12,000 men at strategic points on the Norwegian coast under strong air cover. As long as Weserübung enjoyed priority, other operations had to be held back – and Raeder was growing increasingly impatient. He needed a decision, but Hitler continued to waver.

'He liked to put off difficult decisions,' wrote Heinz Linge, a former bricklayer who had risen in the SS to the rank of captain and served as the Führer's valet and confidant. 'The threatened British invasion of Norway forced his hand. He had to act at once if he were not to come too late.' Hitler questioned Raeder further about coastal fortifications in Norway and the Royal Navy's state of preparedness. But the Grand Admiral had little to add to what he had already said, and time was fast running out.

Later that evening, Hitler finally made his choice. His naval adjutant, Rear Admiral Karl-Jesko von Puttkamer, wrote in the minutes: 'The Führer agreed that Operation Weserübung had to go ahead. It was to start with the coming of the new moon, Sunday 7 April.'

A mere two days later, on Thursday 28 March, the Supreme War Council in London resolved to mine the Norwegian shipping channel. It was the third time since the turn of the year that an attack on ore exports from Narvik had been prepared for. This time, the Allies were determined that no heed would be paid to protests from the neutrals.

The endgame was on, but the warring parties operated on totally different premises. Churchill and the other members of the British War Cabinet wanted to liberate Europe from the evil of Nazism and in so doing protect freedom and democracy in Europe and the world at large. As is the way with democracies, the decision had been preceded by months of doubt and deliberation. The mining of Norwegian waters was, of course, technically a breach of international law, but the intention was a noble one: to put an end to tyranny.

Hitler saw things differently. He had nothing but contempt for democracy and international law. He had only one object in mind – to pre-empt the Allies in order to safeguard his supply of iron ore, a metal vital to the armaments industry by means of which he aimed to put the rest of Europe in chains. Resistance in Denmark and Norway was to be put down brutally and the two countries crushed beneath the jackboot. For the German dictator, this was a war of conquest, and it was to be waged without mercy.

The Führer's aim was, therefore, the direct opposite of the Allies'. He was out to replace democracy with Nazism's perverted ideology and plunder Scandinavia's wealth and resources. His glib talk and promises were nothing but lies and propaganda – a screen for the barbarity and violence soon to come.

PART II

5

OMINOUS RUMOURS

Germany, Britain and Scandinavia, Friday 29 March to Saturday 30 March 1940

Although guardedly worded, the communiqué issued by the Allied Supreme War Council created quite a stir throughout the world. Leaks were rife, and the official French news agency Agence Havas asserted that the Allies intended to take a firmer line with Norway and Sweden – an opinion clearly based on sources in Reynaud's new government:

> The Allied Supreme Council decided to take a stiffer attitude toward Europe's neutrals and to intensify the force of blockade. Under the new policy Sweden was expected to be told to stop providing Germany with iron ore. Over Norwegian waters the Allies would exercise closer supervision.

The Paris newspaper *L'Intransigeant* was equally perceptive:

> We have been patient for far too long. Out of respect for international law we have taken our scruples so far as to tolerate false pretences and a great deal of hypocrisy. The Germans daily exploit Norway's professed neutrality to continue their hostile traffic. Their ships follow the usual route right through Norwegian territorial waters carrying iron ore from Narvik to German ports. If pursued by British warships, they simply take refuge in Norwegian anchorages, which the Oslo government does nothing to stop them using.

The conclusion was a veiled threat: 'From now on we intend to differentiate between genuine and specious neutrality. The Allies have had more than enough of being deceived in this manner. They have been far too lenient and understanding, and Germany has had no difficulty in finding accomplices.'

The progress of the war was a prime topic in newspaper offices all over the world. The leaks and official bulletins from London and Paris were generally taken as a sign that the Allies were becoming more resolute and intended to do something about Narvik and ore shipments to Germany. The *New York Times* was of the opinion that British and French warships would soon start patrolling Norway's coastal waters, and CBS journalist William Shirer agreed in his daily broadcast from Berlin. 'Some people here believe the war may spread to Scandinavia. From here it looks as if the neutrals, especially the Scandinavians, may be drawn into the conflict after all.'

The Norwegian press gave full coverage to these speculations and a banner headline on the front page of the liberal Oslo newspaper *Dagbladet* proclaimed: 'Heightened blockade off Norway's coast after London meeting. Ore transport via Norway prime topic.' This was the second time in only a few weeks that the world press had been overflowing with speculations about an impending Allied move against the ore traffic. The reports were a widespread source of discussion, though no one seemed to realise just how serious the situation was.

'It is far from pleasant to be so often in the limelight, and still more unpleasant to be surrounded by such martial lovers as the western allies and the Germans,' declared a leading article in the Narvik newspaper *Fremover*. 'But there is nothing to be done about it. The ore is so valuable to the armaments industry that it is only reasonable that it should be a source of contention.'

There was a lot of wishful thinking in most of what was said and written on the subject, and leading commentators seemed inclined to believe in a continuation of the status quo. There had been too many false alarms, making it difficult to take the new rumours too seriously.

'In reality, from a trading point of view, Norway's neutrality is far more advantageous to Britain than to Germany,' declared a typical leading article in *Dagbladet* on 29 March:

> And with regard to ore shipments from Narvik to Germany, a prime bone of contention, it should be borne in mind that when spring comes, the bulk of this traffic will proceed more securely via the Gulf of Bothnia and the Baltic Sea. For Britain, these practical considerations must weigh heavily, along with the purely idealistic and principled aspects of the matter, for which reason

> Britain will surely refrain from violating such a peaceful and friendly neutral as Norway.

Hopeful words they may have been, but in London the War Cabinet and Chiefs of Staff were hard at work on the final details of the forthcoming attack on the iron ore traffic.

'This action would give us a last opportunity to try to get to the Swedish ore fields via Narvik before the ice breaks up,' Rear Admiral Tom Phillips had written to Churchill after the Supreme Allied War Council meeting. A short, tough officer of a peppery disposition, Phillips was nicknamed Tom Thumb and widely regarded as a pocket Napoleon – it depended on who was doing the talking. He was undeniably extremely competent, but also stiff-necked and opinionated. However, it needed someone of his calibre to stand up to Churchill, who, brilliant speaker and leader though he was, could at times act like a pig-headed adolescent – not to mention show himself to be vindictive and display a complete lack of empathy. As the First Sea Lord, Admiral Dudley Pound, so pithily put it, 'At times you could kiss his feet – at others you felt you could kill him.'

There was often quite a lot of friction in the higher echelons at the Admiralty, but on the matter of minelaying Churchill and Phillips were of one mind. Their intention was obvious: to force the German ore carriers out into the open sea, where they could be sunk or commandeered as prizes by the Royal Navy. An underlying motive was to provoke a German counter-strike that would compel Norway and Sweden to renounce their neutrality and seek Allied help. Such a request would in turn open the way to the ore fields, which is why the vice admiral so favoured immediate action. 'I feel that it would be absolutely vital to seize the opportunity immediately and to improvise an expedition with what we could make available in the time taken to load the ships and to send them off at once.'

Phillips was roused to action by news from Stockholm suggesting that Hitler's plans to attack Norway were nearing completion. 'Swedish staff believe that Germans are concentrating aircraft and shipping for operation which Swedish intelligence consider might consist of seizure of Norwegian aerodromes and ports,' the British air attaché had telegraphed from the Swedish capital earlier in the week.

Snippets of intelligence from other sources said much the same thing, which added to the sense of haste. So far, both the Swedes and Norwegians had flatly refused to allow British and French troops to set foot on their territory. Faced with the threat of attack by Nazi Germany, many thought they would change their minds and welcome an Allied force. Mining of Norway's coastal channel would therefore no longer suffice, Phillips declared. It was necessary to hold a landing force in readiness should the Germans move northwards. As it was, the troops earmarked for Avonmouth had been stood down and dispersed about the country, and it would take time to reassemble them. 'I do not consider that any considerations of proper organization and preparation of the expedition should be allowed to stand in the way of this,' he wrote. 'The expedition, starting at this late hour, would be a gambler's bid for a really vital stake which, if successful, might lead to the end of the war within a measurable period.'

In the course of Friday 29 March, the newly augmented plan was adopted by the Chiefs of Staff Committee and the War Cabinet, both declaring themselves in agreement with the Admiralty's reasoning. A provisional three-part timetable was drawn up under which, already on 1 April, the Norwegian and Swedish governments would be handed notes in which the British and French governments would make known their views on the ore traffic in no uncertain terms. Three days later, on the night of 4 April, hundreds of mines were to be sown in the Rhine as part of Operation Royal Marine before, early next morning, Friday 5 April, three minefields were to be laid in Norwegian territorial waters, an operation to be code-named Wilfred. No one knew what might happen once the mines had been laid. There was only a week left and immediate action would be called for if Hitler responded the way Churchill and Phillips thought he would.

The alarm was sounded at the 20th Destroyer Flotilla's base in Harwich late that same evening. The Royal Navy had very few purpose-built minelayers and these had been working at full stretch since the outbreak of war, mining the North Sea, Britain's coastal waters and the channel between the Faroe Islands and Iceland.

To relieve the pressure, a number of modern 1,400-tonne E- and I-class destroyers were converted for minelaying and placed under the command of one of the navy's most eminent destroyer captains, Captain Jack Bickford, who was destined to make his name in the withdrawal from Dunkirk. Two gun turrets were removed, along with the torpedo batteries, to make room for the launching rails, which ran aft on both sides of the superstructure.

'They pulled our offensive teeth, and instead, we got 62 mines, each containing 150 kilos of amatol,' said Torpedoman Thomas Chilton, who served on board the *Ivanhoe*, which, together with the *Esk*, *Icarus* and *Impulsive*, had been entrusted with the rapidly approaching operation. A belt of 240 mines was to be laid in the Landego fjord north of Bodø to block the southern exit from the Vestfjord. A few days earlier, the flotilla's flagship, the *Express*, had collided with a trawler and had to be docked for repair. Bickford transferred his flag to the *Esk*, and with no time to lose, on Saturday 30 March set about the task of loading the mines at Immingham on the Humber. It would take four days to get to the Vestfjord, so work proceeded apace.

The British Home Fleet under Admiral Charles Forbes, a highly capable if somewhat cautious officer, had been put on standby in Scapa Flow at the same time, and on Sunday evening the 2nd Destroyer Flotilla was ordered to chaperone the minelayers through the Norwegian Sea. 'Part of the 2nd D. F. was to escort five minelaying destroyers and then stay in the neighbourhood to warn shipping,' wrote Paymaster Lieutenant Geoffrey Stanning, secretary to Flotilla Commander Captain Bernard Warburton-Lee on board the flagship, HMS *Hardy*. 'The Captain (D) was to be senior officer of the whole operation which was to be simultaneous with at least one other minelaying effort to the Southward.'

Forty-four-year-old Welshman Warburton-Lee was the personification of the Royal Navy's younger captains. Broad-shouldered and over 6ft tall, with his brushed-back, sandy hair, he was a dedicated and resourceful naval officer, professional to his fingertips; what is more, he excelled at cricket, tennis and polo. As his service record put it, he was an 'exceptional officer in every way. He is gifted and well-read, has a strong character and a well-developed talent for leadership.'

Warburton-Lee was the youngest of four children and had grown up in a well-to-do family of lawyers and estate managers in Flintshire in the golden years around the turn of the century. 'He seems to have had an almost idyllic childhood, growing up in a close, financially secure family and living in the beautiful rolling countryside of the Flintshire–Shropshire border, straddling two cultures, Welsh and English,' wrote Alistair Williams in a biographical sketch.

The family farm would pass to his elder brother Philip, and Bernard was determined to go his own way. 'From an early age, Bernard was destined to break with the family tradition of the law and seek a career at sea and he entered the Royal Naval College in Isle of Wight in 1908, at the age of 13.'

Warburton-Lee later passed out top of his class from Dartmouth to serve as a cadet on board various cruisers and destroyers until, towards the end of the First World War, he was promoted to lieutenant and given his first posting as first lieutenant on board HMS *Wrestler*. By the time he met the tall, elegant redheaded Elizabeth Campbell-Swinton, some years later, he was one of the Royal Navy's up-and-coming 'band of brothers', a seasoned elite of young officers who were at their happiest in rain and storm on the open bridge of a destroyer, far removed from the more formal and leisurely life of a big battleship in peacetime.

'My own darling, we have really come to September at last and have started on our way home. In three weeks today I shall be in England! It all seems too good to be true,' he wrote to Elizabeth in 1924 after several months' absence serving with the Mediterranean Fleet. 'Don't you think you will get an awful shock when you see me again after so long? Distance lends enchantment, you know. You will probably have one look and say, "Good God am I really going to marry that!!"'

But Elizabeth had answered 'Yes', and the couple had set up house in an old farm, Soberton Mill in Hampshire, just north of Portsmouth, though the years they spent there were interrupted by many a posting to Malta.

In the summer of 1939 they were again on their way back to the Mediterranean, where Warburton-Lee was to take over the responsible and demanding position of Commander of the 2nd Destroyer Flotilla – nine destroyers with a total complement of 1,400 officers and men. Despite twenty years' unblemished service, during which he had amply demonstrated his leadership qualities, there were still times when he was beset by doubt and a lack of faith in his own abilities.

'I have an established immediate aim – to make an unqualified success of a somewhat exacting appointment which I am to take up in 5 months' time,' he wrote that same winter in response to a questionnaire issued by the Pelman Institute, which offered courses devoted to the 'Scientific Development of Mind, Memory and Personality'.

> What I do lack is a long-distance aim. I am not ambitious and cannot at all say that I want to reach the highest ranks in the Navy. I am conscientious up to a point and hate to do things badly. I have the ability but require the tenacity. My

> memory is defective and deteriorating. Particularly bad at names of people and places. Faces make only small impression and I forget people. My vocabulary was good – now I am often at a loss for the right word.

Few would have concurred with such a candid, self-critical assessment. Two of Warburton-Lee's fellow officers and challengers for promotion in the exclusive destroyer fraternity, Lord Louis Mountbatten and Captain (later Admiral of the Fleet) Philip Vian, famed for his boarding of the *Altmark* in the Jøssing fjord to release close on 300 British merchant seamen held prisoner in the hold, considered him to be one of the Royal Navy's youngest admirals-to-be. 'He was the grandest leader any man could wish to serve under, a certain C-in-C plus 1st Sea Lord of the future,' Mountbatten wrote.

Warburton-Lee assumed command of the 2nd Destroyer Flotilla on 28 July 1939, only five weeks before the outbreak of war. At the time Mussolini was still neutral, waiting on the sidelines to see how things developed, and the Mediterranean was far from the likely battle zone. The flotilla had sailed from the Dardanelles in the east to Gibraltar in the west without encountering an enemy ship. In October the destroyers were ordered to Freetown in Sierra Leone to join the hunt for the pocket battleship *Admiral Graf Spee*, which was wreaking havoc among Allied shipping in the South Atlantic, but to no avail.

By the time the *Hardy* reached Montevideo on the Uruguay side of the mouth of the River Plate in December, the hunt was over, the trapped German raider had been scuttled by its own crew and the honours and medals had gone to Commodore Henry Harwood and his cruisers. The scattered ships of the fleet had sailed thousands of miles in all weathers, with the result that shortly after New Year 1940 they were recalled to British ports for a much-needed overhaul. Mountbatten had his links with the royal family to fall back on and Vian would soon bask in glory after his daring exploit in the Jøssing fjord, but all Warburton-Lee and the men of the 2nd Destroyer Flotilla could do was to disperse to their homes on leave – without having heard a shot fired in anger.

'As a warship we were not allowed to stay in the harbours of South America more than 24 hours, and in Freetown in Sierra Leone there was nothing to do,' said Able Seaman Charles Parham, who served on HMS *Hostile*. 'Even Christmas Eve was spent at sea, and the postcards and oranges from South Africa did not do much to alleviate the boredom. When the cook ruined the Christmas dinner turkey he was almost lynched.'

Although the flotilla had nothing of note to show for its months at sea, the time had not been wasted. Perfectionist that he was, Warburton-Lee made exceptional demands of himself and his men. Every spare moment had been spent in training and still more training: gun practice, boat drill and PT. 'He was a real taskmaster,' recalled Frederick Mason, a torpedoman on board the *Hardy*:

> He was uncompromising in his search for excellence and intent on maximum efficiency. Many times I fell foul of him when he was taking his walking exercises on the upper deck adjacent to the torpedo tubes. Seeing something secured that displeased him, he would blast me with verbal abuse: *Tied up like a bloody bunch of flowers!* I lived in mortal fear of him.

Another torpedoman, Cyril Cope, lamented:

> It was as if nothing could be done good enough or quickly enough, and when the same exercise was repeated for the tenth time, many growled: Why the hell are we doing this again and again? We got the answer at Narvik. Training meant the difference between life and death.

In February 1940 the flotilla was ordered to Scapa Flow, where it came under the command of the Home Fleet. The winter of 1939–40 was the coldest and stormiest in living memory and the men of the 2nd Destroyer Flotilla found the transition from the heat of West Africa to the biting winds and snowstorms of the Norwegian Sea a severe trial.

'Darling, here we are again after 8 days out,' Warburton-Lee wrote to his wife on 27 March, when the *Hardy* and the rest of the Home Fleet returned to Scapa Flow after their Easter incursion into Norwegian waters:

> We had an extremely cold trip and some pretty poor weather ending up with a northerly gale (still blowing) and snow blizzards. It is really amazing the contrast and luxury of one's first few hours in harbour … The change, and being able to relax for a bit, is just heaven.

The destroyers had encountered some exceptionally heavy seas and there were times when Warburton-Lee feared for the welfare of his cabin, which was tastefully equipped with a beige carpet, mahogany furniture and a glass-fronted cabinet containing porcelain and silverware:

> We ended up with filthy dirty weather as I said and this morning the ship did some really good rolls. Luckily I am pretty fussy about securing my cabin (!!!!) so nothing got damaged – but the Wardroom who are considerably less particular fairly bought it! At breakfast-time today the Wardroom table took leave of its legs and transported itself and its contents to the other side of the mess, breaking most of the furniture on the way. So the W. R. ate their breakfast in the galley, full pitch out of the frying pan!

While he was on leave at the end of January and early February, Warburton-Lee and his wife manifestly grew closer and their daily letters are full of endearments and practical advice. With their only son, Philip, away at boarding school, life at Soberton Mill was lonely for Elizabeth, exposed as she was to the day-to-day worries of wartime Britain, with its ever-stricter rationing, so it is not to be wondered at that her husband should show such concern for her well-being. He ordered 20 tonnes of coke, enjoined her to look for a new puppy and to procure a number of empty drums of petrol for the farm vehicles and machinery. The all-pervading tone of Warburton-Lee's letters to his wife was one of longing and tenderness, as is borne out by his final words: 'All my love, darling one. Life is a very second-rate affair without you.'

At about the same time as Warburton-Lee was being briefed on Operation Wilfred, late on Saturday 30 March, Major General Pierse Mackesy was called to the phone and received the first hint of what was in the offing. 'Very late at night on Saturday I got a carefully worded telephone message to say that Avonmouth was on again,' he wrote. 'The Director of Plans, Brigadier Ian Fairplay, drove from London to Suffolk on Sunday 31 March to tell me what was in the wind.'

It was not surprising that Mackesy should again have been selected to lead the expeditionary force. Known to his intimates as Pat, the 56-year-old Royal Engineers officer, who was of Irish-Scottish descent, was highly regarded as one of the army's most gifted officers. 'An officer with a brilliant brain: quick, imaginative and yet thoroughly practical,' wrote Major General John Dill, who was later to become Chief of the Imperial General Staff, in an effusive character assessment in 1934. 'In the past years he has frequently been called upon to prepare papers on large strategical questions of great importance, and in doing so he has shown a rapid grasp of essentials and great lucidity of expression.'

Mackesy was widely looked upon as one of the British Army's rising stars, and Dill's glowing assessment was endorsed by a number of other high-ranking officers. 'I agree with all Major-General Dill says in his report,' noted the then Chief of the Imperial General Staff, Field Marshal Sir Archibald Montgomery-Massingberd. 'I have the highest opinion of Mackesy's ability, character and qualifications for either command or staff.'

After close to forty years' service in Africa, India, the Middle East, France and northern Russia during and after the First World War, during which he won a Military Cross, Mackesy could be proud of an unblemished record. The only thing that could be held against him was a certain lack of tact and social graces – a serious handicap in the snobbish class-conscious society of the time. Among his friends, however, he was accepted for what he was: a hard-working, hard-drinking and popular officer. Outwardly, though, thanks to his bristling moustache and rather off-putting monocle, he came across as rather formal and overbearing.

'Although my father had many firm friends, he also made enemies,' wrote his son, Piers Gerald Mackesy, in a private letter many years later. 'Friends say that he did not tolerate fools gladly, and perhaps his solitary childhood had denied him the schooldays lessons in what one can say that is acceptable and what will cause hurt and resentment. He was not good at handling difficult superiors.'

Towards the end of March 1940, however, all such considerations lay well in the future. Mackesy was still assumed to be in the running for one of the army's top jobs, not least because earlier that winter he had overseen the planning of Avonmouth to the satisfaction of all concerned. Asked whether he was prepared to give the operation a second try, Mackesy said yes. In his personal account of the operation, he wrote:

> According to Playfair, the object this time was to safeguard Narvik and the railway to the Swedish frontier. It was hoped subsequently that an opportunity might arise to go on to and deny the Gällivare ore fields to Germany. The cooperation of the Norwegian government was hoped for, but the general conditions of possible opposition at Narvik remained almost exactly as before. Early the following morning I packed my bags and went to London.

At the Foreign Office, the lights remained on all through the weekend.

'No Cabinet, so Halifax had nothing to do but waste our time with one of his dreadful meetings,' wrote Alexander Cadogan, Permanent Under

Secretary at the Foreign Office and the Foreign Minister's indispensable and chronically overworked right hand. 'The longer they last, the more niggling and ineffective they become. Hitler doesn't do this! We were drafting the various communications to Scandinavians, about fluvial mines and Narvik mines etc. Didn't get away till after 1.30.'

The day before, the Foreign Office had received an unexpected visitor in the shape of the Norwegian ambassador, Erik Colban, who had been sent by Foreign Minister Halvdan Koht to enquire how much truth there was in the alarming press speculations. At the meeting of the War Cabinet that same morning, Lord Halifax had been party to the decision to mine the mouth of the Vestfjord. Now, without batting an eyelid, he convinced the ambassador that the rumours were untrue. Reassured, Colban naively reported back to his superior in Oslo: 'I personally believe that the British government has definitely *not* decided to enter Norwegian territorial waters to put a stop to German ore shipments.'

Sweden's prime minister, Per Albin Hansson, wasn't greatly worried either. The end of the Winter War in Finland had come as an immense relief and the government had decided to stand down and send home the thousands of men who for several months had guarded the border with northern Finland during the conflict. 'The weeks following the coming of peace appear in his diary as having been pleasant and carefree all round,' wrote Hansson's biographer, Anders Isaksson, in his book *Per Albin*. 'The pressure was off.'

In the extensive encampments surrounding the frontier town of Boden, weapons were returned to armouries and from 27 March on, southbound trains were packed with demobilised conscripts, all of whom were looking forward to a return to civilian life after a long, dark winter in Lapland.

After an Easter break, the prime minister himself attended a Social-Democratic congress in Karlstad, where discussions centred on matters far removed from the war on the Continent. 'I spent five happy hours doing crosswords and reading detective stories and went about humming and singing,' Hansson confided to his diary. 'I'm still not quite sure why I'm so happy.'

Not even the ominous rumours of Allied action against Narvik and the ore fields were enough to disturb the prime minister's new-found state of euphoria, and he saw no reason to countermand the decision to send the troops home. 'We are calmly waiting to see what transpires. Demobilisation in the north is to be completed.'

In Narvik, too, the prospect of a brighter spring to come seems to have dispelled much of winter's forebodings. As the sun rose higher in the sky, true to custom, thousands of people made their way to the ski slopes bordering the Norwegian–Swedish frontier.

It had never occurred to Mayor Theodor Broch that war might one day engulf his peaceful little town, and the controversial commander of the local garrison, Colonel Konrad Sundlo, likewise seems to have been oblivious to the overhanging threat – although for years he had been predicting a major conflict. 'There's going to be a world war before long,' he had written to a friend as early as 1932:

> When it comes, all the top people will be strung up and then *they* will have to beg *our lot*, which means you and me, to take over and put the sewing basket in order. I'll see you on the battlefield when we go to pick up our medals and listen to the orations.

This 50-year-old colonel must be one of the weirdest characters to be found in the pre-war Norwegian officer corps. An odd fish altogether, Sundlo was teetotal, uncommonly disputatious, rabidly anti-communist, good-natured, a lover of the outdoor life and a highly respected officer; but he was also an ardent Nazi and supporter of both Quisling and Hitler.

'He was a strange man with strange ideas,' Theodor Broch said. Himself a radical, Broch was Sundlo's political opposite and opponent. Despite this, he had never exchanged a discourteous word with the colonel, who had taken command of the Narvik garrison in 1933, the year before Broch was elected mayor.

After the war, many other people made similar remarks on Sundlo's ebullient character. 'He was amazingly buoyant,' said Colonel Sverre Hermansen, who had been the colonel's second-in-command for four years. 'I had the impression that Colonel Sundlo was a born fighter. He loved to pick a quarrel with the press and never took it amiss if they hit back hard.'

But concealed behind Konrad Sundlo's seemingly imperturbable façade and bonhomie was a darker side which often found expression in spite and vindictiveness. He lived out his fantasies in his private correspondence, in which he dreamed of mowing down members of parliament, 'Bolshevist Russians' and other political opponents – as in the letter Quisling had shown to Rosenberg.

'As a matter of fact, I only say *Heil og Sæl* [an old Norse greeting, literally meaning 'healthy and happy', adopted by Quisling's National Union Party] and Long live Hitler. I can only say how happy I am that the Bolshevists' deadly enemy is currently marshalling Europe under his banner in the fight against Satan,' he wrote in a letter to a fellow officer after the Munich Agreement of 1938:

> We are now moving towards a general and also Norwegian rising against the devilry in Russia, and if there is something I'd like to be a part of, it is to be in command of troops firing down a street thronged with Russian Bolshevists. But back to my friend Hitler. *Magnificent, magnificent, magnificent!* Patriotism will now have far better prospects than in the past and the Bolshevist movement in this country will go straight to hell on well-waxed skis! *Heil and Sæl!*

In retrospect, it is difficult to judge how deep Konrad Sundlo's dreams of violent action really went, but there can be little doubt that his superiors had chosen an extremely unsuitable person to defend one of the country's most important and vulnerable seaports. Since Sundlo had been not only a supporter of both Hitler and Quisling but also the National Union's leading representative in northern Norway for many years, it should have been easy to see that if Nazi Germany were to invade in order to safeguard its iron ore supplies from northern Sweden, Sundlo would find it hard to decide where his loyalty lay.

Konrad Sundlo himself was fully aware of Narvik's strategic importance to the warring powers. 'The ore from Kiruna will be of inestimable importance to the armaments industry,' he had written in the winter of 1937 to the commander of the 6th Division in neighbouring Harstad, General Carl Erichsen. 'It will be so important that it must be assumed that both the belligerents, right from the start and without warning, will try to take Narvik, one to put a stop to ore exports, the other to safeguard them.'

Sundlo's letter was a plea for help against attack by air and sea at a time when the money allotted to defence was dangerously low. He had repeatedly urged that appropriate measures be taken against air raids, anti-aircraft guns installed, artillery brought into position and military training intensified – all with a view to protecting the town and blocking entry to the Ofot fjord.

Matters had slowly begun to improve and, starting in September 1939, the new divisional commander, General Carl Gustav Fleischer, had done all he could to put the north of Norway on a war footing, albeit first and foremost directed against a feared Soviet invasion from the east. An infantry battalion, a territorial force and an anti-aircraft battery equipped with 40mm Bofors pom-poms with some 1,200 men had been earmarked for Narvik, but the troops were badly short of equipment. One example is the paucity of guns to repel an attack from the sea. Narvik had only one field gun, a 75mm Schneider-Creusot mounted on a railway wagon. The essential heavy artillery to repulse an intruder further out in the fjord had never been put in place.

'On the seaward side there was nothing,' Sundlo explained after the war:

> But during the last war, work was begun on fortifications in Ramsund, 50km west of Narvik. That was beyond my jurisdiction and came under the coastal defence forces, but I felt that, in my capacity as defence chief in Lofoten, I ought to have been kept informed of what was being done out there.

The mouth of the Ofot fjord was 3km wide and could easily be commanded from Ramnes, on the north side of the fjord. In the First World War, emplacements had been blasted out of the mountainside and three quick-firing 15cm cannons with a range of 19,000m were ordered from Vickers-Armstrongs Ltd in England. The guns were delivered in 1920, but the government never provided the money to pay for their installation. When, in autumn 1939, Colonel Sundlo turned up on an informal inspection tour, it was to find nobody there but a watchman; the three cannons were still in storage on the dock:

> I asked the man what they were going to do with the guns. He said that the intention was to incorporate them into a battery that could fire in the direction of Ofoten. This sounded fine, but when New Year dawned the guns were gone, never to be replaced.

Having rusted in store for nineteen years, in March 1940, despite protests from the division, the three cannons were sent south for installation in a west-coast fort. This left the approach to Narvik wide open, and at Ramnes, the bare concrete emplacements lay buried deep in snow.

'We kept bombarding the central authorities with letters pointing out how important Narvik was and what needed to be done to defend the town. We also demanded that the Ofot fjord fort be completed,' wrote the chief of staff of the 6th Division, Major Odd Lindbäck-Larsen in his post-war memoirs, *The Road to Disaster*:

> We made a final attempt to get something done on 2 February 1940, when we offered to let our Pioneer company finish the job. We believed we could have the cannons in place in two months at a cost of 200,000 kroner. Later, they were taken away for use in Bergen. That may have been a blessing in disguise. Had our proposal been adopted, installation of the battery would have been completed – but it wouldn't have been manned when the Germans came.

It did not take a military genius to realise how difficult it would be to defend Narvik with infantry alone against a heavily armed naval force, and a few weeks after the guns had been moved, steps were taken to restore the balance. On Saturday 30 March – as Captain Warburton-Lee and General Mackesy were starting their preparations – the ironclads *Norge* and *Eidsvold* were ordered out from Tromsø and transferred to Narvik, to strengthen the defence of the Ofot fjord.

The officer in charge of these two outmoded vessels, Captain Per Askim, was on his way back to Tromsø after an extended Easter holiday at Gratangen, a small tourist resort on the fjord of the same name, when the order reached him. 'We drove all that Saturday on roads banked a metre-high with snow,' wrote his wife Signe in her account of the family's wartime experiences, *From Narvik to Washington*. 'In places it was almost impossible to get through as the road was blocked by snowdrifts. The amount of snow that fell in the county of Troms that winter was beyond belief.'

When the bus reached Tromsø late that evening, the two ironclads were already busy coaling. Signe Askim wrote:

> As we couldn't leave the luggage unattended, I went on board with Per for a short while. I shall never forget the hustle and bustle, the screech and clatter of the cranes and chutes, the sailors and stokers, their faces black with coal-dust, the powerful floodlights and the piles of snow that lined the dock.

The *Norge* and *Eidsvold* were the pride of the Norwegian navy, despite being over forty years old and relics of an age long past. Their steel decks supported an amazing assortment of weapons: two 21cm guns fore and aft, six 15cm guns along their sides and fourteen smaller-calibre cannons dispersed on steel platforms. With a displacement of 4,233 tonnes and 15.2cm-thick armour-plated hulls, they reminded Signe of two wild beasts tensed to spring. That was an illusion. Ungainly, hard to manoeuvre and hopelessly outdated compared to modern warships, in reality they belonged on history's scrapheap. For the 270 men who manned them, the two ships were iron coffins, and Signe Askim felt increasingly uneasy about them:

> At the time, the problem of Narvik and iron ore exports was very much to the fore in the British and French press, and we all had a foreboding that something disastrous was about to happen. After those carefree days in Gratangen, the unexpected move to the Ofot fiord came as a complete change, and it was a very concerned and thoughtful lady who drove up to her lodgings in the town. At about seven o'clock on Sunday morning 31 March, I stood at the window in my nightdress and watched the two ships glide away to the south through Tromsøy Sound.

6

THE CALM BEFORE THE STORM

London, Berlin and Narvik, Saturday 30 March to Wednesday 3 April 1940

At a quarter past nine on Saturday evening – at about the same time as in faraway Tromsø, in the north of Norway, Signe Askim was trudging through the snow that still lay deep in the streets – tense and silent, the people of Britain were gathered around their wireless sets. The blackout curtains were drawn, lights were low and every set was tuned to the BBC Home Service programme *From the Front Bench*. Two minutes later Winston Churchill's gravelly voice, with its characteristic intonations, came from the loudspeakers, causing many a heart to beat a little faster. His words, convincing and uncompromising as they were, seemed to be directed at each of his listeners personally. 'It seems rather hard with spring caressing the land, and when after the rigours of winter our fields and woodlands are reviving, that all our thoughts must be turned and bent upon sterner war.'

There was little comfort to be found in what Churchill had to say, and he held out no hope of an early peace. 'We do not conceal from ourselves that trials and tribulations lie before us far beyond anything we have so far undergone, and we know that supreme exertion will be required from the British and French nations.'

As he went on to point out, prospects would have been brighter if all the democracies had joined in the crusade against Hitler's evil regime:

> It might have been a very short war – perhaps indeed there might have been no war – if all the neutral states, who share our convictions upon fundamental matters, and who openly or secretly sympathize with us, had stood together at one signal and in one line. We did not count on this, we did not expect it, and

> therefore we are not disappointed and dismayed. We trust in God, and in our own arms uplifted in a cause which we devoutly feel carries with it the larger hopes and harmonies of mankind.

However intimate and personal it may have seemed to his listeners, every word and every sentence of the First Lord's speech had been carefully chosen, and tried out before his secretaries, as, an unlit cigar clenched between his teeth, he had paced to and fro across his workroom in a red and yellow dressing gown embroidered with Chinese dragons. His reference to neutral countries was a mere introduction to the main thrust of the speech, in which, with rising passion, he proceeded to address the nation:

> The fact is that many of the smaller states of Europe are terrorized by Nazi violence and brutality into supplying Germany with the material of modern war, and this fact may condemn the whole world to a prolonged ordeal with grievous, unmeasured consequences in many lands. We have the greatest sympathy for these forlorn countries, and we understand their danger and their point of view, but it would not be right, or in the general interest, that their weakness should be the aggressor's strength, and fill to overflowing the cup of human woe.

After pointing out that, since the outbreak of war, no fewer than 150 neutral vessels had been sunk by Nazi Germany, with the loss of over 1,000 seamen's lives, he continued:

> Hardly a day passes without fresh outrages of a barbarous character being inflicted upon the shipping and sailors of all European countries. Their ships are sunk by mines, or by torpedo, or by bombs from the air, and their crews are murdered, or left to perish, unless we are able to rescue them. Swedes, Norwegians, Danes and even Italians, and many more I could mention, have been the victims of Hitler's murderous rage.

This was a form of warfare unparalleled in history, and it prompted Churchill to conclude his speech in such a way that left those to whom it was addressed with little to be proud of and still less to hope for:

> This is the monstrous power which even the neutrals who have suffered and are suffering most – this is the power which they are forced to supply with

> the means of future aggression. This is the power before whom, even while they writhe in anger, they are forced to bow, and whose victory they are compelled to aid, even though, as they well know, that victory would mean their own enslavement.

In its entirety, Churchill's speech was a scathing denunciation of the neutral nations' refusal to face facts. Not surprisingly, it resulted in another rash of banner headlines the world over. Few were in doubt that his criticism was mainly directed at the ongoing ore shipments from Sweden and Norway, and the *New York Times* considered the speech to be of such overwhelming importance that it printed it in full. As the paper so perceptively remarked, 'Coming as it did, immediately after the meeting of the Supreme War Council, which decided drastically to extend contraband control regardless of its effect on neutrals, Mr. Churchill's speech had its fullest meaning.'

The First Lord's attack on their policy of neutrality sent shock waves through Scandinavia, but leading political and intellectual circles there remained as blinkered as ever. 'Swedish exports of iron ore loom ever larger in these pronouncements, but nothing is said about how it is intended to stop them,' noted the Oslo daily *Dagbladet* in a leading article on Monday 1 April. 'There is nothing in Churchill's speech to suggest that Britain has any desire to transform Norway's territorial waters into a war zone by taking action against German merchant ships.'

In Berlin, the response to Churchill's speech was quite different. 'Churchill has delivered nothing but a pack of lies!' fumed Hitler's Minister of Propaganda Joseph Goebbels in his diary. 'Violent attacks on the neutrals! He admits, though, that the war will be both long and hard. He's learned something, at least.' The master liar nevertheless grudgingly acknowledged that the First Lord had expressed himself with style. 'He is an outstanding man, but lacks character and resolution. A burned-out genius and as such not overly dangerous.'

Hitler's assessment of his principal British adversary was by no means as condescending, however – at least not to judge by his emotive response to his speeches. 'Churchill's broadcasts used to make Hitler angry,' Field Marshal Gerd von Rundstedt told the British military historian Basil Liddell Hart after the war. 'They got under his skin – as Roosevelt's did later. Hitler repeatedly argued to the Army High Command, especially over Norway, that if he did not move first, the British would – and establish themselves in such neutral points.'

It is no longer possible to determine to what extent Churchill's speech influenced the German dictator, but throughout the morning of Monday 1 April a stream of official black cars rolled in from the outskirts of Berlin and parked in the Reich Chancellery courtyard. 'The commanders of all the detachments due to land in Norway were summoned to present their final reports,' wrote Lieutenant Albert Bach, who had drawn up the plan to take Narvik with Lieutenant Colonel Robert Bader. 'We were represented by General Dietl personally and his chief of staff, Colonel Wilhelm Weiss.'

Among the high-ranking officers lining the mahogany-panelled walls were Hitler's top military adviser, General Wilhelm Keitel; his chief of operations, General Alfred Jodl; the commander of Group 21, General Nikolaus von Falkenhorst; and the real brain behind the planning of Operation Weserübung, the 2m-tall infantry officer Lieutenant Colonel Bernhard von Lossberg.

'After lunching together,' wrote the operations officer of Group 21, Lieutenant Colonel Hartwig Pohlman, in his account of the campaign, *Norwegen 1940*:

> [the] presentation of the plan commenced in a room in the Reich Chancellery, where there was a large table strewn with maps. The five-hour-long meeting was held in a business-like manner and the Führer made a strong impression on all who were present by his calmness and confidence. He evinced a profound grasp of the course of events and of the military fundamentals of an operational, tactical and technical nature.

The commander of the 3rd Mountain Division, General Eduard Dietl, had joined the Brownshirts in 1920, not long after their formation, and was a close friend and admirer of Hitler. He had been appointed to lead the attack on Narvik in person, at the head of a contingent of men from the 139th Mountain Regiment.

'There was room for 2,000 men on board the ten destroyers, but from them we had to subtract 150 men belonging to the artillery, wireless service and harbourmaster's staff,' Bach wrote:

> In our opinion it was better to operate with a fairly large number of weak companies than a few strong ones. For this reason each company of mountain troops was pared down to 100 men, while the staff and heavy companies each retained 120 men. This enabled us to select those soldiers who were best-suited and trained for the task that lay ahead.

The plan provided for some 200 men to be assigned to each of the ten destroyers, which would also carry artillery, ammunition for ten days' fighting and provisions for thirty days.

Two of the destroyers were assigned a special task. This was to land two task forces, each of 180 men, on both sides of the entrance to the Ofot fjord, to take the coastal forts, which the Germans erroneously believed to be manned and in a state of readiness. A select band of naval gunners was to accompany the troops and immediately prepare the captured guns to repel the British if they attempted to enter the fjord.

Covered by fire from four destroyers, the main body of infantrymen – the 1st and 3rd battalions less one company – would attack the camp at Elvegårdsmoen, some 20km north of Narvik, overcome the defenders and thereafter march to and secure the airfield at Bardufoss, a further 100km to the north.

Finally, under General Dietl's personal command, from the remaining four destroyers, the regiment's 2nd Battalion, including the heavy units and members of his staff, would go ashore in Narvik harbour itself. Bach wrote:

> It was intended that this force should fan out through the town and take control of key points. It was especially important to get the artillery into position on the mountainside above the harbour, to stave off any counter-attack from the sea. Every effort was to be made to occupy the town without bloodshed. To this end, it was aimed to make contact with the commander of the local garrison, Colonel Sundlo, who was known to have German sympathies. Every possible consideration was to be taken to ensure that the civilian population came to no harm.

Hitler listened attentively to what Dietl had to say and declared himself satisfied. 'Until the occupation is successfully completed, I shall undergo days more nerve-racking than ever before in my life,' Hitler declared as the meeting drew to a close early that same evening. 'None the less, I have every confidence in our victory, for history shows that, as a rule, well-planned operations succeed with small losses.'

The Führer's parting words echoed what had already been said in French and British newspapers, and proved that he was well aware of what the Allies were doing:

> The British want to cut Germany off from her sources of raw materials by blocking the shipping lanes along the Norwegian coast. They also intend to set themselves up as policemen in Scandinavia and conquer Norway, which is something I cannot possibly permit. It is high time that Germany secures her trade routes and casts off the British yoke. We are facing a decisive battle and I shall not flinch.

At about the same time as General Dietl was showing Hitler the defensive positions surrounding Narvik, Lieutenant Colonel Sigurd Nitter-Hauge arrived in the town to inspect those self-same fortifications. Nitter-Hauge, who commanded the Engineer Battalion based in Harstad, had in December 1939 been allotted a sum of NKr. 50,000 by the divisional commander, General Carl Gustav Fleischer, to build six pillboxes overlooking the sea on both sides of the town. After the war Hauge explained that:

> These pillboxes were extremely well built. They were blasted out of the rock of the mountain and reinforced with ferro-concrete. When I went to have a look at them on 1 April, the one on Framnes Point was finished and already occupied. A telephone line had been installed and the floor was littered with empty cartridge cases. The pillbox near Ankenes church was surrounded by scaffolding, and the remainder were still being concreted.

There was room in each pillbox for four men and two Colt machine guns. Their purpose was to cover the shoreline with devastating fire should enemy troops try to land from barges and other light craft.

Local infantrymen shook their heads in amazement at the line of pillboxes, the brainchild of the Divisional Staff in Harstad. Colonel Sundlo and his field officers had no faith in static defence for fighting at close quarters, and had on their own initiative constructed a line of trenches higher up on the mountainside, some 100m or so from the beach. Without a forward defence further out in the fjord, and with no artillery, they deemed it impossible to prevent a landing made under cover of heavy naval guns. For this reason they contented themselves with setting up advanced posts close to the water's edge and retaining the bulk of the battalion behind the town as a mobile reserve, ready to counter-attack when and where it was needed. 'To me, the position of the infantry was more important than the bunkers,' Sundlo said. 'In the trenches, we could station a whole company. That would provide more firepower than a handful of men in a pillbox.'

While Lieutenant Colonel Nitter-Hauge was engaged in inspecting the controversial pillboxes, after a night spent in heavily falling snow at anchor off Lødingen at the mouth of the Ofot fjord, the *Norge* and *Eidsvold* steamed into Narvik harbour. It hadn't taken long for Captain Per Askim, who had been put in charge of the newly formed Ofoten squadron just two days earlier, to grasp the precariousness of his new command. The two ironclads for which he was responsible had been commissioned in 1901 and were the oldest of their class in the world still in service. Even with a full head of steam they could do only 17 knots – half the speed of their potential opponents. In the open sea, neither ship had much chance of survival. This left them with only one practical way to repel an invader – to adopt the role of floating artillery and trust that their heavy guns could be brought to bear and fill the gap left by the coastal defences that had never been built.

'The officers did their best, but compared with when the ships were built at the beginning of the century, they were sadly lacking,' Askim observed in his diary. 'But we were determined to scrape through somehow.'

Per Askim was 59 years old at the time and had retired with a pension after a service career that had begun before the turn of the century. The son of the local bailiff and prison governor, he had grown up in the small town of Moss in the south-east of Norway. Although he was exceptionally bright, his parents could not afford to send him to university, so he opted for a sailor's life instead. In 1896 he went to sea in a sailing ship, and two years later was enrolled as a cadet at the Naval College in the neighbouring town of Horten. Askim passed out top of his class in 1904 and served with the rank of lieutenant in the navy's golden years – first in the conflict with Sweden over dissolution of the Union, then safeguarding Norway's neutrality in the First World War.

As a first-rate and farsighted naval officer and navigator, Per Askim appeared to be on the threshold of a brilliant career; but the Norwegian Navy was pared down to next to nothing in the revolutionary 1920s. Like many of his contemporaries, he resigned his commission, and in the autumn of 1930 he moved to Oslo to take up a post as head of a department of the Lighthouse Authority, with responsibility for maintenance of all navigational aids from the Swedish border in the south to what was then the border with Finland in the north. In his unpublished memoirs, he wrote:

> I was in charge of three steamships with which we inspected, replaced and installed floating seamarks, buoys and the like. From mid-May on I went from

> boat to boat, with the result that in the course of the summer I managed to cover pretty much the whole length of the coastline.

Askim knew the Vestfjord inside out, as he did the rest of the Norwegian coast, which made him an excellent choice as commander of the Ofoten detachment. His qualifications and experience notwithstanding, he was taken aback when, in the autumn of 1939, he was abruptly plucked from retirement to safeguard Norway's neutrality a second time and placed in command of the two antiquated ironclads on which he had first served almost forty years earlier, around the turn of the century, when both were new:

> In 1935 I was transferred to what was known as the Interim Service. The Army and Navy had been drastically cut back – there being no danger of war – and personnel were given an opportunity to join this body with a reduction in pay and for a shorter, theoretical period of compulsory service. Sometime later I resigned my commission and retired with a pension. In view of the circumstances, I found it strange, to say the least, that I should have been recalled from retirement to command the nation's prime coastal defence division and the *Norge*. When I made my views known to the admiral who was chief of staff, all he could say was: 'We couldn't find anyone better.'

The stocky commander was as solid as a rock, and it wasn't in his nature to complain. Immediately upon arrival in Narvik, together with Odd Willoch, captain of the *Norge*'s sister ship, the *Eidsvold*, Askim went ashore. All he could do was roll up his sleeves and set to work.

'In the morning of Monday 1 April, Willoch and I paid a visit to Colonel Sundlo and the town's civic authorities.' Askim wrote in his report:

> In the afternoon I convened all the officers for a meeting on board the *Norge* and issued an order regarding the ships' stations and various other matters. I also ordered that, for the time being, the ironclads should remain at anchor in Narvik, the Submarine Division – two submarines, *B1* and *B3*, and their mother ship – should proceed to the Ramsund Sound, and that the guard ships, the *Michael Sars* and *Kelt*, should make their way to Lødingen and keep a watch on the area between Barøy Island and Tjeldodden Point.

At 13.00 on Monday 1 April, Commander Jack Bickford's minelayers put out from Immingham with a full load of mines in place on their launching rails on deck. They set a course direct for Scapa Flow, where the 2nd Destroyer Flotilla lay waiting, ready to sail at short notice.

'We set to work to make out orders,' wrote Lieutenant Stanning, who had learned German during a six-month sojourn in Berlin in 1936, when it hosted the Olympic Games. 'The final result included pictures of the minefields and instructions in German with phonetic pronunciations for the German ships which, we hoped, would be forced outside territorial waters and captured by us.'

The plan was for the 2nd Destroyer Flotilla to leave port on the morning of Wednesday 3 April while the minelayers topped up their fuel tanks. A rendezvous had been agreed 10 nautical miles south of Skomvær Lighthouse at 23.00 on Thursday, the intention being to enter the Landego fjord and lay the mines six hours later, in the morning of Friday 5 April.

On board the *Hardy*, Warburton-Lee invited his old friend Captain Philip Vian and another officer to dinner. They talked late into the night while the destroyer strained at its anchor chain in the recurring squalls.

'This March doesn't know anything about lulls,' Warburton-Lee wrote in a follow-up letter to Elizabeth from Scapa Flow:

> Gale has followed gale incessantly; one is blowing now. This afternoon, blowing and raining, we had a paperchase amongst the bogs, peat heaps and bottomless mud ashore. I really am old enough to know better, but it did us good ... You know my passion for taking a long view, so I have been making enquiries as to [the] possibility of taking the shooting round here. There are a few grouse and very good rock pigeon and snipe shooting. Even though one would always have to be within easy recall, think of the difference if one could walk about with a gun! Funny to think of you having spring and things growing. Here after yesterday's blizzard it is all under snow again and might be January.

On Monday 1 April he had 'plodded', as he put it, up to the top of a nearby hill with another officer. This gave him an opportunity to give his wife a hint of what was in the offing. 'I fancy it is the last walk I shall get for a while,' he wrote, 'and you probably won't hear of me for a bit either.' In a prophetic postscript the following day, he added: 'Darling I love you more than ever. I wish there was a chance for meeting but fear this war is going to intensify quite soon.'

The flotilla was ready to put to sea, but in Paris Édouard Daladier and his mischief-making mistress Jeanne Crussol struck another blow at their common *bête noire* Paul Reynaud when, in his capacity as Minister for War, Daladier persuaded the government to veto Operation Royal Marine for fear of German reprisals. John Colville observed in his diary:

> The French are making difficulties about the Royal Marine operation and wish to postpone it, possibly because Daladier, who is now Minister for War, does not want Reynaud to get the credit, or possibly because the French fear instant retaliation which they are not in a position to withstand.

As Cadogan remarked to Prime Minister Neville Chamberlain, Royal Marine and Wilfred were designed to counter the moral opprobrium that would inevitably result from infringing Norway's neutrality, by showing the world that the Allies were not afraid to hit back directly against Hitler's Germany. But if one operation were to be shelved, there would be little point in carrying out the other. Chamberlain didn't hesitate. He immediately summoned the French ambassador and told him angrily: 'No Royal Marine – no mining of the Norwegian fjords.'

The note it was planned to deliver to Norway and Sweden was ready and waiting, and in Scapa Flow, Captain Warburton-Lee's flotilla had steam up. Now, once again, underhand dealings in Paris threatened to put paid to the Allies' carefully laid plans. There was nothing else for it: Operation Wilfred would have to be postponed.

'Glad to find P.M. was absolutely firm with Ambassador Corbin,' Cadogan wrote in his diary. 'We really must try to bring them to heel. They talk about vigorous prosecution of war, which means that *we* should do it, provided we remove the war as far as possible from France!'

7

NO TO ROYAL MARINE, YES TO WILFRED

London, Berlin and Narvik, Wednesday 3 April to Friday 5 April 1940

The maître d' at the Ritz in Piccadilly sought out General Edward Spears, who was at lunch in the hotel's restaurant, and whispered into his ear. 'I was called to the telephone and told to be at the Admiralty in 35 minutes with a bag packed for a few days' journey,' Spears wrote in his memoirs, *Assignment to Catastrophe*. 'I was to accompany the First Lord somewhere. On the doorstep of the Admiralty I found we were off to Paris.'

The date was Thursday 4 April and the new crisis in relations between London and Paris threatened to jeopardise the Narvik plan irreparably. Churchill had offered to negotiate between Chamberlain and the two fractious French ministers, and wanted Spears, who spoke French, to accompany him as his adviser:

> The man in whose hands the decision lay was Daladier. The mere fact that Reynaud had agreed to sponsor Royal Marine was enough, apart from Daladier's general objection to anything savouring of bellicosity near the French border, to make Daladier veto it. We were shaken in our old de Havilland as if we were salad in a colander manipulated by a particularly energetic cook. I did my best, as we capered and caracoled our windy way over the Channel, to explain how I thought this tricky question should be dealt with. It was essential not to antagonize Daladier and important to flatter him, but Reynaud alone could be relied on for an honest picture of the political situation in Paris.

Unlike the Allies, Adolf Hitler had no need to abide by democracy's intricate rules. Possessed as he was of unlimited power, his word was law. Thus it was that when, after lunch on Tuesday 2 April, he summoned the head of the Luftwaffe, Hermann Göring, Grand Admiral Erich Raeder and General Nikolaus von Falkenhorst to the Reich Chancellery for a second meeting concerning the projected attack on Denmark and Norway, it was not to ask for advice. By that time, planning of the operation had been completed, and the Führer was most interested to learn what the weather over Scandinavia would be like for flying in the next few days.

After a brief discussion, Hitler announced his decision. As his senior operations officer, General Alfred Jodl wrote in his diary, 'The Führer decides that Weserübung will be launched on Tuesday 9 April.' The operation was set to start at 05.15 German Summer Time – 04.15 Norwegian time. At that hour the naval forces would all be in position off their target ports, ready to land their first wave of assault troops at the same time as the government would be presented with Hitler's ultimatum: *Surrender or die! Capitulation or war!*

With disaster fast approaching, in Oslo the government's strong man, Foreign Minister Halvdan Koht, proved as unwilling as ever to face facts. His political achievements were about to be rendered null and void, but still he continued to cling to a pedantic and formal legal interpretation of the Neutrality Act, in spite of the fact that the international press had long been pointing out that Norway's position was untenable.

Churchill, Chamberlain and Reynaud had for months been demanding that Norway and Sweden choose between freedom and tyranny, and early in April their pleas and threats had been backed by increasing indications that an attempt would soon be made to put a stop to ore shipments.

On 3 April the Norwegian government learned from their emissary in Berlin, Arne Scheel, that in Stettin, Swinemünde and other Baltic ports German ships were busy taking on troops and equipment in readiness for an assault on Norway. The information came from the Swedish consul, Karl Vendel, who had not only seen what was happening with his own eyes but had also talked with soldiers and sailors awaiting their turn to embark.

That same day the Norwegian envoy in London, Erik Colban, telegraphed confirmatory information he had received from Noel Baker, a prominent Labour MP. 'Today Baker made it clear to me that the British government was preparing to take direct action against the ore traffic in Norwegian territorial waters and that this decision enjoyed wide support within the Labour party.'

Finally, on 5 April the Norwegian embassy in Berlin passed on information received from the Dutch military attaché regarding the 'occupation of points on Norway's southern coast ... to further progress of the war and pre-empt the western powers'. Even then, at the eleventh hour, Koht seemed unable – or unwilling – to change course. He secretly appealed to the USA, saw to it that the Norwegian press carried news of a fall in ore exports and adhered rigidly to the same passive line.

'In this country we understand very well the difference between the two parties' war aims, but it is part of our policy of neutrality not to side with one party or the other in matters of this kind,' he told a Reuters reporter who interviewed him in a break during a closed session of the Storting (Parliament) held after Chamberlain had again warned, in a speech to the Commons, that action was imminent. 'My country is neutral, because that is the only course open to us, and we are forced to maintain our policy of neutrality in all aspects.'

Koht could not know it, but his words were to prove the epitaph of a policy that had been doomed from the outset. As the 1945 Commission of Enquiry put it:

> The government failed to warn the Norwegian people of how close war was and what we had to be prepared for at any moment. It did not mobilise what we possessed of military forces to defend our neutrality, or in the cause of peace and freedom. In fact, it was precisely in these critical April days that it allowed the men manning the coastal fortifications to be relieved in accordance with a predetermined plan. When the need was greatest, what we had at our disposal were untrained troops.

The general failure to comprehend what was at stake was also apparent among high-ranking officers in the north of the country, a region that was especially at risk.

Threats directed at Narvik came thick and fast, but on Wednesday 3 April both the commander of the 6th Division, who was in overall command in the north, General Carl Gustav Fleischer, and his chief of staff, Major Odd Lindbäck-Larsen, embarked upon what was, in the circumstances, a most untimely inspection tour of the Varanger area, 1,000km north-east of the danger zone. The following day the commander of the 3rd Naval

Defence Region in Tromsø, Commodore Leif Hagerup, left for a spell of compassionate leave.

With all three commanders in the north absent, it was left to Captain Per Askim, who already had his hands full, to fill the gap. 'On 2 and 3 April I reconnoitred the Ofot fjord in my ironclads to have a look at the positions we might need to take up if hostile forces entered the fjord,' he wrote in his report. 'On Tuesday 4 April I journeyed up to Tromsø to deputise as commander of naval defence after Hagerup.'

Meanwhile, his wife Signe had packed their belongings and was all set to move down to Narvik. 'All of us naval personnel – and I counted myself as one of them – had thoroughly enjoyed our stay in Tromsø. The townspeople were both friendly and hospitable, and did all they could for the men,' she said in her account of the couple's wartime experiences:

> The darkness of the polar night, with its howling winds and blizzards, wasn't at all pleasant, and Per often complained that it was difficult to carry out proper exercises in such conditions. Coming as I did from Horten [a naval base in the south-east], I knew most of the ships' officers and considered many of them personal friends. They were a grand lot and life aboard the two ironclads couldn't have been better.

After a series of staff conferences, Signe and Per Askim left Tromsø on Friday 5 April and reached Narvik the following day. 'I settled in at the Royal, a new and fully modern hotel. At the time, while still retaining his old command, Per was temporarily in charge of naval defence throughout the north of the country and was also in command of the newly formed Ofoten detachment.' There was an enormous amount of work that needed to be done, which left little time for family life. 'I had a brief visit from my husband on Sunday. When I next saw him again, a great deal had happened!'

On the other side of the frontier, the Swedes continued to stand down their forces. The Frontier Guard was back on a peacetime footing and the troops guarding the vital railway line carrying iron ore to Narvik had been reduced to a minimum. 'Today's news is far from encouraging,' Prime Minister Per Albin Hansson observed in his diary on Thursday 4 April. 'We are trying to convince the Germans that we intend to defend our neutrality.'

Despite his misgivings, the Swedish prime minister made no attempt to halt the trains packed with demobilised soldiers that regularly travelled south from the Kiruna region. This may have been because the Swedish government had been careful to keep itself better informed of events taking place in Germany than had its Norwegian counterpart. Two days earlier, the Swedish naval attaché in Berlin, Anders Forshell, had paid a private visit to Grand Admiral Raeder's chief of staff, Vice Admiral Erich Schulte Mönting, which left him in little doubt that the Germans were about to make a move against Scandinavia – possibly with the aid of parachute troops in the case of Narvik.

Forshell left with the strong impression that any such attack would be directed against Norway alone, not Sweden, and informed Stockholm accordingly: 'It is my belief that Schulte Mönting genuinely wished to reassure us that there was no question of German aggression against Sweden.'

At 02.00 on the morning of 3 April, the first three ships of the German invasion force, the 11,000-tonners *Bärenfels*, *Alster* and *Rauenfels*, sailed from Hamburg. Their holds were crammed with guns, ammunition, fuel and provisions, all hidden from view beneath a deep layer of coke. The plan was to sail north to Narvik inside the Norwegian coastal channel with, among other vital weapons of war, all the heavy artillery General Dietl would need to defend the newly occupied ore town against a British counter-attack: three 15cm, four 10.5cm and ten 20mm anti-aircraft guns.

If the clandestine cargo were discovered by a Norwegian guard ship, the Germans would find themselves in a most embarrassing situation. 'I immediately took steps to inform the foreign minister should one of the ships be inspected by the Norwegians,' General Alfred Jodl wrote in his diary. At five that same afternoon Foreign Minister Joachim von Ribbentrop and Chief of the General Staff Franz Halder were told by Hitler himself that Weserübung was in progress. They were the first, apart from those at the heart of the operation, to be let into the secret.

Whereas many Scandinavian military leaders and politicians allowed themselves to be lulled into a false sense of security by unjustified hopes, and some even left the potential battle zone altogether, the international press took the opposite view. Early in April, at least three reporters took the train from Stockholm to Kiruna and thence, by the Ofot line, to Narvik in expectation that something of great moment was about to happen. They were Harold Callender of the *New York Times*, UPI's Peter Rhodes and Giles Romilly, representing London's *Daily Express*.

'Along Germany's winter life-line – the railway from Sweden's iron-mountain of Kiruna – I travelled today to Narvik, a bustling little Norwegian port which has become the focal point of Britain's struggle with Germany,' reported 23-year-old Romilly in a despatch on Thursday 4 April:

> From this port is shipped almost the whole winter output of the vital Swedish iron mining industry. I found the town humming with rumour of Allied activity far out offshore where, it is said, vessels of the naval patrol lie in wait to intercept the ore ships as they creep south along the Norwegian coast towards Germany. But about the ore traffic – not a word is said here.

Dark-haired and well built, in keeping with his aristocratic background, Romilly had attended prestigious Wellington College in the 1930s. A born rebel, at an early age he had embraced the revolutionary fervour of the time, cutting short his studies at Oxford to join his younger brother Desmond, an avowed communist, to fight with the International Brigades in Spain. Churchill followed the doings of his refractory nephews with both fury and delight. At the outbreak of war he was probably instrumental in securing Giles a position with the *Daily Express* through the good offices of his friend Lord Beaverbrook, the paper's owner. As a cub reporter Romilly quickly picked up the *Express* style. He was never lacking a bit of hyperbole, either, as is exemplified by his account of the train journey: 'On the way I got off the train for a second look at Kiruna's iron mountain. A Swedish companion pointed out the terraces which have been quarried in its face. One day's output, he said, would provide sufficient metal to build a 40,000-ton battleship.'

Harold Callender, who was some years older than Romilly, was head of the *New York Times*' Paris bureau. He and Romilly arrived in Narvik together:

> Standing upon the high iron ore dock in Narvik harbor today the writer had a striking glimpse of a dramatic episode of the war as seen from the vantage point of this singular seaport, 140 miles above the Arctic Circle and not far from the northernmost tip of Europe. About sixty feet below were the decks of three large ships. Their hatches were open. From chutes above there poured noisily into their holds a thick stream of what looked like gray-colored rock. It sent up clouds of dust as it piled up in the ships' bottoms. It was iron ore from Kiruna in Northern Sweden, the richest deposit in the world.

Despite persistent questioning, neither Callender nor Romilly were able to ascertain precisely how much ore was shipped out through the port, as such information was classed a military secret. 'Any reporting of names or movements or destinations of the ships is regarded as espionage under a special law adopted soon after the war began.'

Callender described Narvik harbour as jammed with merchant ships – German and British, as well as Norwegian vessels and merchantmen from other neutral nations – and to all appearances relations between the warring nations were cordial and unproblematic:

> It seemed odd to stand upon the deck of a German ship alongside German seamen and to look across a short space at a gun mounted on the stern of a British vessel. If anyone imagines that these British and German seamen laboring side by side in a neutral port are animated by a spirit of mutual hatred or even dislike, he is greatly mistaken. They are workingmen, doing a hard and unpleasant job, and for the British, a dangerous job. They have neither the time nor the inclination for rancor.

Narvik reminded Callender of similar mining towns in the US Midwest and Alaska:

> Standing upon the dock one has a superb panorama of the elongated harbor with the high mountain opposite and a series of rounded summits beyond, their snow-covered slopes meeting the low-hanging cloud under a low-hanging sun. Nearby is a strangely new-looking town of about 10,000 people. It is only 38 years old and a kind of frontier-town largely consisting of wooden houses, half hidden in snow.

Though iron ore exports from Narvik had topped 7 million tonnes in 1938, a record year, the overhanging threat of war prompted the LKAB to ship more of its exports via Luleå in the summer of 1940, when the Gulf of Bothnia was free of ice. Large quantities of ore continued to be shipped via Narvik, but the local population feared that exports would fall to no more than 3 million tonnes that year. 'Thus one paradox of the war is that the greatest iron ore port will not profit, but will suffer from the increased demand for the raw material of munitions,' Callender wrote. He summed up his first impression of the situation with the observation: 'Such is the Arctic seaport where British and Germans now meet in a not-unfriendly manner to carry away ship-loads of iron ore to make guns and shells to kill British and Germans.'

The reports were studied with close attention on the other side of the North Sea, where army and navy planners were putting the final touches to Operation Wilfred, which was already behind schedule, and to the expedition they were preparing to send to Norway.

Although the laying of mines off the Norwegian coast had been postponed indefinitely pending the outcome of Churchill's attempt to mediate in Paris, Captain Warburton-Lee and his destroyer flotilla, comprising the *Hardy*, *Havock*, *Hotspur* and *Hunter*, had been ordered north from Scapa Flow to Sullom Voe in the Shetlands, where it was expected to arrive on Wednesday morning, 3 April.

'Shortly after leaving Scapa we watched an air raid on the fleet anchorage as we were passing East of the Orkneys and saw the very impressive barrage of fire which looked like a ring thrown into the sky and held there,' wrote Lieutenant Geoffrey Stanning.

When the destroyers dropped anchor in the lonely inlet allocated to them, with the exception of the anti-aircraft cruiser HMS *Calcutta*, an oil tanker and a converted steamer, the *Manela*, which was serving as a depot ship for Coastal Command flying-boats, they were alone:

> Sullom Voe was quite pleasant and peaceful in many ways apart from gales each day except one, and air raid warnings about a dozen times a day. We went on making out our orders and had time to have a walk in the hills in a blizzard and also a very amusing paperchase on the Friday. Another amusement was a boarding exercise when each ship had to send a boarding party to the next ship and board it against opposition and cheers from the victim. We 'boarded' *Hunter* and fired a rocket at her to represent a shot across her bows which so nearly hit a Sunderland flying boat which happened to be passing overhead, that we had to make abject apologies to the R.A.F.

After a punishing voyage northwards, Captain Jack Bickford's minelaying force reached Sullom Voe late Wednesday evening; but there was no intimation from government offices in London as to what their next move was to be. Fuel tanks were topped up and the ships were ready and waiting, but Operation Wilfred still hung fire.

In his cabin on board the *Hardy*, Warburton-Lee once again put pen to paper. 'Darling one,' he wrote to his wife, who was feeling very cut off and alone on the farm in Hampshire, 'you will be surprised at hearing from me again – so am I.' By this time their son Philip, now 13, was at Eton and Elizabeth had no close family in the neighbourhood. The couple's attempts to have more children had ended in miscarriages and Elizabeth was probably still not fully restored to health. None the less, she was eager to find a regular job, even if it meant commuting between the farm and London, some 150km distant. Concerned for his wife, Warburton-Lee did all he could to persuade her to stay put:

> I am sorry that you are so bored at Soberton, by yourself. I have been thinking over what you said about getting a job in London for the week. I'm afraid I don't think it would be a good idea at all.
>
> My principal reason against it is that I am sure you couldn't make it and would inevitably do yourself in – that would be very foolish.
>
> To live in London all the week and work full hours would probably do you in, in time, anyway, bearing in mind that you are still very young and require a lot of sleep!!
>
> But added to this you would have to travel back to Soberton weekends, take on all the things that had not been done down there during the week, and [be] back again Monday morning. You might last one month or even two!
>
> Soberton would go to pieces to some extent. It would have no advantage financially because you would spend more by running two pied-à-terres than you would make. Then you wouldn't be able to do any of the amusing things you think you would because you would be too tired.
>
> On the whole it's a rotten idea.
>
> Don't forget that everyone is bored stiff in war and you no more than most. There is no doubt that the thing to do is to comply with the catechism and do your duty in that state of life unto which it shall please God to call you.

In the mountains Warburton-Lee had racked his brains for an alternative, but to no avail – and he himself was far away and helplessly tied up by his responsibilities as a naval officer. There was little he could offer by way of consolation:

> Thinking it out, the logical best thing to aim at is to make more use of Soberton (which happens to be well sited at present) since it has to be kept going anyway.

> How you can do this is more difficult unless you can get anyone to come as paying guests. If of course London were to be attacked then you could have dozens of lodgers soon enough. I hear that lots of people want houses in our neighbourhood because it is clear of air-raids.

This was a typical exchange between husband and wife who, like hundreds of thousands of others, were endeavouring to solve everyday problems in the shadow of a war that was becoming increasingly arduous. Beneath Warburton-Lee's suggestions and admonitions lay hopes and longings which in the circumstances had no chance of fulfilment: 'Mail is going and I will get this away. It is blowing its usual gale. Darling one, I love you, Your own husband.'

At Bedale Hall, his headquarters in Yorkshire, Major General Pierse Mackesy wasn't finding things easy either, and he was still unsure as to precisely what he was expected to do. The chief of the Imperial General Staff, General Edmund Ironside, was on an inspection tour in France, and Mackesy was still awaiting detailed orders. Pending their arrival, pressed for time as he was, he had sent five battalions of conscripts from the far-from-ready 49th Infantry Division to Rosyth, where four cruisers, the *Devonshire*, *York*, *Berwick* and *Glasgow*, lay waiting. Two battalions were earmarked for Stavanger and two for Bergen, and the cruisers were under orders to be ready to sail by Friday 5 April at the latest. The remaining battalion was to be transported to Trondheim by passenger ship, while Narvik was to be taken by more powerful forces, crack troops drawn from the Scots and Irish Guards.

In their provisional directive, the War Cabinet had pointed out that the mining of Norwegian waters might well arouse a German response, for which reason it was resolved to hold further forces in readiness to occupy Stavanger, Bergen and Trondheim in addition to Narvik. There was an important rider to the directive, however: it was *not* intended to land any forces in Norway before the Germans had violated Norwegian territory or provided clear proof of their intention to do so.

The situation was unclear all round and no news was forthcoming from Paris. The situation was reminiscent of how things had been a month earlier, and Mackesy was feeling increasingly frustrated. As the Director of Military Operations, Major General Richard Henry Dewing, noted in his diary: 'Mackesy came in, less thrilled by the present prospects than he had been with his previous show.'

Churchill and Spears had in the meantime landed at Orly airport south of Paris, but all hope of reconciling the two antagonists over a good dinner was dashed on their arrival at the British embassy. Paul Reynaud attended but the prime cause of the trouble, Daladier, had refused outright to sit at the same table as the prime minister. To add insult to injury, Daladier repeated his refusal the following day. As Spears wrote:

> Churchill was greatly disappointed. He had hoped to bring Reynaud and Daladier together by making them realize the pettiness of their quarrels in the light of the gathering storm. This was an illusion. All Paris realized that such a result was improbable unless a bomb eliminated both the Ministers' Dulcineas; an unlikely contingency unless the whole city was blown up, for it was highly improbable that they would ever be at the same place at the same time.

When, at long last, Churchill got to see the haughty Minister for War on the Friday morning, despite his oratorical gifts, he made no progress whatsoever. Daladier was adamant that there could be no question of agreeing to mining the Rhine until France's aircraft factories had been safeguarded against German retaliation from the air – and that would take at least three months. Royal Marine was definitely off and it was a distinctly chastened Churchill who phoned news of his failure through to the War Cabinet back in London.

According to Lord Halifax, Churchill would not recommend applying more pressure on the French, and Chamberlain's private secretary John Colville gleefully noted in his diary:

> Winston went over to Paris to try and convert Daladier to the Royal Marine operation and then telephoned in the middle of the Cabinet to say that he had been converted by Daladier! This much amused the P.M. who said it was like the story of the pious parrot which was bought to teach good language to the parrot which swore, but ended by itself learning to swear.

In a letter to the French government Chamberlain had reiterated the need to launch Wilfred and Royal Marine at the same time. Mining Norway's territorial waters would inevitably upset a lot of people. If Wilfred alone were set in motion, the Allies would not be able to lay claim to the moral high ground.

It was a persuasive argument, but the time for such considerations had passed and the War Cabinet was not prepared to wait any longer. The fleet was ready to sail and the troops were equipped and waiting. Late in the morning of Friday 5 April, the War Cabinet unanimously gave its assent to the operation. The Norwegian and Swedish governments would be handed the already completed notes during Friday afternoon and the leads mined in the early morning hours of Monday 8 April, three days later than originally envisaged.

Discussions relating to action against ore shipments from Narvik had ebbed and flowed ever since September 1939, but now the die was cast. There was no going back. As the Cabinet dispersed for the weekend, teleprinters began to chatter in operations rooms from Yorkshire in the south to Scapa Flow in the north. The issue had been a thorny one throughout and the debate had often been heated; even at this late stage not a few people in government still questioned the wisdom of mining the leads. According to John Colville, in the end the Foreign Office agreed to the operation only because the Winston policy had triumphed over the Halifax policy – and the foreign minister had condoned the mining purely out of loyalty to Chamberlain:

> The P.M. for his part is not over-enthusiastic, but feels that after the expectations aroused by the meeting of the Supreme War Council the other day some effective action must be taken. He does not believe like some people in action for action's sake, but he recognises the importance of the psychological factor in the present war and the necessity of throwing occasional sops to public opinion. The question is will it be only a sop? May not the Germans be stung to retaliate forcibly?

Sir Alexander Cadogan had retired to his country retreat to nurse a bad cold. Spring had come, and with the sun climbing ever higher in the sky, he set about regaining his health by digging the kitchen garden, which was beginning to show signs of life after the long winter. In his diary he made no attempt to disguise his true feelings: 'We lay Narvik mines tomorrow. This I think is silly – unless it induces Hitler to do something sillier.'

PART III

8

THE INVASION FLEET PUTS TO SEA

Scotland, Northern Germany and Scandinavia, Friday 5 April to Sunday 7 April 1940

High above the Atlantic and the Norwegian Sea, warm air from the south was in collision with cold air from the north, and the resulting fronts were sending one deep depression after another across the British Isles and Scandinavia. Banks of grey-black cloud came rolling in from the sea, lashing ships and men with icy rain.

'The flotilla left Sullom Voe in a south-westerly gale at 04.40 am Saturday 6 April and headed for the Lofoten Islands,' wrote Commander Jack Bickford who, in the dim light of early dawn, stood watching the windswept cliffs and shores of Shetland recede from view, blotted out by recurring squalls.

HMS *Esk* and her companion minelayers were built for calmer waters. The destroyers pitched and rolled as they battled their way north, and the heavy seas threatened to wrench the mines lining the decks from their fastenings and wash them overboard. 'The railings broke like matches. The waters crashed over the stern, and *Icarus* lost a man overboard. Another broke his leg.'

On a parallel course some cable-lengths distant, the escorting destroyers – the *Hardy*, *Hotspur*, *Hunter* and *Havock* – were undergoing a similar battering. Below deck, it was chaos. 'We had no idea where we were heading, and the weather turned bad soon after departure,' said Able Seaman Arthur Brown of the *Hotspur*. 'The seas grew into mountains, and the rolling and pitching became truly scary. No stoves could be lit, and the mess-deck was awash in tins, potatoes, cutlery, chairs and other furniture. I was terribly seasick and convinced that I was about to die.'

The flotilla's paymaster, Lieutenant Geoffrey Stanning, tried hard to work, but it was no easy task. 'Although it had been a glorious day on Friday, by the time we left on Saturday morning at 03.00, there was a Southerly gale blowing and, in the dark, going through the unlighted booms was not an easy matter.'

Stanning and his captain had been out sailing the day before and returned with frostbitten hands. 'It was so cold,' Warburton-Lee wrote in his penultimate letter to his wife, 'that it took 20 minutes before I could get any feeling into my hands. Now after a bath I feel grand and that it was well worth it.' The thought of his wife's predicament in the old mill north of Portsmouth occupied Warburton-Lee's every spare moment. But the war had put paid to all hope of a normal life, and he could see no simple solution:

> The war is going to intensify quite soon and will I think be long and gory and by the end of it I doubt if we shall have much left. Again, after the war I may have to or want to leave the Navy and we shall be poorer than we are now.

He clearly had dark forebodings, and he saw only one possibility if they were to save the farm: the longer the war lasted, the greater would be the demand for farm produce. 'Soberton does us very well and it would be a pity to leave it. But to keep it we shall have to try to make some part of it pay – farm a bit – grow something.' What he had in mind was pigs and poultry and vegetables. This prompted him to suggest that Elizabeth should apply for a course in farming. 'Give all this a think over and let me know what are your reactions,' he wrote, before signing off with a jaunty, 'Don't forget the war is going to start quite soon and I am going to start it.'

In the Vestfjord, dawn manifested itself as a wall of thickening snow, so that the 23,000 Lofoten fishermen, following the annual migration of cod in their 7,000-odd boats, were kept very much on their toes. Catches approximated 90,000 tonnes, but the effects of Norway's recently signed trade agreement with Nazi Germany had yet to make themselves fully felt.

Privileged buyers were kept hard at work day and night packing freshly landed cod in crates of ice for shipment to Hamburg, Bremen and other German ports. The fishermen themselves received only 10 øre per kilo, a pittance, and not a few of them were living on the poverty line. The war had driven the price of bait, bunkers and gear through the ceiling, leaving little from gross earnings of 530 kroner (approximately £26) for a whole winter's toil in the worst of weathers. 'If one considers what each crew ends up with when the season is over, one soon realises that this year, as in previous years, the net profit is nil,' lamented the local newspaper, the *Lofotposten*. 'This is because of running costs.'

In Narvik, at the head of the fjord, prospects were equally daunting. 'Here it is not expected that Britain will do anything to cut off this stream of ore except to try to buy more of it herself from Sweden,' reported Harold Callender after a tour of the snow-bound town in the company of fellow journalists Giles Romilly and Peter Rhodes. 'It is believed there will be increasing British pressure on the neutrals, but no direct intervention. Meanwhile Narvik takes its fate with resignation almost amounting to apathy.'

All through the week, ore shipments had continued at the same cracking pace, and at times there were more than twenty ships awaiting their turn to load in the harbour. Stocks of ore had risen to 455,000 tonnes, and at the railhead some 12,000 to 15,000 tonnes of pulp and timber, as well as other commodities in transit from Sweden, stood stacked along the quay.

'Not one of Narvik's 930 dockers is unemployed just now. They are averaging more than 5 pounds a week,' Romilly telegraphed to the *Daily Express* office in London:

> Brilliant lights, which I thought last night were the lights of houses, came in fact from the railway sidings and the loading docks. Loading is going on night and day in three shifts. If the ore traffic is stopped, Narvik as a town will be killed. A docker I asked about this said: We must tighten our belts.

The three newspapermen had followed the Ofoten squadron's movements with interest and reported on the presence of the ironclads in detail – undoubtedly in understanding with the local authorities, who were eager to let the world know that Norway's navy was on the alert. 'Narvik is being well defended. Two submarines came in yesterday to join the two coastal defence vessels, the *Norde* and *Edinbold* [*sic*]. These two warships, heavily armoured, each carry two 8-inch and two 6-inch guns and several anti-aircraft guns,' Romilly wrote. 'The two grey submarines, moored along the quayside, looked insignificant beside the towering bulk of the ore ships. The smartness of their sailors on parade impressed the British Consul here: Jolly good show, he said.'

On Saturday afternoon Romilly, Callender and Rhodes were invited on board the *Norge*, where the commodore served them coffee in the mahogany-panelled saloon:

> In the comfortable sitting-room in the *Norde* [*sic*] I talked yesterday with the commander of the squadron – a small, tired-looking, friendly man. He had just received by telephone the latest report from his headquarters at Tromsø, 150 miles further north. Asked if all was quiet, he replied: Not so bad.

Askim was nothing if not succinct in his report of the meeting: 'I got back to Narvik on Saturday and was visited by four representatives of the international press. They wanted me to answer questions on Narvik and how we intended to preserve our neutrality. I was non-committal.'

Rumours abounded. On Friday, Foreign Minister Halvdan Koht had received further indications that war was coming closer. It made no difference: his mind was made up and he made no attempt to act upon the warnings he had been given.

The information had come from the British and French ambassadors, who had made a surprise visit to his office and in an ominously worded note made it clear that the western powers were close to losing patience with the Norwegian and Swedish governments' policy of neutrality. They emphasised that they were no longer prepared to allow iron ore to pour into Hitler's armaments factories from the mines in Lapland and that they felt justified in taking all necessary measures to put a stop to this traffic.

An Allied attack on ships carrying ore from Narvik would inevitably result in a counter-attack from Germany and extend the war to Norway. This would put paid to the government's pacifist policy once and for all. It was a daunting prospect and Koht was still visibly shaken when, that same evening, he went to dine with the American ambassador, Florence Harriman. 'He excused himself and said the day had been the most nerve-racking of his official life,' the ambassador wrote in her memoirs, *Mission to the North*. 'His face was drawn, and I sensed that the day really had been more tense than usual.'

At an open meeting of the Norwegian Parliament the following morning, Koht could still have assumed the stance of a resolute national leader and a man of consequence. In the event, he not only failed to grasp the opportunity open to him, he never even mentioned the Franco-British note or the warnings he had received from Berlin – neither to the members of the Storting nor to his own government. Norway was teetering on the brink of the greatest and potentially most calamitous event in the nation's history, yet even now Koht did nothing to rally his fellow countrymen and exhort them

↑FAMILY LIFE: Bernard and Elizabeth Warburton-Lee with their baby son Philip, photographed in the garden of their home in about 1928. (Bernard Warburton-Lee's personal archive)

↖↙THE SPORTSMAN: Warburton-Lee excelled at sports, both individually and as a team player. In the photograph of the polo team (top) he is third from the left in the back row. In the bottom picture, he occupies the same position as a competitor in the navy's tennis championship sometime in the interwar years. (Bernard Warburton-Lee's personal archive)

↑THE PERFECTIONIST: Warburton-Lee was highly purpose-oriented and took every opportunity to train both himself and his men to achieve ever-better results. He is shown here ready to take to the polo field in Malta. (Bernard Warburton-Lee's personal archive)

→THE DESTROYER CAPTAIN: Warburton-Lee was given his first command towards the end of the First World War. In the twenty years that followed, he rose to become one of the Royal Navy's foremost destroyer captains and was widely tipped to become one of the Second World War's youngest admirals. He is pictured here with his wife Elizabeth on the deck of a destroyer in the 1920s. (Bernard Warburton-Lee's personal archive)

←**BOY ENTRANT:** By tradition, Warburton-Lee's family were lawyers and landowners, but Bernard opted for a career at sea. In 1908 he was accepted as a naval cadet at the age of 13. (Bernard Warburton-Lee's personal archive)

↑**THE FLAGSHIP:** HMS *Hardy* left the Cammell Laird shipyard in 1936 to become flagship of the 2nd Destroyer Flotilla. H-class, she had a displacement of 1,455 tonnes and was armed with five 4.7in guns.

↓**THE FATEFUL SIGNAL:** The signal sent by Warburton-Lee from the Vestfjord at 17.51 on 9 April 1940 was logged as received at the Admiralty at 18.20. (Bernard Warburton-Lee's personal archive)

SECRET MESSAGE 1751/9th April IN

From Captain (D) 2. Date 9.4.40.

Recd 1820.

Naval Cypher (C) by W/T.

Addressed Admiralty, C. in C. Home Fleet, F.O.C.B.C.S.

<u>MOST IMMEDIATE</u>.

Norwegians report that Germans hold Narvik in force, also six repetition six destroyers and one submarine are there and channel is possibly mined. Intend attacking at dawn high water.

1751/9.

Advance copy sent Ops, O.I.C. and U.W.R.

←CHRISTMAS GREETINGS: This light-hearted Christmas card was printed and sent out by the officers and men of the *Hardy* in December 1939, after they had spent several unproductive weeks scouring the wide expanse of ocean between Africa and South America in pursuit of the German pocket battleship *Graf Spee*. (Bernard Warburton-Lee's personal archive)

↓THE *NORGE*: The ironclad *Norge*, a coastal defence vessel, was the pride of the Norwegian Navy when she was commissioned early in the twentieth century; but by 1940 she had long been ready for the breakers' yard. (Per Askim's unpublished memoirs)

↑FULL SPEED AHEAD: The *Norge*'s sister ship *Eidsvold* was an impressive sight when travelling at top speed, black smoke belching from her twin funnels. But the impression she gave was a false one. Her top speed was a mere 17 knots, only half that of more modern naval vessels. (Per Askim's unpublished memoirs)

←THE NORWEGIAN COMMANDER: In autumn 1939, Commodore Per Askim was plucked from retirement to help safeguard Norway's neutrality and appointed commander of his country's two antiquated coastal defence vessels. He had graduated from naval college top of his entry in 1904 and was one of the Norwegian Navy's most highly esteemed officers. (Chr. Hansen, Tromsø / Ole P. Børmer)

←THE COMMODORE'S WIFE: Signe Askim, born and bred in the naval town of Horten, accompanied her husband northwards when, in March–April 1940, the two ironclads were sent first to Tromsø, then south again to Narvik. (Per Askim's unpublished memoirs)

↑EYEWITNESSES: Both Signe and Per Askim wrote detailed personal accounts of their lives before and during the war, making them important observers of the dramatic events in Narvik. (Per Askim's unpublished memoirs)

←THE COMMANDER: Captain Odd Willoch was one of Norway's most renowned naval officers, not least in consequence of his exploits in the Arctic Ocean in the interwar years. (Ingrid Willoch)

↑THE ORE TOWN: The Swedish town of Kiruna was the site of one of Europe's most outstanding industrial undertakings. The mountains ringing the town hold one of the world's largest and richest deposits of iron ore. (Bundesarchiv, Filmarchiv / Transit Film GmbH)

←THE OFOT RAILWAY: The Ofot railway snakes its way down from the Swedish border to Narvik through tunnels and snow sheds to the export terminal at the head of the Ofot fjord. (Scan from Fritz-Otto Busch: *Narvik. Vom Heldenkampf deutscher Zerstörer*)

↑THE ORE TRAINS: From the Swedish mines in Kiruna, the roughly crushed ore was conveyed by rail across the mountains to the ice-free Norwegian port of Narvik, 160km distant. Every day, twenty to twenty-five heavily laden trains made the journey westwards, carrying ore with an iron content of 60 to 70 per cent. (Bundesarchiv, Filmarchiv / Transit Film GmbH)

↑NARVIK: Early in the twentieth century, iron ore exports created Narvik, and by the early 1930s some 6 to 7 million tonnes of ore were being shipped out annually. Most of it found its way to Hitler's arms factories. (Source unknown)

↑THE ORE QUAY: Built of granite, the 400m-long ore quay could accommodate three ore carriers at a time. A standard 5,000-tonner could be fully loaded in the space of eight hours. (Bundesarchiv, Filmarchiv / Transit Film GmbH)

↑MOUNTAIN FASTNESS: The Ofot railway wound its way through the trackless mountains encompassing the Rombak fjord, making the journey between Kiruna and Narvik a truly breathtaking experience. (Bundesarchiv, Filmarchiv / Transit Film GmbH)

→THE REPORTER: A nephew of Winston Churchill, Giles Romilly was only 23 when he was sent to Narvik in early April 1940 by London's *Daily Express*. (Scan from Giles Romilly, *The Privileged Nightmare*)

→THE WAR LEADER: In the winter and spring of 1940, Winston Churchill rose to become the Allies' foremost war leader and played a large part in the early planning of the Narvik campaign. (Source unknown)

↑THE SUPPLY SHIP: En route from Murmansk, the German whale factory ship *Jan Wellem* dropped anchor in Narvik harbour in the afternoon of Monday 8 April with a full cargo of fuel and provisions on board. For many hours after the German invasion, Churchill and other highly placed people in London erroneously believed that the ship also carried German troops. (Bundesarchiv, Filmarchiv / Transit Film GmbH)

↑'PEACE FOR OUR TIME': On his arrival at London's Heston aerodrome on 30 September 1938, after his visit to Munich, Prime Minister Neville Chamberlain triumphantly holds aloft the agreement signed with Hitler. (Wikimedia Commons)

↑BETRAYAL: Chamberlain, Daladier, Hitler and Italy's foreign minister, Count Ciano, after their negotiations in Munich at the end of September 1938. The Western powers gave in to Hitler's demands and, in the hope of securing peace, handed Czechoslovakia's Sudetenland over to him. When, despite this infamous submission, war came one year later, Britain and France were still mentally and materially unprepared for the trials that lay ahead. (Bundesarchiv / Wikimedia Commons)

↑OUTSIDE THE FOREIGN OFFICE: Britain's Foreign Minister Lord Halifax (right) and his Permanent Under Secretary Alexander Cadogan. Cadogan kept a detailed diary of developments in Britain throughout the war. (Source unknown)

↗HITLER'S RIGHT-HAND MAN: General Alfred Jodl (centre) was the Wehrmacht's Chief of Operations on the Führer's staff and was nearly always present when important decisions were taken. His tersely worded personal diary is thus a valuable key to understanding what went on at the conferences held in the Reichs Chancellery in the spring of 1940. (Source unknown)

→THE CORRESPONDENT: The most famous of the international reporters in Europe up to 1941 was CBS's William Shirer who, in his broadcasts from Berlin, kept his listeners up to date with the progress of the war. (Scanpix / Corbis)

↑THE MILITARY LEADERS: The Allies' top-ranking army chiefs photographed in France in the spring of 1940, together with Winston Churchill. Left to right: Britain's Chief of the Imperial General Staff, General Edmund Ironside; Churchill; General Maurice Gamelin, Commander-in-Chief of the French Army; and the two commanders of the northern sector on the Western Front, Generals Lord Gort and Alphonse Georges. While the British Army was extremely weak, the French had more than 1 million men under arms. In terms of weaponry and morale, however, they were in a sorry state and were quickly routed when the Germans attacked in May 1940. (Source unknown)

←FELL FROM FAVOUR: The British Commander-in-Chief of the land forces sent to Narvik, Major General Pierse Mackesy, was widely thought to possess one of the best brains in the army. Until he became involved in the Narvik campaign, he was tipped for one of its top jobs. (Pierse Mackesy's personal archive)

↑**THE GO-BETWEEN:** General Edward Spears (centre) was an MP and in spring 1940 liaised between London and Paris. His memoirs, *Assignment to Catastrophe*, do much to lift the veil from the activities of the Allied leaders in the critical weeks preceding and following the German invasion of Norway. (Scan from Edward Spears, *Assignment to Catastrophe*)

↑**RESIGNED**: French Prime Minister Édouard Daladier (right) resigned in March 1940 when his policy of appeasement proved an abject failure. He detested his successor, Paul Reynaud, and did his utmost to disparage him. Seen with him here is Nazi Germany's foreign minister, Joachim von Ribbentrop. (Scanpix / akg-images)

↑AGREED TO WILFRED: Prime Minister Paul Reynaud sanctioned both Operation Wilfred and Operation Royal Marine, but the latter was cancelled when Daladier vetoed it. (Scanpix / TopFoto)

↑THE EMISSARY: The Norwegian ambassador, Erik Colban, was assured by the British that they would not act against the ore traffic and seemingly believed what he had been told. (Scanpix / TopFoto)

←THE NORWEGIAN COMMANDER: General Carl Gustav Fleischer distinguished himself in the battle for Narvik in the spring of 1940, but in the first week of April not even he appears to have grasped the gravity of the situation, as he left Narvik on a pointless inspection tour of eastern Finnmark, 1,000km distant. (The Armed Forces Museum of Norway)

↑EMBARKATION: The 2,000 soldiers of Germany's 139th Mountain Regiment boarding the ten destroyers moored alongside the Columbus Quay in Bremerhaven on Saturday 6 April 1940. Few of the men were aware of their destination, for their orders were in sealed envelopes which they were forbidden to open until the ships were at sea. (Bundesarchiv, Filmarchiv / Transit Film GmbH)

→THE CHRONICLER: Lieutenant Hermann Laugs (standing, far right) was gunnery officer of the *Hans Lüdemann*. He has provided a vivid description of his experiences in his book *Kampf um der Erzbahn*, the best of the propagandistic accounts published in Germany after the occupation of Narvik. (Scan from Herman Laugs, *Kampf um die Erzbahn*)

←DESTROYER COMMANDER: Commodore Friedrich Bonte commanded the German destroyer flotilla, flying his flag in the *Wilhelm Heidkamp*. Together with several of the officers on his staff, he was killed when the destroyer was torpedoed in Narvik harbour on 10 April 1940. (Scan from Fritz-Otto Busch, *Narvik. Vom Heldenkampf deutscher Zerstörer*)

↑THE VOYAGE NORTH: The 2,100km voyage from Bremerhaven to Narvik has just begun. Here, in the Jade Bight, the weather is still good. (Scan from Fritz-Otto Busch, *Narvik. Vom Heldenkampf deutscher Zerstörer*)

↑STORM: Both the North Sea and the Norwegian Sea were dominated by the Royal Navy, which meant that the German expeditionary force took an enormous risk in setting out for Norway. Two violent storms, the first from the south-west, the second from the north-west, made the voyage extremely unpleasant for the soldiers crowded below deck. (Scan from Fritz-Otto Busch, *Narvik. Vom Heldenkampf deutscher Zerstörer*)

←ON THE BRIDGE: A sharp lookout was maintained on the *Wilhelm Heidkamp* after the expeditionary force was sighted by a British aircraft off the coast of Jutland on the morning of 7 April. (Scan from Fritz-Otto Busch, *Narvik. Vom Heldenkampf deutscher Zerstörer*)

←POOR VISIBILITY: The blinding snow made it extremely difficult for the German destroyers to keep station as they entered the Vestfjord. (Bundesarchiv, Filmarchiv / Transit Film GmbH)

←HEAVY DESTROYERS: Germany's 1934-class destroyers had a displacement of some 3,300 tonnes, a top speed of 38 knots and carried five 12.7cm guns. This made them considerably larger and more heavily armed than their British counterparts. The painting is of *Z13*, the *Erich Koellner*. (Ullstein Bild / Olaf Rahardt)

↑**A CONTROVERSIAL ISSUE:** Herbert Friedriches's handling of the 1936-class destroyer *Hans Lüdemann*, both as regards her clash with the *Glowworm* and her subsequent performance in Narvik, was severely criticised by his fellow officers. (Ullstein Bild / Süddeutsche Zeitung Photo / Scherl)

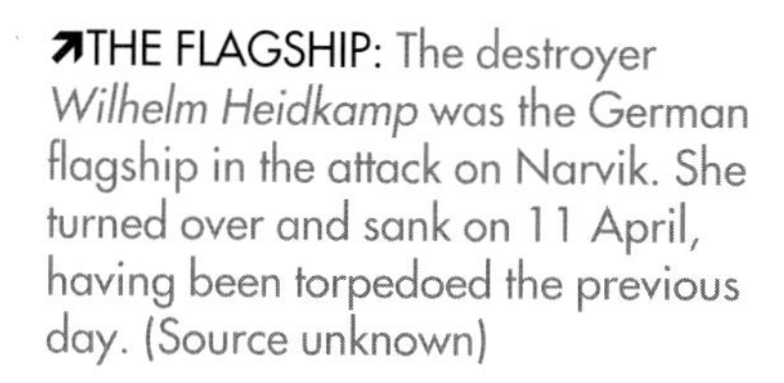

↗**THE FLAGSHIP:** The destroyer *Wilhelm Heidkamp* was the German flagship in the attack on Narvik. She turned over and sank on 11 April, having been torpedoed the previous day. (Source unknown)

→**ONE OF THE ELITE:** Max-Eckart Wolff took his destroyer, the *Georg Thiele*, into Narvik harbour as second in line and subsequently distinguished himself in the engagements in the Vestfjord. Awarded the Knight's Cross of the Iron Cross for his achievements, following his post-war denazification he rose to the rank of admiral in the Bundesmarine. (Scanpix / Corbis)

↑FIRST INTO NARVIK: Commanded by Lieutenant Commander Curt Rechel, the *Bernd von Arnim* was the first German destroyer to enter Narvik harbour, where she sank the *Norge* after a brief engagement. Rechel was a recipient of the Knight's Cross of the Iron Cross when he returned to Germany later in 1940. (Ullstein Bild / Heinrich Hoffman)

←REGIMENTAL COMMANDER: From 1933 onwards, Colonel Konrad Sundlo was commander of the Norwegian forces based in Narvik. An ardent supporter of Nazism and an admirer of both Hitler and Quisling, after the war he was sentenced to life imprisonment for treason. It should be noted that this was because of his activities as a Nazi-appointed district governor during the occupation, not because of his conduct when the Germans invaded. He was acquitted by the Supreme Court on charges of having surrendered Narvik to General Dietl in the morning of 9 April. (Scanpix)

↑↓THE END: Lieutenant Commander Gerard Roope and his gallant shipmates on board the *Glowworm* make smoke in the Norwegian Sea west of the island of Frøya shortly before nine o'clock in the morning of Monday 8 April 1940, as the heavy German cruiser *Hipper* closes in. The *Glowworm* had no chance against her vastly superior opponent and went down a quarter of an hour later. Bottom: Of the 149 men on board, only forty were saved. In a letter to the British authorities after the war, the *Hipper*'s captain, Vice Admiral Hellmuth Heye, praised Roope and his men for their bravery, with the result that in 1945 Gerard Roope was awarded a posthumous VC. (Atle Wilmar's Collection; Scanpix / akg-images)

↑↓THE IRONCLADS: Prompted by veiled threats in the Allied press, on Saturday 30 March the Norwegians decided to transfer their two veteran coastal defence vessels from Tromsø to Narvik, which they reached on Monday 1 April. Despite this precaution, when, one week later, on the instructions of the War Cabinet and Churchill himself, Vice Admiral Tom Phillips informed the Norwegian embassy in confidence of the German fleet movements and the threat they posed to Narvik, Oslo did not take the warning seriously. The men of the ironclads only went to action stations when the German destroyers passed the guard line in the outer reaches of the Ofot fjord shortly before 03.20 on 9 April 1940. (Erling Skjold's Collection; Atle Wilmar's Collection)

←MINELAYING: Four converted I-class British destroyers laid 234 horned mines in the Landego fjord north of Bodø early in the morning of Monday 8 April, thus effectively cutting off supplies of Swedish iron ore to Nazi Germany. Seen here is the *Express*, which took part in this operation. (Source unknown)

↑THE BJERKVIK LANDING: Three German destroyers, the *Wolfgang Zenker*, *Erich Koellner* and *Hermann Künne*, set 600 mountain troops ashore in Bjerkvik Bay in the morning of 9 April without meeting resistance. This was primarily because the majority of the Norwegian troops stationed at nearby Elvegårdsmoen Camp had been transferred to Narvik a few hours earlier. Reinforcements from Indre Troms, further to the north, were held up by snowbound roads and failed to arrive in time. The German regimental commander, Colonel Alois Windisch, and his battalion commander, Major Wolf Hagemann, were thus able to occupy the two depots without a shot being fired. The photograph was taken aboard the *Erich Koellner*, which ran aground, delaying the landing of men and equipment until 18.00 on 9 April, when the destroyer was hauled off by the *Erich Giese*, a straggler. (Scan from Fritz-Otto Busch, *Narvik. Vom Heldenkampf deutscher Zerstörer*)

➔THE OCCUPATION OF NARVIK: From five in the morning until late in the afternoon of 9 April a total of 1,000 German and Austrian mountain troops were set ashore in Narvik – 600 in the first wave, from the *Bernd von Arnim, Georg Thiele* and *Wilhelm Heidkamp,* followed by a further 400 at about 14.00 hours from the *Anton Schmitt* and *Hans Lüdemann* (which had been engaged in a vain search on both sides of the entrance to the Ofot fjord for coastal fortifications that had never been built). The smaller vessels moored alongside the quays are the Norwegian guard ships *Kelt, Senja* and *Michael Sars,* which had surrendered without offering resistance and returned to Narvik. (Bundesarchiv)

➔DIETL GOES ASHORE: General Eduard Dietl (right) and his operations officer, Lieutenant Colonel Robert Bader, on board a pinnace taking them to the steamship quay in Narvik. The photograph was probably taken at about half past five in the morning of 9 April. Lieutenant Hans Rohr and some of his fellow mountain troops are seen here lowering themselves into the waiting pinnace from the deck of the *Wilhelm Heidkamp.* (Bundesarchiv, Filmarchiv / Transit Film GmbH)

←THE MOUNTAIN GENERAL: As a youthful lieutenant, in about 1920, Eduard Dietl, a fanatical Nazi, gave Adolf Hitler, who was then virtually unknown, an opportunity to deliver his first public speech in a military encampment near Munich. It was a gesture the future dictator never forgot, and as a result Dietl rose rapidly through the ranks when Hitler came to power in 1933. It was widely thought that Dietl had been promoted far beyond his true capabilities and that, after his taking of Narvik, his depiction as a military genius was sheer propaganda. (Bundesarchiv)

→THE LANDING: It took the German troops a mere two hours to occupy all strategic positions in the ore town – in a lightning manoeuvre that amazed the journalists who witnessed it. The defenders, traumatised by the brutal sinking of the *Eidsvold* and *Norge*, made no attempt to halt the landing. (Scan from Herman Laugs, *Kampf um die Erzbahn*)

→UNDER GERMAN GUNS: The Norwegian ore carrier *Cate B* (8,000grt) had unloaded 8,000 tonnes of grain from Buenos Aires in ports along the west coast before putting into Narvik on Monday 8 April. The *Cate B* was set ablaze and sank on 13 April. (Erling Skjold's Collection)

↑↗FEVERISH ACTIVITY: With the exception of the *Jan Wellem*, none of the German supply ships sent north reached Narvik, with the consequence that all the equipment and provisions that could be spared were taken ashore from the German destroyers. The quays were the scene of frantic activity all day on 9 April.
Left: (Bernard Warburton-Lee's personal archive)
Right: (Bundesarchiv, Filmarchiv / Transit Film GmbH)

↑INSIDE THE HERJANG FJORD: The *Wolfgang Zenker* at anchor off Bjerkvik in the safety of the Herjang fjord. (Erling Skjold's Collection)

↑THE ARMY COMMANDERS: General Eduard Dietl in conversation with the men of Major Wolf Hagemann's battalion. The photograph was probably taken on the small quay at Bjerkvik. On the left is Colonel Alois Windisch, veteran commander of the 139th Mountain Regiment. (Scan from Fritz Otto Busch, *Narvik. Vom Heldenkampf deutscher Zerstörer*)

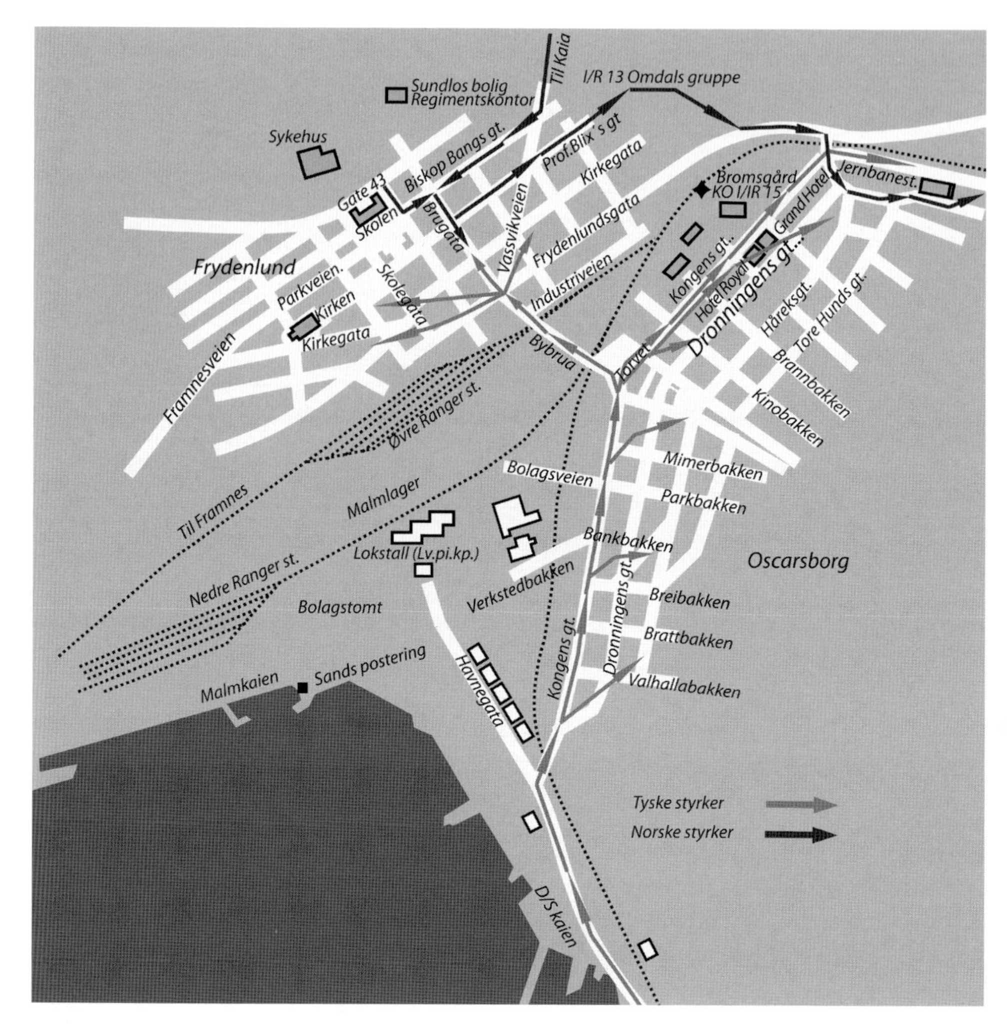

↑STREET PLAN OF NARVIK: The main German force landed at the three jetties jutting out from the steamship quay and quickly made their way to the marketplace, where the Norwegian commander surrendered. The foreign journalists and Norwegian Army officers in bed at the Royal and Grand hotels in King's Street (Kongens Gate) were taken completely by surprise by the speed of the German advance. The Norwegian positions on the ore quay and around the pillboxes on Fagernes Point (not shown, but probably located in the lower right-hand corner of the map) were armed with machine guns and manned by some fifty to 100 infantrymen. They failed to open fire when the Germans landed and surrendered without resistance. (Map: Alvin Jensvold, *Narvik 1940*)

↑THE *SCHARNHORST*: Together with her sister ship *Gneisenau*, the battlecruiser *Scharnhorst* escorted the German destroyer flotilla from Bremerhaven to Bodø, where both turned north-westwards to take up station between the islands of Senja and Jan Mayen. Off the Røst Bank the two were surprised by the British battlecruiser *Renown* and Warburton-Lee's destroyers, but after a brief engagement they made their escape to the north in a storm. (Bundesarchiv, Filmarchiv / Transit Film GmbH)

→HOME FLEET COMMANDER: Admiral Charles Forbes commanded the British Home Fleet, but failed to discern the Germans' intentions when the alarm went on Sunday 7 April. In consequence, his superior force was unable to intercept the attackers before they reached their destinations in Norway. (Source unknown)

↓HMS *RENOWN*: The British battlecruiser *Renown* was distant escort for Warburton-Lee's destroyer flotilla and the minelayers under its protection, and from the night of 8 April it was cruising off Lofoten Point. She was armed with six 38cm guns as opposed to the nine 28cm guns carried by the *Scharnhorst* and *Gneisenau*. But the *Renown* was notorious for her poor seakeeping properties, and in the storm that was raging at the time was unable to keep up when the Germans increased speed following an engagement on the Røst Bank on the night of 8–9 April. (Scanpix / TopFoto)

S. 1320f. **NAVAL MESSAGE.** (Established—May,) (Revised October, 1935.

For use in Signal Department only.

Originators Instructions: (Indication of Priority, Intercept Group, etc.) MOST IMMEDIATE.

No. of Groups.

TO: B.C. One (R) C-in-C H.F., C.S. One., C.S. 18., C.S. Two.

FROM: ADMIRALTY.

Write across

The force under your orders is to concentrate on preventing any German forces proceeding to NARVIK.

1850/8.

↑THE DECISIVE ORDER: At 18.50 on Monday 8 April Churchill ordered the commander of the battlecruiser squadron, Vice Admiral William Whitworth, flying his flag in the *Renown*, to cordon off the Vestfjord. But Whitworth did not believe that the Germans would dare to enter the fjord in the prevailing storm and decided to ride it out until the wind died down. This was a tactical error that would cost the Allies dear. (Bernard Warburton-Lee's personal archive)

↑NARVIK HARBOUR: A German destroyer can be seen far left behind the German ore carrier *Altona*, which masks the whale factory ship *Jan Wellem*. On the right is the British steamship *Blythmoor*. The photograph was taken in the morning of 9 April. (Erling Skjold's Collection)

to take up arms to defend their homeland. Instead, his hour-long report was more a plea for the defence – justification of *his* policy of neutrality and *his* interpretation of international law.

'We hope that the Great Powers will respect this, our right, in this war and that they will abide by it when the war is over,' he said in his final appeal, which was directed at politicians who were, in his eyes, cynical exponents of *realpolitik* in London, Paris and Berlin. 'We believe that lasting peace in the world is inconceivable on any other basis. We ourselves will do everything in our power to safeguard our national independence. It is our duty to our country and our duty to the future.'

Pious words they may have been, but nothing was done to back them up. When, that same morning, the Chief of the General Staff, Colonel Rasmus Hatledal, begged for permission to mobilise, the government rejected his plea outright.

A few hours later, Koht was offered another opportunity to change course. The President of the Storting, Carl Joachim Hambro, received a telephone call from Prime Minister Johan Nygaardsvold, who was worried by the foreign minister's silence and aloofness: 'He never talks with us, but now and again he tells you something,' he said.

'Hambro phoned Koht Saturday evening and asked him if there was any news that should be communicated to the Standing Committee on Foreign Affairs,' wrote the President's nephew, Johan Hambro, in his post-war biography of his uncle, *C. J. Hambro: Life and Dream*. The leader of the Conservative Party was becoming increasingly anxious and had asked members of the committee to be ready to attend an emergency meeting on Sunday. To no avail: not even the President of the Parliament could persuade the foreign minister to see reason. 'Koht answered in the negative,' he wrote bluntly.

At just about the same time as the minelayers and Warburton-Lee's escorting destroyers were weaving their way through the anti-submarine nets guarding Sullom Voe, two blacked-out trains left Berlin heading north across the flat expanse of the North German Plain. General Eduard Dietl and his 3rd Mountain Division had been cooped up in barracks and encampments around the capital since early March, and most of the men were relieved that the waiting was at an end.

'Saturday morning the weather was glorious and the spring sunshine warmed the men in the two long trains chugging across Lüneberg Heath towards the distant North Sea,' wrote Gerda-Luise Dietl and Kurt Herrmann in their joint biography of the general, *General Dietl, Das Leben eines Soldaten*. 'Looking out through the windows of the train could be glimpsed the faces of incredulous Austrians who had never seen the sea or the northern regions of Germany before. But they were all in high spirits and most of them were looking to the future with confidence.'

Ten hours later the two trains came to a halt before Lloyd Hall on the Columbus Quay in Bremerhaven, from which, around the turn of the century, millions of emigrants had bade Europe farewell and boarded ships bound for the New World. Now the terminal was sealed off, and along the kilometre-long wharf, not a civilian vessel was to be seen, only the grey superstructures of ten sleek destroyers.

'The men of the 139th Regiment clambered stiffly down from the train in growing amazement,' wrote Lieutenant Albert Bach who, together with his opposite number on the navy staff, Commander Heinrich Gerlach, had drawn up the detailed embarkation plans. 'They still had no idea of what lay ahead, and it was only at this moment that the company commanders were handed the folders containing the actual operations orders. But the folders were sealed and it was strictly forbidden to break them open until the destroyers had put to sea.'

Throughout the afternoon and evening, the 2,000 soldiers were divided among the destroyers, which were under the command of Commodore Friedrich Bonte on board the flagship, the *Wilhelm Heidkamp*. Bach wrote:

> Bonte was a great bear of a man, good-looking and possessed of many endearing qualities. He made no attempt to downplay the difficulties facing us because of the Royal Navy's supremacy at sea. But at the same time he radiated calm and was optimistic about our ability to achieve our object. He hoped that the British would be taken by surprise and that luck would be with us.

While hundreds of sailors and infantrymen were engaged in stowing ammunition and provisions below deck, motorcycles, mortars, field guns and other heavy equipment were lashed to the rails:

> With a displacement of 3,400 tonnes and a complement of some 300 men, every destroyer was a fighting machine pure and simple; every space, every passageway, was utilised to the maximum. For landlubbers like us, it was already terribly cramped. But we had no choice: we had to find room for 200 men with their backpacks and small arms.

Whereas Bach and his immediate superior, Lieutenant Colonel Robert Bader, were fortunate in being able to share a cabin, for the rank and file there was no such luxury. 'They were packed on the orlop deck like sardines, squeezing out the sailors, who slept in shifts on the deck, which in some places was inch-deep in swirling water.'

Not surprisingly, after several days without proper rest, the young lieutenant was worn out. In the confines of the cabin he fell into a deep sleep the moment his head touched the pillow and thus missed the ship's departure at 22.00 that same Saturday. 'But I knew we were setting out on one of the boldest voyages in the annals of war, 2,100km through waters dominated by the enemy. For me, though, there was more to it than that: it was the first time I had been to sea.'

On the neighbouring destroyer, the *Hans Lüdemann*, the ship's gunnery officer, Lieutenant Herrmann Laugs, had buckled to with a will and helped with the loading. 'It was ten before we cast off,' he wrote in his account of the Norwegian campaign, *Kampf um die Erzbahn*. 'The sky above us was glassy clear, like a sheet of silk. The stars were out, but all we thought about was going into action.'

Shortly after leaving port, the voice of the ship's captain, Lieutenant Commander Herbert Friedrichs, came over the loudspeakers: 'The task facing us is both great and formidable. The Führer has ordered that Norway must be safeguarded. We are bound for Narvik. We shall execute his order to the best of our ability – secure in the knowledge of how grateful the Führer will be. Long live Adolf Hitler!'

Silence reigned in cabins and mess rooms throughout the ship. In the semi-darkness, the only sound was an occasional whisper: Narvik? Why? What are we going to do there?

'Fatigue overcame our bewilderment, and as always at sea, most of the men soon fell sound asleep. On the bridge stood the few, watching over the many. All were dreaming of the same thing: their homes, fast receding into the distance.'

Only an hour earlier, similar scenes had been enacted at London's Euston station. Not until 13.00 on Saturday afternoon did Major General Pierse Mackesy receive the Chiefs of Staff's instructions following the War Cabinet's long-overdue decision of the previous day. Once again he was forced to improvise.

Since December 1939 Mackesy's main force of some 4,000 men had been designated the 24th Guards Brigade. It comprised the 1st Battalion Scots Guards, 1st Battalion Irish Guards and 2nd Battalion South Wales Borderers under the command of Colonel William Fraser, a highly experienced Scot who had seen service in the First World War and won the DSO and Military Cross at Ypres and Cambrai. With troops drawn from some of Britain's oldest and most illustrious regiments, on paper the brigade had the appearance of an elite force. But the two Guards battalions had only served in London and the South Wales Borderers had just returned from India, after which they had been stationed in the north of England. The brigade's HQ staff was quartered at Aldershot in the south, where it was manned by recruits who had only very recently been called up.

'The result of this arrangement was that I had never seen my battalions until we met in Norway, although of course I knew the officers of the two Guards battalions,' Colonel Fraser wrote in his unpublished memoirs. 'The time at Aldershot was spent in teaching them to drill, to shoot with the rifle and bren gun, to march, to clean their equipment, to dig, or to put it shortly, in trying to give them some smatterings of general military knowledge and training.'

When Mackesy's marching orders reached Aldershot on Saturday lunchtime, the brigade staff hastily entrained for Waterloo station, whence it was transported by bus and lorry to Euston:

> The battalion HQ and half the 1st Scots Guards, together with certain other oddments, were in the same train. As a great concession my wife and Pat Barttelot were allowed on to the platform to see us start. We had a great send-off. General Boy Brooke, Bill Balfour and a lot of others were there, and I know that some of them at any rate never expected to see us come back.

The Scots and Irish Guards officers set off to war in jubilant mood. Fortified though they already were by many a parting toast, whisky and champagne seem to have flowed freely in the crowded coaches.

At a quarter past nine in the evening of Saturday 6 April – at about the same time as the German destroyers were slipping their moorings in Bremerhaven – two crowded trains steamed out of Euston. It took them twelve hours to reach their destination, Glasgow, where Major General Mackesy was anything but pleased by the orders he had been given. 'The Chiefs of Staff's instructions were that the force was to be prepared and embarked for a purely peaceful landing at an organised port,' he wrote in his report some time later. 'The folly of such a ruling, which was carried out to the full, became painfully obvious at a later stage.'

Some of those who had witnessed the troops' departure on the platform in London had other things to worry about. 'Scandalous rumours have been received about the circumstances in which Mackesy and his senior staff officers left London to embark for Narvik,' the Director of Military Operations, Major General Dewing, wrote in his diary a few days later. 'The A.T.S. driver has reported that they were drunk, shouting "to Narvik" and similar phrases, and would have left papers in the car had she not followed them to the train.'

9

RACE TO THE NORTH

The North Sea and the Norwegian Sea, Sunday 7 April 1940

On board the German destroyer *Wilhelm Heidkamp*, Albert Bach slowly shook himself awake in the grey light of that memorable Sunday morning. 'The ship forged steadily ahead, but I could feel the vibrations of the hull and hear the dull thump of the turbines and boilers labouring away in the engine room below.'

Twenty-nine years of age, Bach had been born in a village in the southern Austrian state of Kärnten in the Austrian Alps. His life's ambition had been to become a soldier, and on completing his secondary education in the autumn of 1930, he had immediately enlisted as a cadet in the Austrian Army – and as a group leader in the local branch of the aggressive, anti-Semitic and fast-growing Nazi Party, whose declared aim was the unification of Germany and Austria. A renowned mountaineer and skier, in the 1936 Winter Olympics Bach had captained his country's national team to fourth place in the military biathlon – after Italy, Sweden and Finland.

When, two years later, Hitler incorporated the diminutive republic into the German Reich, Albert Bach soon reaped his reward. He was promoted to 1st lieutenant in the Wehrmacht, appointed aide-de-camp to General Dietl's Mountain Division and offered a place at Germany's prestigious military academy in Berlin. He still had to wait some months before he could start his training, but his feet were nevertheless firmly planted on the first rung of the ladder leading to a successful military career. He thus had every reason to be satisfied with life when he emerged onto the deck and felt the fresh south-westerly breeze on his cheeks.

'The weather was gorgeous,' he wrote. 'The sun was already above the horizon and the sea was as placid as an alpine lake. But just below me the water was streaming past. I felt quite giddy. The stern wave built up by the propellers seemed to be several metres high!'

The escort, in the shape of the battlecruisers *Scharnhorst* and *Gneisenau*, flagships of Hitler's fleet, had rendezvoused with the destroyers at 02.00 that morning off the Frisian island of Wangerooge, outside the Jade Bight. Shortly afterwards they were joined by the cruiser *Hipper*, along with four destroyers carrying the force earmarked for Trondheim.

The seventeen ships were a majestic sight as they headed north some 30 nautical miles off the coast of Jutland. Sailing line astern in three columns, 1,500m between each column and at a speed of 23 knots, their combined wake seemed to reach the horizon. Bach could see, stretched out on a life raft amidships, one of his shipmates, a man of his own age who happened to come from the same village, basking in the spring sunshine.

'The golden orb of the sun rose ever higher in the sky, bathing the scene in red,' wrote Lieutenant Hans Rohr in his unpublished autobiography, *Tagebuch eines Gebirgsjägers im II. Weltkrieg*. 'Ahead, astern and alongside us we could see the dark hulls of the squadron's warships, while above, the silver birds of the Luftwaffe, there to provide air cover out into the Skagerrak, flew to and fro.'

Rohr, a convivial 28-year-old, was a qualified mountain guide and on his left breast pocket proudly bore the emblem of his calling, a badge comprising an enameled shield with an edelweiss in gold and silver. He had been selected to serve as a platoon commander of the Seventh Company and was destined to accompany his hero, General Eduard Dietl, when the troops were put ashore in Narvik harbour. The enormous risk the landing entailed had been strongly emphasised at that morning's briefing; but it had also been pointed out that fortune favours the brave and the general himself, cheerful and unassuming as always, had strolled about the deck offering words of encouragement. 'He seemed quite at home on the destroyer and chatted and joked with all of us. He was solicitous of our welfare and showed a keen interest in where each of us was from. He carried a bucket in case, he said, "anyone needed to throw up".'

On the bridge it was a different matter. The flotilla commander, Commodore Friedrich Bonte, and the skipper, Lieutenant Commander Hans Erdmenger, studied the bright spring sky with mounting anxiety. Early that same morning the unmistakable sound of a British reconnaissance aircraft had been heard in the distance, and shortly afterwards the flotilla's wireless operators had picked up a signal from the plane reading: '09.48 hours cruisers, destroyers and aircraft at 55.30 north, 7.37 east. Course 350 degrees.'

Dark-haired and ambitious, 36-year-old Erdmenger was one of the few regular officers in the Kriegsmarine to have been born and grown up as far from the sea as it is possible to get in Germany – in Bavaria, in the deep south. It is not surprising then that, early in the 1920s, he should have applied to join the infantry – by coincidence under a young and, at the time, relatively unknown captain by the name of Eduard Dietl. 'But one day the young cadet's yearning for a life on the seven seas grew so strong that he approached his instructor with a request for a transfer to the Navy,' wrote Gerda-Louise Dietl and Kurt Herrmann.

Dietl had approved the transfer, and the young Bavarian would later prove himself worthy of his confidence. Erdmenger was given his first command in 1926, and in the years that followed he gained rapid promotion in the torpedo-boat arm. Tough, enterprising and aggressive, by the spring of 1940 he was looked upon as one of the German Navy's most talented destroyer captains, and his reunion with his former tactics instructor at the Military Academy was a truly warm one. 'By way of thanks, Erdmenger had promised Dietl a pleasant promenade on a proper ship's deck, and he kept his word.'

There was no means of knowing whether, and for how long, the squadron would be allowed to proceed in peace. On Sunday morning it was still west of Esbjerg, with Horns Reef to starboard, and light clouds were beginning to appear on the horizon. The weather was ideal for flying, so there was every reason to believe that the British would do what they could to intercept them. If they were to lose the advantage of surprise, the rest of the voyage was likely to be lively, to say the least.

As Erdmenger wrote in his war diary: 'The wireless signal we picked up reveals that the squadron has already been sighted by the enemy, although the position given differs considerably from our actual position. I ordered the lookouts to keep an extra-sharp watch.'

Erdmenger's anxiety was well-founded. The signal reached the Admiralty in London shortly before 10.00 on Sunday morning and alerted the RAF from Kinloss in the north to Great Yarmouth in the south-east. It wasn't long before the first wave of Bristol Blenheim bombers of 107 Squadron, led by

Wing Commander Basil Embry,[3] took off and set a course for Skagen on the northern tip of Denmark. 'Twelve Blenheims took off from Yarmouth at 11:40. A Hudson reconnaissance aircraft will be over their last position at 12:30, ready to shadow the squadron,' read a signal sent from the Royal Navy base at Rosyth to the Admiralty and Home Fleet.

Churchill had returned to his quarters just before midnight on Saturday after his taxing – and abortive – flight to France, but, although he was over 65, his vitality and capacity for hard work seemed unimpaired. 'Mr. Churchill lived in the top flat of Admiralty House, and he was working almost continuously by day and night,' wrote Captain Richard Pimm, who had converted the library in the floor below the First Lord's bedroom into a private map and conference room, known as the Upper War Room:

> His day started with a visit in his multi-coloured dressing gown to the War Room, generally soon after seven in the morning. With the exception of about two hours' rest each afternoon, he continued hard at it with a short respite for meals until one or two o'clock next morning when he used to pay us a final visit on his way to bed.

The walls of the War Room were covered in enormous maps of the world's oceans, which could be concealed behind heavy curtains. Three officers were on duty around the clock, their task being to plot the last recorded position of every Allied and German naval vessel, convoy and merchant ship, each with an appropriate symbol, accompanied by information relating to enemy attacks, sinkings and shipments that had reached a British port. 'The positions were plotted from signals which came in day and night in a continuous stream. If any signal of importance arrived, a very few moments would elapse before he arrived in the War Room and was in complete possession of all the facts.'

The First Lord set a cracking pace, and many were impressed by the copious draughts of champagne, wine and whisky that accompanied his meals – with no discernible effect on his command of the situation, judgement or vitality. Possessed as he was of seemingly inexhaustible energy, Churchill was an

3 A legend in the RAF, after the war Embry rose to the rank of Air Chief Marshal and was knighted.

outstanding personality who came into his own when Great Britain and the whole of the free world needed a leader of his calibre. He devoted himself wholeheartedly to the task in hand and acted like a shot in the arm for the Admiralty and War Cabinet. When the outlook was blackest and Nazism seemed to be invincible, he kept the flame of hope alive in the mind of the public throughout Europe in a succession of broadcast speeches: *We shall never surrender!*

But Churchill was not infallible, as was to become evident in the next hours and days, following his visit to the War Room that portentous Sunday morning, when he was able to see with his own eyes the marker plotting the position of the German fleet west of Jutland.

Month after month, with unfailing zeal, he had pressed for mining of the Norwegian leads, to be followed by occupation of Narvik and the ore fields in northern Sweden – not only to cut off supplies of ore to Nazi Germany, but also to provoke a German response. Now, at last, Warburton-Lee's and Bickford' s ships were under way, and the mines would be laid within twenty-four hours. Suddenly the German fleet had appeared out of the blue, steaming northwards – without provocation. But against which target? And for what purpose?

'The Admiralty's attention was still singularly concentrated on the possibility that the German battlecruisers would break out into the Atlantic between Shetland and Iceland, threatening the trade routes,' wrote Captain Stephen Roskill in the official naval history of the Second World War, *The War at Sea*, in which – the first to do so – he ventured to criticise Churchill's grasp of the situation and subsequent conduct. Roskill had worked at the Admiralty during the war and derived support from the diaries of Captain Ralph Edwards, who disliked Churchill's overzealous attempts to interfere in matters that, by rights, were the responsibility of officers such as himself. 'WS is taking a great personal interest and tends to interfere with the sailors' business. He is an extraordinary man and has an astonishing grasp of the situation, but I wish he would keep to his own sphere.'

The man ultimately responsible for naval operations was the First Sea Lord, Admiral Sir Dudley Pound. But he had taken the weekend off to fish for salmon at Broadlands, Lord Mountbatten's estate in Hampshire. As officer of the watch, Edwards was alone in the War Room with Churchill and Pound's fiery deputy, Rear Admiral Tom Phillips.

'Rather an uninteresting day except for mutterings from Denmark & the DNI's creatures about movements in North Germany, Kattegat etc. No one except me very interested, but they always think I am an alarmist. It isn't fair really!!' Edwards wrote in his journal that Saturday evening. 'The evening reports tend to show some indications of a German move in the not distant future against Norway. My own personal view is that it's only a matter of hours before it occurs, but I am in the minority.'

Tall and dark, and with the looks of an American film star, Ralph Edwards found it no easy task to handle Phillips and the brilliant and volatile Churchill. However, he had stuck to his guns and given the order that led to aerial reconnaissance of the Jade Bight that Sunday morning. When the report of the northbound German squadron came in, orders were issued to attack it, and Edwards tried to get the mining of the Norwegian leads called off. 'I recommended that Operation *Wilfred* be postponed, but the 1st Lord and Phillips would not agree. Winston is taking a great personal interest. He wants to nurse the fire, but I'm sure he's wrong. An astonishing man.'

Along with Oslo and Stockholm, London had received a number of diplomatic and military warnings of impending German action against Scandinavia but, despite prolonged discussions on the subject of iron ore shipments via Norway, the men who analysed these reports failed to see the overall picture. However, the general alarm, which was despatched on Sunday morning, was specific enough, reading as it did:

> Recent reports suggest a German expedition is being prepared. Hitler is reported from Copenhagen to have ordered unostentatious movement of one division in ten ships by night to land at Narvik, with simultaneous occupation of Jutland. Sweden to be left alone. Moderates said to be opposing the plan. Date given for arrival at Narvik 8 April.

The information was amazingly accurate, but the analysts were not convinced and added a fateful rider: 'All these reports are of doubtful value and may well only be a further move in the war of nerves.'

The Admiralty's principal weapon was the Home Fleet, then lying at anchor in Scapa Flow. It was under the command of Admiral Sir Charles Forbes, who read the report in the comfort of his cabin on board the *Rodney*, later drily noted: 'In light of the later events, it seems reasonable to state that it was extremely unfortunate that the last sentence was included in the message.'

In the Norwegian Sea, Warburton-Lee's destroyers and minelayers were making steady progress as they headed for the island of Røst. A strong wind, which now and again reached gale force, was still blowing from the south-west, so speed was reduced to prevent mines being swept overboard.

'We steered towards the position 67° N 10° E, where our intention was to part company with the minelayers on Sunday evening at 8 o'clock,' wrote Vice Admiral William 'Jock' Whitworth on board HMS *Renown*, which was serving as distant escort. The aging battlecruiser had twice undergone reconstruction and had a bad reputation for its seakeeping properties. Whitworth had himself commanded the 2nd Flotilla, and the *Hardy* and many of the other destroyers had operated with the *Renown* in the Mediterranean and South Atlantic. 'We had no idea that the battlecruiser was nearby and were glad to see her,' Stanning noted.

In spite of frequent squalls of rain and sleet, on Sunday morning Warburton-Lee held a church service on the quarterdeck, though for some unexplained reason the ship's organ was missing. 'Afterwards, he assembled us on the lower deck and disclosed that we were soon going to cross the Arctic Circle,' wrote Torpedoman Leslie Smale. 'Our final destination was a little south of Narvik, where we were to lay mines at dawn on Monday morning. The sea was very heavy and so was the rain, and one couldn't help but feel the extra nip in the air.'

In Scotland, Major General Mackesy and Colonel William Fraser had had a busy morning. The two trains carrying the 1st Battalion Scots Guards, the brigade staff and assorted administrative personnel had arrived in Glasgow that morning after a long and well-lubricated all-night journey. Over on the east coast, in the Firth of Forth, some 3,000 men of the 49th Division were waiting on board four cruisers for Hitler's response to Operation Wilfred – with Bergen and Stavanger as their primary objectives. Meanwhile, destined for Narvik, 1,500 men of the 24th Guards Brigade were embarked on the *Batory*, a luxurious Polish liner anchored in the Clyde estuary at the Tail of the Bank. 'I had a very comfortable cabin on the port side,' wrote Colonel Fraser. 'The *Batory* is a fairly modern ship, and in normal times she plies between Poland and the USA.'

Together with his orderlies and staff, Mackesy, who was in overall command, was quartered on board the cruiser *Aurora*, where Admiral Sir Edward Evans, who was married to the daughter of a Norwegian paper wholesaler and spoke Norwegian, was already installed. Evans, one of the most renowned sailors, adventurers and polar explorers of the early twentieth century, had been second-in-command on Robert Falcon Scott's ill-starred expedition to the South Pole and had barely escaped with his life. 'He is a real fire-eater,' Fraser wrote. 'Some sailors seem to think he is something of a swashbuckler, but they all admit that he is a fine sailor and a fighter. I like him.'

The feelings were not always reciprocated. When, some days later, Evans got to London, Major General Dewing noted in his diary that 'Evans had formed a very bad opinion of Mackesy, who was, I think, in his flagship ready for the old Narvik plan.' What aroused Evans's animosity was the way the Scot drank. Dewing seemed to be less concerned. 'Unless Evans is prepared to make at least a semi-official report, I cannot see that I can take any action.'

The approaching British bombers were spotted at precisely 13.38 on Sunday 7 April by the *Wilhelm Heidkamp*, which by this time had reached a position west of Skagen on the coast of Denmark. 'The air-raid warning was suddenly sounded and the sirens wailed,' wrote Albert Bach, who was standing on the destroyer's open bridge. 'But the planes weren't coming from the west, as we had expected. Instead, they appeared from the clouds in the east, heading straight for us. There were about fifteen British aircraft in tight formation at 10,000 feet, flying on a course at right-angles to our own.'

When the order to open fire was given, the barrage enveloped the ships in a wall of steel. In the course of the next few minutes the *Scharnhorst* alone fired 625 shells of varying calibre at the oncoming aircraft, which, with death-defying courage, continued unwaveringly on their course. 'They released their bombs as though on command. We could see them coming down – probably aimed at the big ships. Enormous fountains of water rose into the air, but none of the ships were hit.'

By two in the afternoon it was all over. The Blenheims pulled up and disappeared into the clouds, which were becoming ever thicker. 'We'd come through all right but now it was a case of steeling ourselves to meet the renewed attacks that were bound to come. We were all aware that it was one hundred per cent sure that the British had discovered that we were on the way north.'

Back at the Admiralty it was nearly 17.00 on the afternoon before the report from Embry's pilots reached Captain Edwards, and a further forty minutes were to elapse before a copy was handed to Admiral Forbes on board HMS *Rodney* at anchor in Scapa Flow.

Close study of the aerial photographs taken during the attack suggested that the German force consisted of at least a battlecruiser, a pocket battleship, three cruisers and twelve destroyers steering north at high speed. The cream of the German Navy, by then they had covered a further 100 nautical miles and were most likely somewhere off the coast of Rogaland in south-western Norway. Four valuable hours had been lost, but interception was still possible, and the admiral acted promptly.

'All ships in harbour were ordered to raise steam,' Fraser wrote. At 20.15 the three battleships, three cruisers and twelve destroyers of the Home Fleet put to sea from Scapa Flow with orders to rendezvous with three more cruisers and eight destroyers at 07.00 on Monday morning.

A vastly superior force was gathered to do battle with the German squadron but, like his superiors Churchill and Rear Admiral Phillips, Forbes seemed to be in a kind of mental straightjacket. The vital importance of Swedish iron ore to Nazi Germany's war effort had been central to most discussions on strategy since well before Christmas, but it never seemed to occur to the admiral that Hitler might take steps to protect his supply lines, and therefore had despatched his Kriegsmarine to conquer Narvik, Trondheim and other ports along the Norwegian coast. Instead, it appears that he assumed that the heavy units were intending to break out into the Atlantic, which was why he accorded priority to closure of the gap between the Faroes and Iceland. As a result, the thirty or so ships at his disposal were directed to the position 61° N 1° E, directly north-east of Shetland, far away from the German invaders, who continued on their way north, close to Norway's west coast.

'What happened was a complete fiasco,' Stephen Roskill wrote in *The War at Sea*. 'The significance of the available intelligence was not understood and much less translated into a powerful and timely counter-offensive.'

In London, Captain Edwards was feeling tired and frustrated after a succession of prolonged discussions with Churchill and Phillips, who were opposed to intervening in Forbes's plans. 'They strongly advised against ordering him into the middle of the North Sea, which would have been the correct strategic position if we were concerned about Norway,' Edwards wrote in his diary. When Pound arrived at around 20.00, the conversation became quite pathetic. 'The old man had been fishing all day and was dead beat, Phillips was tired and the 1st Lord well dined. The result was that they all failed to come to any useful decision. I tried to interest them in Norway, but they were only interested in the battle cruiser problem.'

In Narvik, Giles Romilly spent most of the day at the Royal Hotel with a number of other journalists in an atmosphere of fatalistic calm. 'Expecting disaster, fearful of the counter-warnings and threats which poured from the Third Reich the Norwegians braced their spirits with pessimistic, melancholy courage,' he wrote in his memoirs, *The Privileged Nightmare*:

> In Narvik they said: We must make the best of whatever comes. Sunday was a day of rest, silence and peace. The younger officers of the coastal defence ship *Norge* went skiing into the mountains, hurtling down slopes headlong 30 miles beyond the Swedish border. They gave a party afterwards in the Royal hotel. Wet skis parked against the walls, they sprawled in deep chairs wearing thick sweaters, glowing with zest and health. It was the last holiday they ever took. Less than thirty-six hours later they lay dead, one and all, at the bottom of Narvik harbour.

The crews of the German cruisers and destroyers were ordered to action stations at 19.30. All guns were manned, and on board the *Scharnhorst* the prototype of the first German ship's radar was switched on. 'We are now approaching the breakthrough gap between Norway and Shetland,' the war diary records. This area was viewed as the most dangerous part of the voyage, and the bombing attack was proof that the British were on the alert.

The next six or seven hours would be decisive, and soldiers and sailors alike were on their toes. The wind was blowing harder from the south-west and the destroyers were already finding it hard going. Seasickness was rife and men were lying helpless in the passageways. 'The waves were growing ever bigger, and the ship was tossed about like an eggshell,' wrote Hans Rohr. 'When I was thrown from my bunk for a third time, I could stand it no longer. I remained lying on the deck, oblivious to what was going on around me. I'd never felt so miserable in all my life.'

On the bridge, Albert Bach was also fighting seasickness, but he couldn't stand the stench and stifling atmosphere below deck. 'Somewhere or other in the blackness to starboard lay Bergen, and it was only 160km to Shetland. This was where the danger of a British attack was greatest. All had gone well so far, but what would the night bring? I remained standing on the bridge, where all I could do was to wait – like everyone else on board.'

10

THE MINING OF THE VESTFJORD

Norwegian Sea, Monday 8 April 1940

The mining of the Vestfjord, north of the town of Bodø, began at 04.30 on the morning of Monday 8 April. After battling driving rain and gale-force winds for forty-eight hours, the *Esk*, *Icarus*, *Ivanhoe* and *Impulsive* approached as close as they dared to the shore, then steamed westwards on parallel courses as the mines they carried slid along the launching rails to disappear over the stern.

Three-quarters of an hour later, the task was finished. Six months after Churchill had first broached the question of putting a stop to the ore traffic, a rectangular area 5 x 13 nautical miles in extent had been sown with 234 deadly horn mines, effectively blocking the southern outlet of the Vestfjord. Henceforth ships carrying iron ore from Narvik to Nazi Germany would be compelled to leave the safety of Norway's inshore channel and venture out into international waters, where the Royal Navy lay waiting.

'The weather got much better that evening especially as we turned North inside the Lofoten islands and were sheltered by them,' wrote Lieutenant Geoffrey Stanning on board the *Hardy*:

> Our four ships took up positions at each corner of the area. We steamed up and down at 10 knots waiting for something to happen and admiring the scenery. To the east of us there were snow-covered mountains as far as we could see, and as it got lighter we could see the blue of glaciers. We were all wearing all the clothes we possessed and then were not warm, and one could not help contrasting this life with the sweltering existence in the South Atlantic which we had left only three months before.

On board the Norwegian Navy's guard ship *Syrian*, which happened to be in the neighbourhood, Captain Bernhard Kaaveland reacted immediately when the lookout spotted the minelayers and their destroyer escort. He ordered the 'neutral waters' signal to be hoisted on the old steam trawler's foremast, seized a signal lamp and signalled to the nearest vessel: 'I protest. Leave Norwegian waters.'

The first wireless message reporting the incident was logged at 3rd Naval Defence District HQ in Tromsø at 04.45. In the next few hours a flood of similar signals brought naval defence forces to a state of alert from one end of the country to the other. The destroyer that had received Kaaveland's first warning to the south of the minefield was the *Hunter*, whose youthful South African captain, Lieutenant Commander Lindsay de Villiers, had been given orders to stay put. Accordingly, he hoisted the signal 'Minefield ahead. Heave to for instructions' and followed up by Aldis lamp with 'Do not intend to leave area'.

A few hours earlier, far away to the south, the seventeen ships of the German force had run into a gale that was to test the soldiers' and sailors' endurance to the limit. 'During the night a full south-west gale blew up,' wrote Lieutenant Commander Hans Erdmenger on board the flagship *Wilhelm Heidkamp*. 'The sea was extremely rough. With the wind coming in from astern, the destroyers yawed and rolled violently – up to 40 degrees each way.'

They were under orders to sail in close formation, and the squadron continued to race northwards in the howling wind from 22.00 on at a speed of 26 knots, about 30 nautical miles from the Norwegian coast. In two parallel columns close to the battlecruisers, the destroyers fought desperately to maintain station, but the heavy seas breaking over their sterns continually threatened to drive them off course. 'The destroyers refused to answer the helm and there was an ever-present risk of collision to both port and starboard. It didn't help that we were under orders to maintain wireless silence. It was as black as pitch and it was impossible to see the shapes of the other ships. Bonte had given permission to switch on the stern lights, but in the heavy seas these were mostly under water.'

Below deck, where conditions were just as bad, if not worse, soldiers and sailors alike clung on as best they could and tried to snatch a little sleep on decks overflowing with seawater, vomit and pieces of equipment. In the captain's cabin, Albert Bach was afraid the ship wouldn't last the night:

> At times we had a list of more than 45 degrees, and it took an unbelievably long time before the destroyer righted itself. At least once I was sure that we approached the end. The waves thundered and crashed against the hull and the whole ship shuddered. The stern had been lifted clear of the sea and the propellers were thrashing uselessly in empty air.

In the first grey light of dawn Bach gave up all hope of sleep. At risk to life and limb, he made his way to the bridge to be met by an amazing sight: several lengths of the destroyer's railing had been torn away and most of the heavy equipment stowed on deck had been swept overboard. Only two ships, the *Wilhelm Heidkamp* and *Anton Schmitt*, had managed to remain in contact with the battlecruisers; all the other destroyers had disappeared. 'The sea had taken on a luminous blue-green colour. I estimated that it was 2km between the waves, which were enormously high and capped with angry foam. Whenever we plunged into a trough, the mast tops of the cruisers disappeared from sight.'

It was a totally mind-shattering experience. The only good thing about it was that they had all survived the night and were by then off the coast of Trøndelag, well to the north. The hazardous stretch between the Shetlands and the Stad Peninsula was behind them, and there was still no sign of the Royal Navy.

In Oslo, Foreign Minister Halvdan Koht had been notified of the British mining of the Vestfjord by phone at 06.00 the same morning. The *Syrian*'s alarming message had by then reached the Admiralty staff and the British and French ambassadors had handed over their final notes.

'I immediately rang Prime Minister Nygaardsvold, who had a bedside phone,' Koht wrote in his memoirs, *For Peace and Freedom in Wartime*. 'I said that I thought we ought to have a meeting of ministers at once.' As Koht himself expressed it, 'an avalanche had engulfed the country,' after it had been under threat for months, and German counter-action could be expected any minute. The risk of war was acute but the prime minister would not be hurried. 'He was thinking on more parliamentary lines and said that the government needed to have a joint meeting with the Foreign Affairs Committee in the Storting.'

In the meantime, the officer in overall command, Admiral Henry Diesen, had discussed the delicate situation in the Vestfjord with Commodore Per

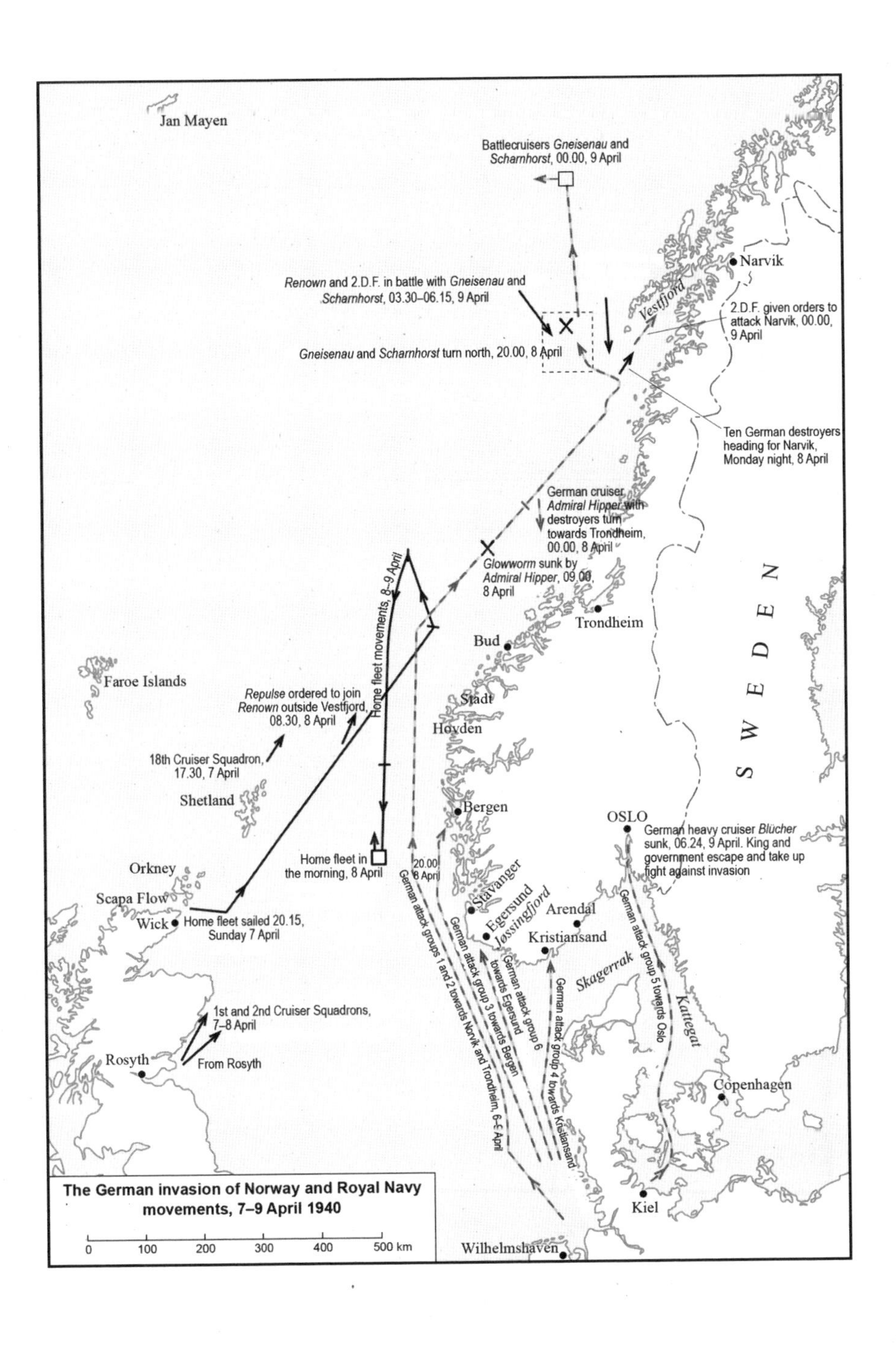

Jan Mayen
Battlecruisers Gneisenau and Scharnhorst, 00.00, 9 April
Narvik
Vestfjord
Renown and 2.D.F. in battle with Gneisenau and Scharnhorst, 03.30–06.15, 9 April
2.D.F. given orders to attack Narvik, 00.00, 9 April
Gneisenau and Scharnhorst turn north, 20.00, 8 April
Ten German destroyers heading for Narvik, Monday night, 8 April
German cruiser Admiral Hipper with destroyers turn towards Trondheim, 00.00, 8 April
Glowworm sunk by Admiral Hipper, 09.00, 8 April
Home fleet movements, 8–9 April
Trondheim
Bud
SWEDEN
Faroe Islands
Stadt
Repulse ordered to join Renown outside Vestfjord, 08.30, 8 April
Hovden
18th Cruiser Squadron, 17.30, 7 April
Shetland
Bergen
OSLO
German heavy cruiser Blücher sunk, 06.24, 9 April. King and government escape and take up fight against invasion
Orkney
Home fleet in the morning, 8 April
20.00 8 April
Stavanger
Scapa Flow
Egersund
Jøssingfjord
Arendal
Wick
Home fleet sailed 20.15, Sunday 7 April
Kristiansand
German attack groups 1 and 2 towards Narvik and Trondheim, 6–8 April
German attack group 3 towards Bergen
German attack group 6 towards Egersund
German attack group 4 towards Kristiansand
German attack group 5 towards Oslo
Skagerrak
Kattegat
1st and 2nd Cruiser Squadrons, 7–8 April
Rosyth
From Rosyth
Copenhagen
Kiel
Wilhelmshaven
The German invasion of Norway and Royal Navy movements, 7–9 April 1940
0
100
200
300
400
500 km

Askim,[4] who, from the *Norge*, had a telephone link with the mainland. All shipping had been brought to a standstill and there was a strong possibility that the British destroyers would launch an attack on the ten German ore carriers at anchor in Narvik harbour.

'Diesen asked if he should open fire on them,' Koht wrote:

> I thought for a moment before telling him that he should. Faced with such an infringement, it was necessary to offer resistance – though that didn't have to mean that we would be at war with Britain. I immediately phoned Nygaardsvold and told him what I had said. He declared himself in agreement.

In Narvik, Askim continued to ponder the alternatives before him. He had immediately given the order to take up action stations when the news from the *Syrian* reached him. But the belligerent order from Koht and Nygaardsvold was never passed on by the Admiralty staff, which instead, at 08.35, telegraphed the commodore as follows:

> If the mines have already been laid, lodge a protest on the spot if this has not already been done. If the mines have *not* been laid or laying is still in progress, act in accordance with clause 17 of the Instructions for the Defence of Norway's Neutrality.

Clause 17 laid down that violations of the nation's neutrality were to be prevented 'by all available means – though not if faced with a substantially superior force'. But the mines had long ago been laid, a protest lodged and the opposing force was overwhelmingly superior to the armed trawler's sole armament, a 76mm cannon. For this reason Askim opted for a compromise solution. He despatched his two submarines, *B1* and *B3*, together with their mother ship, the *Lyngen*, to Liland on the northern shore of the Ofot fjord and ordered Captain Kaaveland to set up a patrol line to the north of the minefield. He himself remained in Narvik with his two venerable ironclads, while retaining a sufficient head of steam to enable him to put to sea at short notice should the need arise.

---

4 Captain Askim had just been promoted commodore as commander of the newly formed Ofoten squadron.

In the vicinity of the minefield in the scenic archipelago north of Bodø, relations between the British destroyers and Norwegian craft were almost convivial. 'A fishing boat was stopped and hailed in English and German but with no result,' Stanning wrote. 'So we wrapped a picture of the area round a potato and threw it onboard and left them to it.' With the passage of time, some five or six cargo vessels approached the cordon and the *Hardy*'s men offloaded many more potatoes. But it is doubtful whether they had any effect for the Norwegians kept the potatoes and threw the paper in which they were wrapped overboard.

Further out to sea, west of Trondheim, two of the German destroyers, the *Hans Lüdemann* and *Bernd von Arnim*, were lagging far behind the rest of the squadron. Both had suffered badly in the night's gale and had had to reduce speed. 'Never in my many years of service on board torpedo boats and destroyers have I experienced such a difficult passage,' Lieutenant Commander Curt Rechel wrote in the *Bernd von Arnim*'s war diary. The 37-year-old Westphalian destroyer captain had spent eighteen years at sea and knew what he was talking about. When, later that morning, the steering gear broke down, leaving the destroyer broadside-on to the still heavy sea for twenty long minutes, Rechel was forced to use all his skill to avoid disaster. 'Only by a concentrated effort and with the aid of the propellers was it possible to right the ship and get her back on course.'

A 1934A-class destroyer with a displacement of 2,200 tonnes, the *Bernd von Arnim* was armed with five quick-firing 12.7cm guns. But her builders had provided the forward sections with too little buoyancy, making her top-heavy. The consequence was that she had a tendency to dig herself down and take on inordinate quantities of water over the forebody. 'What happened that night was a clear indication of the ship's lack of stability and how poor were its seakeeping properties – coupled with the low power of the helm on destroyers of this class,' wrote Rechel, who had survived some nasty hours.

The 2,800 tonnes *Hans Lüdemann* was of the newer and more modern 1936 class and a better ship all round. If there was any doubt attaching to her performance, it had to do with the captaincy and navigational skills of her skipper, Lieutenant Commander Herbert Friedrichs. Round about midnight the destroyer had veered away to starboard and only avoided ramming her neighbour by a hair's breadth. After that, Friedrichs no longer dared to maintain the same high speed and slowed to 21 knots. 'To avoid the danger of a collision, I am bearing away to starboard and falling astern,' he wrote in his war diary.

At 08.00 on the morning of 8 April, Friedrichs was still trying to catch up with the rest of the squadron, but there wasn't another ship in sight. 'Then, dead ahead, I caught a glimpse of a shadowy shape! Or did I? In the rain that was pouring down it was there one moment, gone the next,' wrote gunnery officer Hermann Laugs. The sea was still running high but the wind had dropped a little. 'After a while we could see the other ship more clearly. It was a destroyer proceeding on a parallel course in the opposite direction, as forlorn as ourselves and equally battered by the waves.'

When the other vessel was some 5km away, it suddenly changed course and took up a position parallel to the *Hans Lüdemann*. Only after several unsuccessful attempts to establish each other's identity by signal lamp did Friedrichs and Laugs realise that the destroyer was British:

> Alarm bells rang throughout the ship. Fifty seconds later we had our guns ready to fire. For the first time we were face to face with the enemy in the bright light of day. I felt an inner calm. I knew that we had to get in the first shot. We had to destroy our opponent.

The ship the *Hans Lüdemann* had so unexpectedly encountered was HMS *Glowworm*, which had left Scapa Flow late on Friday evening as part of the battlecruiser *Renown*'s close escort. Due east of the Orkneys, the destroyer had lost a man overboard and Admiral Whitworth had given the *Glowworm*'s captain, Lieutenant Commander Gerard Broadmead Roope, permission to leave the formation and try to find him. The gale had blown the 1,300-tonne destroyer off course and for long periods at a time she was forced to reduce speed to a minimum and ride out the storm where she was. The gyro-compass had been damaged, and it was only late that night that the *Glowworm* had been able to set out on the long voyage that would take her from Halten Bank to Lofot Point – more than two days late.

The encounter with the German destroyer in the midst of a raging sea had come as a surprise, but Roope immediately ordered his men to action stations. At 08.07 the wireless operator transmitted the following resolute signal: 'Engaging enemy destroyer.' It was a gallant gesture in the best traditions of the Royal Navy, but on board the *Hans Lüdemann* the commander of the 3rd Destroyer Flotilla, Commander Hans-Joachim Gadow, had intervened. 'In view of the main task, it is necessary as long as possible to avoid any engagement before reaching Narvik. We must therefore withdraw.' Frustrated, Friedrichs had no option but to increase speed to 35 knots and flee the *Glowworm*'s salvoes, which fell harmlessly into the retreating destroyer's wake.

Just minutes later, the *Bernd von Arnim* unwittingly entered the scene from the south-west. With the *Glowworm* dead ahead to starboard, Curt Rechel had no choice: 'The distance between us was rapidly decreasing,' he wrote in his war diary. 'It was impossible to avoid battle. I opened fire at a range of 6,000 metres.' For the next hour the two destroyers continued to exchange fire, with the *Hans Lüdemann* as an idle spectator. 'I would really have appreciated it if she had come to our aid,' Rechel wrote. 'Instead I received a signal reading: You should think of your prime task!' This unexpected admonition only served to increase the young skipper's exasperation, causing him to append an acid comment to his own report: 'Even without this admonitory finger I was very well aware of what my prime task was. But in the circumstances I was forced to give battle.'

At about 08.30 Rechel made smoke and increased speed to 35 knots. 'But we had just reached 33 knots when the forebody was engulfed by a breaking wave. The bridge plating and the portholes in the wheelhouse were staved in, while on the port side the controls of the torpedo battery had been wrenched loose. The air was full of glass splinters and the bridge was half a metre deep in water. We heeled so far over that it seemed as though the destroyer was going to capsize and plunge into the depths.' After several nerve-racking minutes, Rechel managed to regain control of the stricken vessel and resume the battle. He was laying a second smokescreen when the muzzle flash of a bigger ship momentarily coloured the horizon red. 'Because of the smoke we first took it to be another enemy vessel. Our attempts to make contact elicited no response. Only when it could clearly be seen through the rangefinders did we realise that it was the *Hipper* coming to sort things out.'

With the appearance of the heavy cruiser, it was only a matter of time before it was all over. In the next fifteen minutes shells rained down on the *Glowworm*, which fought heroically against a vastly superior opponent. Hits on the superstructure soon transformed the destroyer into a blazing inferno. Lieutenant Commander Roope fought to the last and continued to fire torpedoes until, emerging from the smokescreen he had laid, he found himself close up against the *Hipper*. Without hesitation he rammed her, stripping off 40m of the heavy cruiser's armour plating and her starboard torpedo tubes, causing 500 tonnes of water to enter the *Hipper*'s hull. But for the *Glowworm* and the men aboard her, the collision was the beginning of the end. The bow was gone and the whole forepart of the ship was on fire. When, ten minutes later, the boilers exploded, the destroyer disappeared beneath the waves in seconds.

Forty of the ship's complement of 149 were rescued by the *Hipper*, but Roope himself, cold and exhausted after swimming in the icy water, lost his grip as he strove to climb to safety and sank helplessly into the depths. Thirty-five years old at his death, he was posthumously awarded a well-deserved VC.

At the Admiralty, Churchill, Pound and Phillips had followed the agonising signals from the *Glowworm* with mounting dismay. The final signal came in at about 09.00 on Monday morning: 'One unknown ship bearing 000 steering 180, in 65.06, 6.20.' After that, nothing more was heard from the stricken destroyer and there was every reason to fear the worst. 'At 0904 she made her last signal which faded out,' wrote Admiral Charles Forbes on board the *Rodney*, which was then between Shetland and the Stad Peninsula, 500km south-west of the battle. 'I thought it probable that she had been sunk.'

The formal and always immaculately dressed Forbes was considered by many to be a first-class administrator, but not a bold and innovative commander-in-chief. Air reconnaissance was made difficult by the atrocious weather in the Norwegian Sea, but radio direction finding and the reported position indicated that the German ships that had been in action against the *Glowworm* to the west of Trondheim could well have been part of the fleet that had been sighted off Jutland the previous day. 'If so, they would have had to make good over 27 knots, which was unlikely but not impossible,' the admiral wrote.

Despite being aware of the enemy fleet's probable position, Forbes stuck to his original belief that the Germans were intending to break out into the Atlantic and allowed the bulk of the Home Fleet to continue on its current course at a rate of 22 knots, under orders to observe strict wireless silence. The battlecruiser *Repulse* was sent ahead to the *Glowworm*'s estimated position, together with the light cruiser *Penelope* and four escorting destroyers, while the battlecruiser's sister ship, the *Renown*, sailed southwards past Lofotodden Point at her best possible speed. The ships were the arms of a pincer movement, and Forbes was optimistic as to its outcome: 'If bound for the Vest fiord, the enemy [should be] met and cut off at 13.30.'

Back at the Admiralty, opinions were divided and the discussion grew heated. New information regarding the position of the German fleet kept coming in. Edwards was convinced that a full-scale invasion of Norway was in progress, but the others present disagreed with him. 'A lack of firm decision,' he scribbled on his desk calendar. 'All the Senior officers very tired, and DCNS Phillips, who normally has a masterly grip, allowed himself to be carried with the crowd. The fleet is still steaming madly to the north. I wanted to cram the Kattegat with ships, but was outvoted and made to look rather stupid.'

At a quarter to eleven, another order was issued from the Admiralty, directing all destroyers, including those patrolling the newly laid minefield, to join the *Renown*. The intentions were of the best, as the battlecruiser was alone off the Lofotens, apart from one destroyer, the *Greyhound*. But the consequences were disastrous: the order left the Vestfjord open to the German squadron fast approaching from the south. Forbes wrote: 'This message, which led to the Vest fiord being left without any of our forces in patrol in it, had a very far-reaching effect.' Vice Admiral Whitworth put it more strongly: 'That there was such a mess, was in my opinion chiefly due to the manner in which the Admiralty mishandled the whole situation.'

Lieutenants Geoffrey Stanning and Edward Clark had just returned from a visit to a large cargo vessel, where they had handed over a chart showing the position of the minefield, when the Admiralty's order reached the *Hardy*. 'We did not know why this was, and I cannot be certain now that we knew either of the loss of *Glowworm* or the German expedition to Norway,' Stanning wrote. The wind was shifting and a new storm centre was building further out to sea. 'There was still a very heavy sea when we got outside the Lofoten islands. The visibility was bad, and we did the heaviest rolling I have ever experienced.'

As soon as the *Glowworm*'s signals started coming in at about 08.00, on his own initiative Vice Admiral Whitworth, another cautious man, had turned the *Renown* about and set a course south. With the wind dead ahead, the battlecruiser soon came up against the full force of the waves. 'It was reported that the ship was working heavily,' Whitworth wrote in his report of proceedings. 'The upper strake of the port bulge was peeling away from the ship's side. Speed was therefore reduced to avoid extension of the damage.' The *Greyhound* and *Renown* continued to fight against wind and wave for a few more hours before the vice admiral gave up. 'In the visibility which was now reduced to two or three miles there was little chance of intercepting an enemy force with only one destroyer in company, and I decided to turn to the north-eastwards at 13.30 and rendezvous with the minelaying force.'

Off the Helgeland coast, the German squadron had been fortunate to experience a few hours' improvement in the weather after the night's ordeal. As afternoon gave way to evening, all the destroyers – with the exception of the *Erich Giese*, whose gyro-compass had been damaged by a breaking wave and was lagging far behind – caught up with the *Scharnhorst* and *Gneisenau*.

The ships' officers had been warned by wireless that the Vestfjord had been mined and that the British Home Fleet was at sea. But the squadron commander, Vice Admiral Günther Lütjens, a seasoned sailor of the old school, adhered to the original plan with undiminished zeal. Even when the wind veered north-west and again increased to gale force, he continued to forge ahead at a speed of 25 to 27 knots. 'After a brief interval the wind shifted to the north-west and soon increased to force 10 in the squalls,' wrote Lieutenant Commander Erdmenger in the *Wilhelm Heidkamp*'s war diary. 'There was a nasty sea coming in on the beam, and the soldiers were suffering badly from seasickness. Snow showers and hail did much to reduce visibility and the bridge was drenched with spray. Maintaining station was quite a challenge.'

Churchill had been in an ebullient mood at the staff meetings held in London that same morning. 'Winston is back from France full of blood,' General Ironside wrote in his diary. 'He was like a little boy this morning describing what he had done to meet the Germans.' At the meeting of the War Cabinet held at 10 Downing Street at 11.30, the First Lord was still quite elated:

> It appeared that the German force was undoubtedly making towards Narvik. It was calculated that if they were unopposed, they could reach there about 10 PM, but they would no doubt be engaged by His Majesty's ships *Renown* and *Birmingham*, and the destroyers which had been laying the minefield, and an action might take place shortly.

He prudently added: 'It was impossible to foretell the risks of war, but such an action should not be on terms unfavourable to us.'

Not a few of the men in the British government were wondering what the Germans' intentions might be. 'It was thought quite possible that Herr

Hitler might have ordered Narvik to be seized, as a preparatory measure to the occupation of Luleå when the ice melted,' the minutes said. 'It might also be the intention, when the force had been landed, to send the *Gneisenau* out into the oceans as a raider. In any case, the whole operation seems to be a most hazardous venture.'

For months, Lord Halifax had opposed Churchill's wish to mine Norway's coastal waters and he had only reluctantly assented to the operation. He now suggested that the Norwegians should be warned of what was in the offing. 'They might be told what was going on, not through the diplomatic channel, but by the Admiralty.' In the minutes, the government's unanimous decision read: 'The War Cabinet invited the First Lord of the Admiralty to pass on to Norwegian naval authorities the information we had received as to German naval movements.'

It was 13.00 on Monday 8 April when the Norwegian counsellor, Ingvald Smith-Kielland, was requested to present himself at the Admiralty without delay. Churchill had passed the Cabinet's injunction on to Rear Admiral Tom Phillips, who didn't mince his words:

> German naval forces were yesterday observed in the North Sea with at least one merchant vessel, probably a troop transport. This morning advanced forces were seen off the West coast of Norway, heading northwards. It is our firm opinion that operations against Narvik are intended, and that the Germans may enter the port before midnight, probably around 10 PM.

At 15.00, as soon as he got back to the embassy in Kensington, the shaken counsellor phoned the Ministry of Foreign Affairs in Oslo and informed them of the alarming news in a coded message. 'The Legation's telegram this afternoon must be dealt with immediately. It concerns reported German naval movements in the direction of Narvik,' noted the man who took the call in Oslo. The urgency of the matter notwithstanding, it took three hours for the deciphered telegram to reach the Foreign Minister and another two hours for the news to get through to Commodore Askim on board the *Norge*, still lying at anchor with steam up in Narvik harbour. By then it was 20.00 and, by Rear Admiral Phillips's calculations, only two hours before the Germans would reach the Vestfjord. Countermeasures needed to be taken immediately, but for some strange reason, neither orders nor comments were forthcoming from the admiral in command. The explanation was eventually given over the phone by a junior officer on the admiral's staff: 'No one here believes in the probability of an attack on Narvik.' This was a case of gross negligence and, in consultation with Captain Odd Willoch, commander of the *Eidsvold*, Askim decided to act on his own initiative:

> I despatched the *Eidsvold* to take up a position at the entrance to the harbour, while I myself stayed where I was to maintain a telephone link with the mainland as long as possible. The submarines I ordered further inshore, closer to Bogen, so that they could not be seen from the fjord, and I sent the guard ships, the *Kelt* and *Michael Sars*, further out.

The general atmosphere in Narvik was tense. None of the twenty-five or so ships in the roads were allowed to leave, loading of iron ore came to a standstill and the air was thick with rumour. 'The town itself today wore a Sundayish calm,' Giles Romilly reported in the *Daily Express*. 'There were no ore trains standing on the dock. I missed the deep, rumbling sound of the ore being tipped down the 200-foot chutes. A few workmen were taking snow from the tracks.'

At the Royal Hotel, Romilly had run into Theodor Broch, who was having dinner there with his wife Ellen after a visit to the cinema. 'The news bulletin on the wireless was relayed to the cinema at seven o'clock,' Broch wrote. 'The main item was the sinking of a German troop transport off the south coast and of the bodies of drowned horses and soldiers drifting ashore. The soldiers all had close-cropped hair and were of the same age-group.'

The majority of the diners were foreigners. According to the landlord, this was because the men of the *Norge* and *Eidsvold* had had their shore leave cancelled. As Broch observed: 'We had seen the storm building up on the horizon but failed to realise that it might reach us. We had seen the signs but not read them correctly.' Broch was highly critical of the minelaying when he spoke to Romilly:

> We can't understand why England should do this. What can you gain in comparison with what you will lose? It must be part of a bigger move. We are in danger – yet in spite of all we cannot understand why you must do it. Yes, we say – Norway is one of your best friends. Why should you begin with us?

Among those listening to this exchange in the dining room was Signe Askim, who had been awakened early Monday morning by a phone call from the reception desk:

> I dressed quickly and ran down to the telephone box. Per was brief and military: 'Something very serious has happened. The British have laid mines in the Vestfjord. I have been at it since five this morning. I'm sending a man ashore with money so that you can do what we agreed on yesterday. I can't keep the phone engaged for long. I'll ring you when I have time.'

Worried by what she had just heard, the commodore's young wife had then gone in to breakfast:

> I found it hard to get anything down. I kept looking out of the window, where sleet was falling from a lowering black sky. I felt lonely and ill at ease. What did it mean? Were the British planning to raid Narvik to destroy the German ships? The war had come closer.

Later that same morning, a sailor entered the hotel with the promised money and a small case containing two silver fox furs Signe's husband had bought her in Tromsø. 'I thought I ought to do something useful, so I made my way to the post office and sent off the last instalment on the tax we owed in Oslo!'

Signe Askim waited by the phone all day, but it was after eight that evening when her husband phoned again. This time too he barely had time to talk:

> 'Hello. Don't ask me anything. I'm very busy and I can't tell you anything. Things are becoming serious and if you hear gunfire this evening, it'll be from us. Thank you for all the good times we've had together. Look after yourself. Get yourself off to bed and stay calm.' 'Yes, all right. But Per –,' I cried. But he had already put down the phone. The silence was ominous. There was no reply.

Signe Askim returned to the lounge fearful and confused:

> What did he mean? He'd as good as said goodbye to me forever! Why might there be firing from the ironclads tonight? I was in a daze and a little annoyed, too, that he couldn't tell me what it was all about. There were a lot of people in the lounge, commercial travellers, foreign journalists and a number of army

officers. The last-mentioned didn't seem any more concerned about the situation than usual. I couldn't help being surprised that they should be sitting there so carefree when Per was clearly getting ready for battle and firing could start at any moment.

In London, Churchill was still pacing backwards and forwards with an unlit cigar in his hand and a broad smile on his face. 'The First Lord who at last sees a chance of action, is jubilant,' wrote John Colville in his diary. 'He maintains that our failure to destroy the German fleet up to the present is only due to the bad visibility and very rough weather in the North Sea. If the German ships fly for home, they will leave their garrisons exposed to our expeditionary forces.' Churchill had been equally forceful when he addressed the War Cabinet: 'The Admiralty had judged it desirable to do everything they could to ensure that the German ships would not be able to return home. Everything possible had therefore been ordered out.'

Once again, Churchill had taken upon himself the role of commander-in-chief – albeit in agreement with Pound and Phillips. In the course of Monday morning all remaining ships of the Home Fleet had been rushed to sea. They were the cruisers *Devonshire*, *York*, *Berwick* and *Glasgow*, all of which were anchored off Edinburgh with the expeditionary force destined for Bergen and Stavanger on board. The soldiers were swiftly disembarked and their 360 tonnes of equipment offloaded, whereafter the cruisers headed east across the sea. The *Aurora* outside Glasgow was despatched in the same direction.

'We lay all day in the Clyde, but our naval escort, including the Admiral, departed to take part in naval operations in the North Sea,' wrote Colonel William Fraser. Vice Admiral Evans had been appointed naval commander of the landing in Narvik, but preferred to take part in the expected battle off the Stad Peninsula. 'He was only allowed to go on the condition that he hauled down his flag and went as a passenger. He wasn't going to miss a good scrap for a thing like that, so down came the flag and off he went.'

Mackesy and Fraser thus lost both their escorts and their admiral, but there was nothing they could do about it. They had to start again from scratch.

North of the Shetlands, the commander of the Home Fleet, Admiral Charles Forbes, regarded the stream of orders issuing from the Admiralty with an apparent blend of amazement and indulgence. In the course of the next twenty-four hours the greatest and most powerful fleet ever seen in these waters would be ready for action: five battleships, an aircraft-carrier, some fifteen cruisers and thirty destroyers.

The British force's superiority would be overwhelming once battle was joined, but there was a problem. Where were the Germans, and what were their intentions? There was certainly at least one enemy battlecruiser in the north, but fresh information from submarines and aircraft appeared to indicate that there was another battlecruiser in the Skagerrak, along with two pocket battleships. At about 20.00 that evening Forbes finally decided to break wireless silence. At the same time he made a new and highly controversial decision: he turned the whole fleet about and set a course southwards – away from Narvik.

Off the Lofotens, Captain Warburton-Lee's destroyers had caught up with the *Renown* at 17.15 after a gruelling day's sailing in the rising gale. A patrol line was established west of Skomvær Lighthouse, but the destroyers found it extremely difficult to take up and maintain station. 'It took some time to form the screen,' wrote Stanning on board the *Hardy*. 'The whole evening and night were acutely uncomfortable, and I don't suppose anyone in the ship slept even if they had a chance.'

Later that Monday evening, the Admiralty reiterated its view that Narvik was a potential target. At 19.15, in another signal to Vice Admiral Whitworth, an overarching order in line with the thinking in the Upper War Room was issued: 'Most immediate. The force under your orders is to concentrate on preventing any German force proceeding to Narvik.' Whitworth never hesitated. 'I decided to proceed up West Fiord with the object of placing myself between the enemy and his objective.'

But the storm centre was now rapidly nearing Lofotodden Point and the wind from the north-west, accompanied by driving rain and sleet, had risen to full gale force. The destroyers had to contend with one towering wave after another with the wind on the quarter. The more Whitworth thought about the plan, the more uncertain he felt. Once he was within the confines of the fjord, he would have limited room for manoeuvre. Moreover, in the darkness and driving snow his ships would find it hard to get their bearings. 'The sudden deterioration in the weather decided me to change my plans,' he wrote in his report. 'I felt that the enemy would make little progress and not try to make West Fiord during the dark, and would probably stand to seaward during the dark hours. I decided to do the same.'

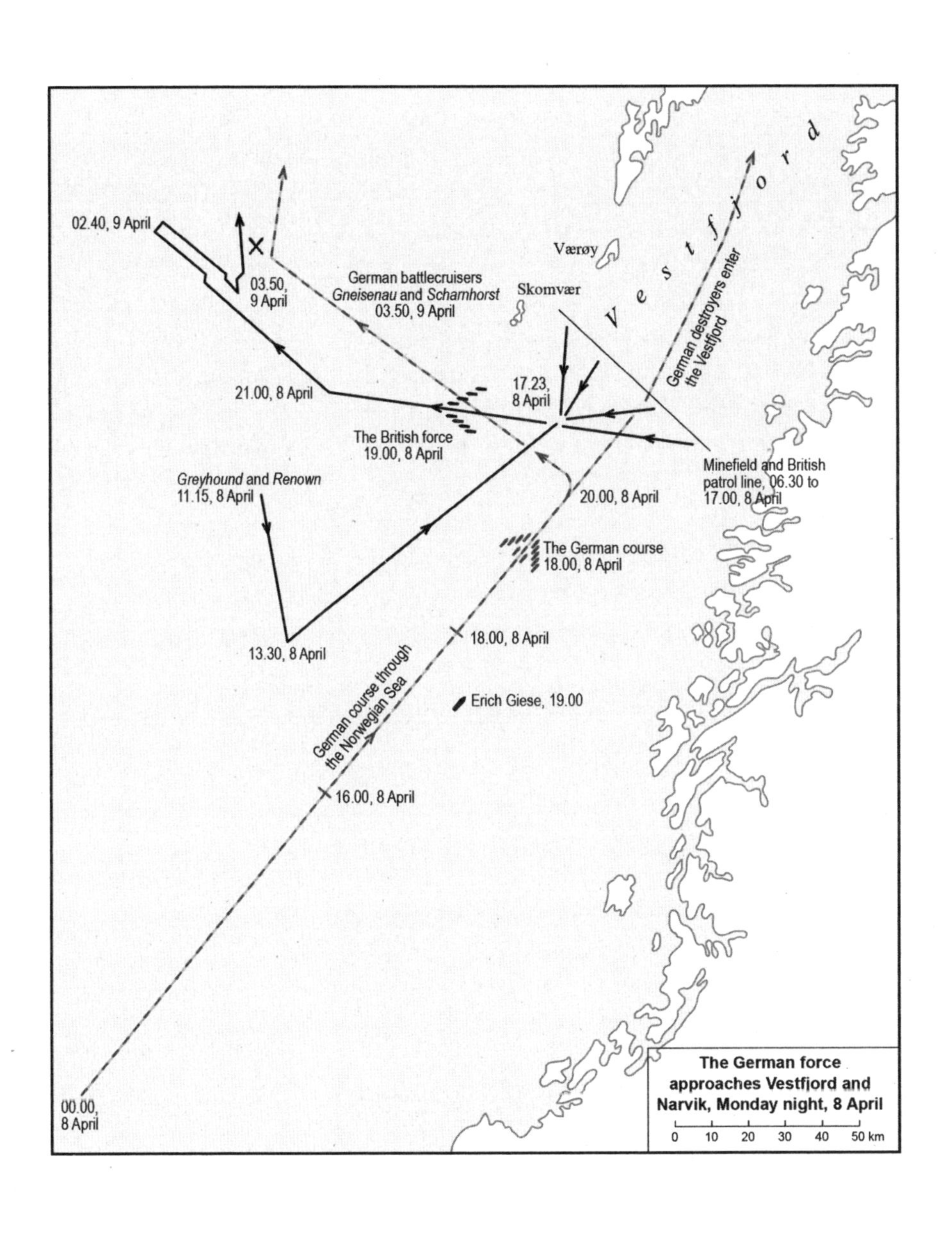

02.40, 9 April
03.50,
9 April
German battlecruisers
Gneisenau and Scharnhorst
03.50, 9 April
Værøy
Skomvær
V e s t f j o r d
German destroyers enter the Vestfjord
21.00, 8 April
17.23,
8 April
The British force
19.00, 8 April
Minefield and British
patrol line, 06.30 to
17.00, 8 April
Greyhound and Renown
11.15, 8 April
20.00, 8 April
The German course
18.00, 8 April
13.30, 8 April
18.00, 8 April
German course through the Norwegian Sea
Erich Giese, 19.00
16.00, 8 April
00.00,
8 April
The German force
approaches Vestfjord and
Narvik, Monday night, 8 April
0 10 20 30 40 50 km

It was another fatal miscalculation and one destined to cost the Royal Navy and the Allies dear. At the same time as Vice Admiral Whitworth and his destroyers were riding out the storm west of the small island of Skomvær, the *Scharnhorst*, *Gneisenau* and their destroyers were nearing the mouth of the fjord a few nautical miles distant after an exhausting struggle with the storm. The German ships passed Bodø at 21.00 and a few minutes later the two battlecruisers changed course to the north-west, to await events between the islands of Senja and Jan Mayen in the Arctic Ocean.

The German destroyers continued alone, battling their way against the continuing snow squalls and howling wind in the hope that they were in the right position. But these were treacherous waters, full of islets and submerged rocks – and it was pitch dark into the bargain. None of the ships were equipped with radar, and the plot had not been updated for more than twenty-four hours. 'We steered a course that we expected would take us more or less down the middle of the fjord,' wrote Hans Erdmenger on board the *Wilhelm Heidkamp*. 'We were out to avoid the minefield and any patrolling British ships.'

The flotilla approached the eye of the storm at a speed of 23 knots. With the wind on the beam, the destroyers were blown hard to starboard. Visibility was nil and they couldn't see the land. It was only thanks to the flagship's highly experienced navigator, Captain Lindemann, that they got through without mishap. Lindemann had been brought in from the Merchant Navy, in which he had sailed as captain of an ore carrier plying between Germany and Narvik. When he got a bearing on the beacon on the island of Skrova, he knew that the flotilla was on the right course. 'The problem was that the signals we could pick up were so faint that we might well have been three to five nautical miles east or west off course,' wrote Erdmenger, who was glued to the echo sounder. 'Thanks to his experience, Lindemann did us a real service. He operated the direction finder himself all the way in.'

It was only after five hours of sailing more or less blind that the Germans felt sure that they had made it – after a taxing voyage of 2,000km. The lurching and rolling gradually died away and on the starboard bow they could see the welcome light of Tranøy Lighthouse.

It was nearly 03.00 on the morning of Tuesday 9 April. The flotilla had successfully completed one of the most hazardous voyages in recent naval history. Ahead of them lay Narvik. The order was given for action stations.

PART IV

11

THE SINKING OF THE IRONCLADS

The Vestfjord and Narvik, Tuesday 9 April, 04.00 to 08.00

On board the *Hardy*, Lieutenant Geoffrey Stanning was still hunched over his desk in the paymaster's cabin when a thunderous crash brought him to his feet. 'I had spent the whole night deciphering messages and trying to make sense of any number of long telegrams which were coming in very mutilated,' he wrote in his personal report. 'I did all this in my cabin which though dry was rather a shambles, and things which I had not seen for ages and thought were lost kept reminding me of their presence by dropping on my head.' It was 04.00 and the men had just taken up their stations with the breaking dawn:

> The ship's company had not been at action stations more than a minute before a ship near us opened fire – presumably *Renown* – and we did the same. For a moment I thought we were doing a practice firing on the spur of the moment as we had done several times before.

Stanning stormed out onto the deck with Torpedoman Les Smale, both men slipping and sliding on the ice-covered plating and ladders. When they reached the open bridge, it was to see the horizon lit by intermittent flashes of red and orange. 'I could just make out the enemy – two ships – but no one could see them except for a second after they fired. Spotting was out of the question. One sea in two or three was coming right over the bridge, and it was all very uncomfortable.'

The *Renown* and Warburton-Lee's destroyers had come up against the *Scharnhorst* and *Gneisenau* just off the Røst Bank. The two German battlecruisers were sailing slowly north-westwards towards their waiting positions and were clearly unprepared for battle. Several minutes were to elapse before they returned the rain of fire from the *Renown*'s 15in guns. The distance between the two squadrons was about 15km. Because of the constant pitching and rolling, no hits were scored by any of the ships, but at 04.15 the British battlecruiser at last appeared to have got the range. 'With the fall of our sixteenth salvo, a bright orange flash was observed near the enemy's fore superstructure,' Vice Admiral Whitworth noted in the log.

One of the *Renown*'s heavy shells had struck the front of the *Gneisenau*'s 'A' turret, severely damaging the main fire-control system, along with the range finders, radar and parts of the central communication system. The first gunnery officer, Commander Hans-Georg von Buchka, and five other men were killed instantly and another nine were wounded. 'Fire control from the turret no longer working,' wrote the *Gneisenau*'s captain, Harald Netzbandt, in the ship's log. Water flooded in from the seas which continued to engulf the foredeck. The electrical systems short-circuited and, amid a shower of sparks and rising steam, the turret ceased to function.

Far away to the west, Warburton-Lee and the flotilla's gunnery officer, Edward Clark, had together hit upon an ambitious and novel idea. They ordered the four destroyers to fire a simultaneous and concentrated salvo – which, because of the way the destroyers were being tossed about, was virtually impossible. 'Wash complimented us,' wrote the captain of the *Hotspur*, Commander Herbert Layman. 'Most others thought it was a waste of ammunition.'

There is no record of what went through the German squadron commander's mind, but after half an hour it was obvious that Lütjens had had enough. The German ships turned north and increased speed to 27 knots.

In the deeper reaches of the Vestfjord, the ten German destroyers were racing all out for Narvik. They were scheduled to reach the town at 04.15 and their commander, Commodore Bonte, was determined not to be a minute late.

'I woke at half past two and had a proper shave for the first time since leaving Berlin,' Albert Bach wrote. When he made his way up onto the destroyer's bridge shortly afterwards, the first faint streaks of dawn were beginning to appear in the east:

> We were in a kind of dark, narrow corridor. On either side, mountains thrust their way upwards into the low clouds. The fjord was quite calm and there wasn't a light to be seen ashore. It was snowing a little. Astern I could just make out the other destroyers sailing line astern at about 30 knots, their bows cleaving the water to leave a wave of white foam on either side.

The German intelligence service had recorded the Norwegian government's purchase from Britain of three heavy guns in 1920 and, marked in the Kriegsmarine's manuals were the estimated positions of the coastal forts on the north and south sides of the entrance to the Ofot fjord.

'We crouched down and waited for a flash of light from the shore,' Bach wrote. 'But there was no firing. Nothing happened and it wasn't long before we found ourselves in the inner reaches of the fjord – a small inland sea ringed by snowclad peaks. We were enveloped in fog and snow and it was difficult to see anything.'

Meanwhile, Lieutenant Hans Rohr had assembled his 100 men of No. 7 Company on the quarterdeck.

'Weapons, equipment and ammunition were brought up from below. As we were to be the first to go ashore, with the intention of taking Colonel Sundlo prisoner, I took the precaution of issuing the men with hand grenades,' Rohr wrote in his personal account of the operation. He and his men were exhausted by seasickness and lack of sleep, and many of them found the wild and unaccustomed surroundings both frightening and forbidding:

> The mountains plunged sheer into the darkness of the fjord. Snow lay deep all over and there wasn't a sign of human habitation in the fog and swirling snow. Although the task ahead of us helped to keep our imaginations from running wild, most of us felt chilled by thoughts of what was to come.

At about 03.10 a small steamer came into view not far from the southern shore. 'Bonte ordered us to leave it in peace,' wrote Hans Erdmenger on board the flagship, the *Wilhelm Heidkamp*. 'He didn't want to give it an added reason to use its wireless.'

Bonte's pious hope was soon dashed. A few minutes later the wireless operators picked up the following signal, which was transmitted in plain language on the international distress frequency, 500kHz: 'Nine German destroyers have entered the Ofot fjord.' The flotilla had been sighted by the steam trawler *Kelt* and the *Michael Sars*, both of which, since early Monday evening, had been patrolling the fjord, one on each side.

'The weather was pretty thick, south-west breeze accompanied by frequent, though not particularly dense, snow showers,' reported Captain Bjørn Jackwitz from the *Michael Sars*, which carried two 4.6cm cannons but had orders not to open fire:

> At 03.10 an unidentified cruiser [*sic*] was observed heading into the fjord, more or less in the middle, at high speed. This information was immediately passed on to the *Norge*, with which the *Michael Sars* happened to be in wireless contact at that moment. Next to appear was a destroyer, followed by several more, all sailing in line astern at high speed. Their presence was reported as they passed, two or three at a time. In all, nine destroyers went by in the course of ten minutes.

On board the *Norge*, which was still at anchor in Narvik harbour with a telephone link to the shore, Commodore Askim didn't hesitate. 'At about 03.20 on 9 April, news was received that nine German destroyers had entered the Ofot fjord at great speed,' he wrote in his official report. 'I gave orders to cast off and sounded the alarm. All guns were loaded with live ammunition.' In a more intimate account compiled for his family, Askim was more personal and outspoken:

> It was strange that I wasn't more nervous from the time we went to action stations on Monday morning, 8 April. It was probably because I had too much to do all the time. From eight o'clock in the evening I was pretty sure that something was going to happen in Narvik, but I had no means of knowing whether it would be British or German ships that would make the first move. I rang Signe and prepared her for all eventualities. I told her that if she heard firing in the night, it would be us who were doing the shooting.

Several of the ship's officers made their way to his cabin to phone their families who, understandably, were worried by the day's events – the mining of the Vestfjord and the presence of a German naval force off the Norwegian coast. Askim wrote:

> My worst moment was when, at half past three on Tuesday morning, I gave the order to sound the alarm. It's a most eerie sound. The men were out of

> their bunks and cabins, fully dressed, in seconds. Then it was up to the bridge in the semi-darkness and snow. We had our work cut out raising the anchors, surrounded as we were by merchantmen. We slowly made our way past the *Jan Wellem* and *Planet*, both of which were showing special lights – no doubt because they'd been notified that the Germans were on their way.

As the day wore on, tension in Narvik had risen. Loading of ore was still at a standstill and the ore carriers lay idle at anchor. The news bulletins were full of alarming reports of German naval movements in the Danish straits, and the military staffs and government had been informed in confidence by their Danish and Swedish contacts that no fewer than ninety-six vessels were heading north – in addition to the squadron that Rear Admiral Phillips had warned of and which was expected to make Narvik before midnight. This was just about all the naval forces Hitler could muster at the time, but neither Norway's senior politicians nor the country's high-ranking military officers seemed to grasp how acute the danger was.

'Round about midday the general gave me permission to interrupt my tour of inspection to make a phone call,' wrote Major Odd Lindbäck-Larsen, chief of staff to General Carl Gustav Fleischer, who had been appointed Supreme Commander of northern Norway for the duration of hostilities. 'I made my way down from the mountains to the shop at Gornitak, where I lost no time in phoning the District Commander in Harstad.'

For reasons hard to understand, General Fleischer had elected to complete his inspection of troops stationed deep within the wild expanse of the Varanger plateau instead of doing all he could to get back to the potential area of conflict in the southern part of the county of Troms. The roads were covered in snow, and it was 20.00 before the general reached the local boarding house, from where it was no easy task to prepare for war over an unreliable 1,000km-long telephone line.

> As there was no talk of mobilisation, we had to assume that the central authorities did not associate the German transports with operations in Norway. However, I did order that District Command should move its headquarters to Målselv, and that a sufficient number of machine guns and men should be stationed in the pillboxes outside Narvik.

The situation was very muddled, and the government's disastrous refusal to mobilise at 22.00 that night did nothing to help. Fleischer felt very uneasy and on his own initiative gave orders to prepare for local mobilisation and reinforcement of the Narvik sector. This entailed moving two lots of troops in tandem: a battalion from the 15th Infantry Regiment and a motorised field battery to be transferred inland from Troms to the camp at Elvegårdsmoen, near Bjervik, some 20km north of Narvik as the crow flies. At the same time, the remainder of the local battalion was to be moved from Elvegårdsmoen to Narvik, to bring the number of troops in the first line of defence up to about 1,200.

By this time, however, the after-effects of the storm at sea had begun to make themselves felt in the shape of snow showers and a rising wind. The roads had been poorly cleared, which meant that it would take a long time to complete the planned transfers. In the meantime, Elvegårdsmoen, with its stores and barracks, would be left empty, apart from a skeleton staff of non-combatants.

General Fleischer's plan was completely at odds with the thinking of Colonel Sundlo, who immediately voiced his disagreement. 'When the order reached Colonel Sundlo via District Command', wrote Major Lindbäck-Larsen, 'he retorted that he had no wish to fill the town with infantry.'

This was yet another manifestation of the time-worn division of opinion over how Narvik was to be defended. Sundlo and his local field officers wanted to retain the battalion as a mobile reserve, while the staff in Harstad wanted it in a forward position close to the shore.

Many people saw the colonel's protest as a manifestation of his Nazi sympathies and reluctance to fight to repel a German invasion force, but Sundlo himself maintained that his protest was based solely on military considerations. 'I was opposed to the order,' he wrote at a later date:

> I was of the same opinion as I had always been – that it was impossible to defend Narvik against a naval force with nothing but rifles. What were needed was cannons. That is why I did not intend to move the battalion to Narvik. In the town it would have been of no use at all.

When, after the war, he was arraigned before a military tribunal, Colonel Sundlo further developed his argument:

> If the defence forces had been deployed west of the town and close to the shore, they would have been blown to bits by an enemy fleet inside the Ofot fjord. It wouldn't have helped in the slightest. That is why troops shouldn't have been

> there. They needed to be on the eastern side of the town and in the mountains. From the heights they would have commanded views of the entire Narvik area and could have swept the whole peninsula, as far out as Framnes, with machine gun fire. Forces positioned in the mountains would have made it hard for an intruder to hold the town and it would have been difficult to encircle them. If things got too hot, they could have retreated deeper into the mountains.

But confidence in the refractory officer was by then wearing thin, with the result that General Fleischer ordered the area commander to put Sundlo in his place. 'He did so with no little high-handedness,' Major Lindbäck-Larsen wrote:

> Sundlo maintained that the task was impossible. Colonel Mjelde retorted that that didn't interest him but that he wanted to know whether the colonel was aware of what he had to do. Sundlo responded by saying that he knew what his duty was and that he intended to do it.

The crux of the matter was that Narvik was to be held no matter the cost and that this was to be done in the way the Divisional Commander had determined. In thickening snow that same evening, the disputed orders were duly implemented. The trenches on Framnes Ridge and the pillboxes on the point west of the town, and at Fagernes to the east, were manned and a snow-clearing detail was ferried across the 4km-wide Rombak fjord to the ferry terminal at Øyjord to open a path for the main body of the advancing battalion.

But it was 13km by ski from Elvegårdsmoen to Øyjord, and the first ferry was not due until midnight. This meant that much of the night would be spent in getting the whole battalion to Narvik. In the meantime, many of the officers decided to turn in; there had been no alarm, either from military sources or from the municipal authorities. As a result, after midnight much of the town was deep in slumber.

Despite the acrimonious exchange with his senior officer, Colonel Sundlo appears to have remained calm. When, in the course of the afternoon, he chanced upon Giles Romilly, he was to all appearances his usual affable self:

> I heard the latest news this afternoon in the comfortable sitting-room and private office of Colonel Sundlo, commander of Narvik's military garrison while his men paraded with gas masks in the streets. This is all an affair for the Norwegian government, he said, smiling amiably. We military men simply have

> to obey orders. We are ready for all emergencies. He added: England has a very good standing in Norway.

However, at his post-war trial Sundlo gave vent to his true feelings: 'I might just as well have attempted to stop a heavy lorry by putting a matchbox in front of its wheels as to have tried to stop the Germans with the forces I had at my disposal.'

It was snowing more heavily than ever when, at 04.15, the *Wilhelm Heidkamp* slowly approached the entrance to Narvik harbour. 'Suddenly we saw the outlines of a ship a bare hundred metres away,' wrote Lieutenant Commander Hans Erdmenger in the destroyer's log. 'It was the coastal defence vessel *Eidsvold* at anchor off Framnes Point. We immediately signalled her that we were sending over a boat with an officer.' But on board the *Eidsvold* Captain Odd Willoch had been awaiting the intruders for close on three-quarters of an hour, having been warned of their approach by the *Kelt* and *Michael Sars* shortly before 03.30 that morning. He immediately fired a warning shot and signalled the German destroyer that she should heave to.

The 55-year-old captain was one of the Norwegian Navy's most popular and respected commanders. Where his friend and superior officer Per Askim had made his name in the Lighthouse Authority, Willoch had established himself among the nation's fishermen and trappers as the intrepid commander of the fishery protection vessels *Michael Sars* and *Fridtjof Nansen*, after years spent patrolling the ice-filled waters between Jan Mayen, Spitzbergen and Novaya Zemlya. 'He was always in a good humour, full of initiative and determined to see that everything went smoothly,' wrote Per Askim, who shared his younger colleague's interest in cutting-edge technology, most notably in regard to communications. Willoch was head of the Technical Section of the Naval Corps, a signals instructor at the Naval College, and had written a manual for radio hams, while Askim had studied wireless telegraphy in London and served on the International Code of Signals Committee, which published books of signals for the Merchant Navy. They were both family men of the old school, principled and conscientious but, after years of being pumped full of pacifist propaganda, they were poorly equipped to combat the evil and brutality of Nazism.

When the German flagship reversed her engines and came to a standstill a cable's length from the *Eidsvold*, deep down, the men on board her already knew what the outcome would be. The ironclads were too slow and cumbersome to cope with a modern warship like the *Wilhelm Heidkamp*. They needed time to get up steam, not to mention to reach their top speed of 17 knots; it took them even longer to turn and fire their massive cannons – and time was something they most decidedly did not have. The men on the *Eidsvold*'s deck were well aware of what was at stake: life and freedom – for themselves, for the young sailors crammed together beneath the armour-plated deck and for the hundreds of thousands of their fellow citizens in towns and villages throughout the country who were about to wake up to life under the iron heel of Nazi Germany. If they fired, it had to be with intent to kill. The knowledge weighed heavily upon these men imbued from childhood with respect for life and democratic principles. As Askim, in other respects a rather reserved man, so graphically put it in what was very much an understatement: 'It was strange preparing to open fire at live targets. We simply weren't used to it.'

The *Wilhelm Heidkamp*'s senior officers, who were gathered on the bridge scanning the aged ironclad through powerful binoculars, were of a far different stamp and could look back on a much sterner tradition: a lost world war followed by an ignominious peace, street fighting and the social turmoil of the short-lived Weimar Republic before the Brownshirts took over with their batons and bloody ideology.

It was common knowledge in the German officer corps that the 43-year-old Commodore Friedrich Bonte was anti-Nazi and that the same was probably true of the men closest to him – first staff officer Lieutenant Commander Rudolf Heyke and his principal assistant, Lieutenant Commander Heinrich Gerlach, who was deeply religious. 'Bonte was a torpedo officer and a veteran of the First World War,' recalled Karl-Theodor Raeder, son of Grand Admiral Erich Raeder, who was later to serve in the Bundesmarine and was for a time West Germany's naval attaché in London. 'Resolute and brave, he was held in high esteem by all who knew him.' 'In moral terms, Bonte was a first-class man, firm as a rock,' added the captain of the straggling *Erich Giese*, Lieutenant Commander Karl Smidt, who was destined to attain the rank of rear admiral in the Bundesmarine after the war and, like his commander, viewed Adolf Hitler with distrust. 'From the outset Bonte was strongly opposed to the Nazis.'

Bonte ordered 33-year-old Gerlach to present Willoch with the Führer's ultimatum, but to the chagrin of the officers assembled on the destroyer's bridge, there was an unforeseen delay. 'The derrick arm snapped as we were lowering the pinnace,' wrote an irate Erdmenger. 'It took between five and ten minutes to get a new boat onto the water.'

On board the *Eidsvold*, the men were busy preparing the ship for action. Anchors were weighed, boats lowered and extra ammunition brought up from the magazines. 'Everyone was very much on edge and the officers were quite agitated,' reported Quartermaster Leidulf Holstad, who was in charge of the 21cm aft turret. 'It was snowing and the snow was blowing straight in on us, so that we could barely see the land some 600–700 metres to the east.'

Only a few minutes earlier an ashen-faced and clearly flustered Captain Willoch had dashed past, shouting that there were German destroyers in the fjord. Holstad immediately ordered the ten men manning the gun to don their life jackets and start loading. When he reached the deck, the German pinnace was about to make fast to the stern ladder on the starboard side of the ship. 'An officer of commander rank and a signaller with flags tucked under his arm clambered on board. I remember remarking that of all things, he had brought us a German flag!' The German emissary was greeted by the *Eidsvold*'s second-in-command, Captain Leif Jansen, who had recently turned 47 and normally worked in the Legal Department of the Ministry of Defence, and the newly married Second Lieutenant Bjørn Aas. On the bridge, the four men were received by Captain Willoch and the duty navigator, 38-year-old Captain Sverre Kvande.

'Gerlach reeled off the usual hollow phrases about the Germans having come to Norway as friends to help us defend our neutrality against British aggression,' wrote Erik Anker Steen in *Norges Sjøkrig 1940–45*. 'He then urged the captain to show his loyalty by cooperating with the German forces.' The cooperation Gerlach was asking for was in reality a demand for complete and abject capitulation: the ship was to be surrendered to the Germans, all breech blocks had to be removed and the engine rendered useless. It was a demand totally at odds with all the Norwegian officer stood for and Willoch turned it down flat.

'The commander said that the Norwegian government had already issued orders to offer resistance,' Erdmenger wrote in the destroyer's log some time later. 'When our emissary pointed out that resistance would be futile, the Norwegian asked for ten minutes in which to discuss the matter by wireless with the commander-in-chief on board the *Norge*.' Without further ado Gerlach then broke off the discussion and left the *Eidsvold*, while Willoch hurried down to the wireless room.

According to Per Askim's memoirs, the ensuing exchange was brief and to the point:

'There's a German officer here demanding that I should surrender the ship,' Willoch said. 'What do you want me to do?'

'Open fire!' I told him.

'Right, I will,' came the answer.

A gentleman to the last, Captain Willoch called the Germans back and informed them of his decision. Gerlach reacted immediately. Once he was a fair distance away from the *Eidsvold*, he raised his signal pistol and pulled the trigger. The time was about 04.45. A few seconds later the ironclad and the sea around it were bathed in a scarlagen glow.

Some few kilometres distant, Colonel Konrad Sundlo had a little earlier been awakened by a phone call from District Command. The duty officer relayed the news from the *Kelt* and *Michael Sars* that unidentified warships had entered the fjord. The message had come via Harstad, where it was logged at 03.37. 'On receipt of this information Sundlo immediately made preparations to resist,' says the official Norwegian history of the war. From a purely formal point of view, this was correct, but in practice it meant little. Most of the field officers, who for several months had been training to repel an attacker from the pillboxes along the shore, were fast asleep in their hotel rooms and had to be roused from their slumber.

'I was feeling somewhat uneasy and didn't go to bed until half past one that night,' recalled Captain Peder Langlo, a dentist in civilian life who had been called up under the provisions of the Neutrality Act to command No. 2 Company of the Trøndelag Battalion. 'After a brief sleep I was sent for to attend a meeting called by the colonel.' Langlo's second-in-command, Captain Sverre Dalsve, was fetched from his room at a nearby boarding house at about the same time. 'I asked what it was all about,' said the company's administration officer, Anton Sjåstad, a 62-year-old farmer, who was sharing a room with Dalsve. 'He said: We're off out, but you're not.'

Langlo and Dalsve were key figures in the much-disputed plan for an advanced defence of Narvik, and in the course of six weeks had strengthened the forces at their disposal by some 190 men – a rifle company and machine gun section – to man the front line at the water's edge. Armed with machine guns and 120 rounds per man, since the previous evening some fifty to sixty of them had stood guard around the pillboxes on Framnes Point and at Fagernes. Between the two pillboxes were positioned a further twenty men who, from vantage points close to where the ore was loaded, could enfilade the wharf direct.

On Colonel Sundlo's order, the rest of the men in the company were despatched by lorry to reinforce the front line. Exactly what this pro-Nazi said and did not say can no longer be ascertained, but there seems to be no doubt that he was torn between his admiration for Hitler and loyalty to the land of his birth – a fact of which he had just been reminded. After the war he stubbornly maintained that his order could not have been misunderstood: 'I said that it was better to shoot too much than too little.'

On board the *Wilhelm Heidkamp*, which was still lingering in the harbour mouth, Erdmenger ordered full speed ahead the moment he saw Gerlach's red flare. 'The ironclad suddenly increased speed,' he wrote in the ship's log. 'I assumed that the idea was to ram us. We were in a dangerous position as, in the course of the negotiations, we had drifted quite close to the *Eidsvold*.'

The destroyer's sudden burst of speed forced Lieutenant Albert Bach on the bridge back against the steel bulkhead:

> The powerful force exerted by our engines was absolutely amazing. We leapt forward and the *Eidsvold* receded astern – 100 metres – 300 metres – 500 metres. We all had our eyes glued to the Norwegian ship. Would they open fire? Would they blast off with their heavy guns – and blow our fragile hull to bits?

As Gerlach's pinnace pulled away, Captain Willoch raced from the quarterdeck to the bridge and shouted: 'Now we're going to give 'em what for, lads!' The *Eidsvold*'s gunnery officer, 45-year-old Captain Knut Thorkelsen from Oslo, who was standing with his back to the mast, responded immediately: 'Salvo! Fire!'

But it was a clash of two totally different worlds, past and present, the modern versus the antiquated, belligerence opposed to fundamental pacifism hammered in by decades of anti-military propaganda. Before the ironclad's cumbersome guns could be brought to bear, the sleek destroyer had disappeared into a snow squall. When it reappeared a few minutes later, it was to starboard of the *Eidsvold* and some 1,500m astern.

To Erdmenger, watching through his binoculars, it seemed that the Norwegian ship was again hove-to. Fearing attack by the ironclad's devastating 21cm guns, he didn't dare wait. 'I asked for permission to torpedo her,' he wrote in the destroyer's log. But Flotilla Commander Bonte was

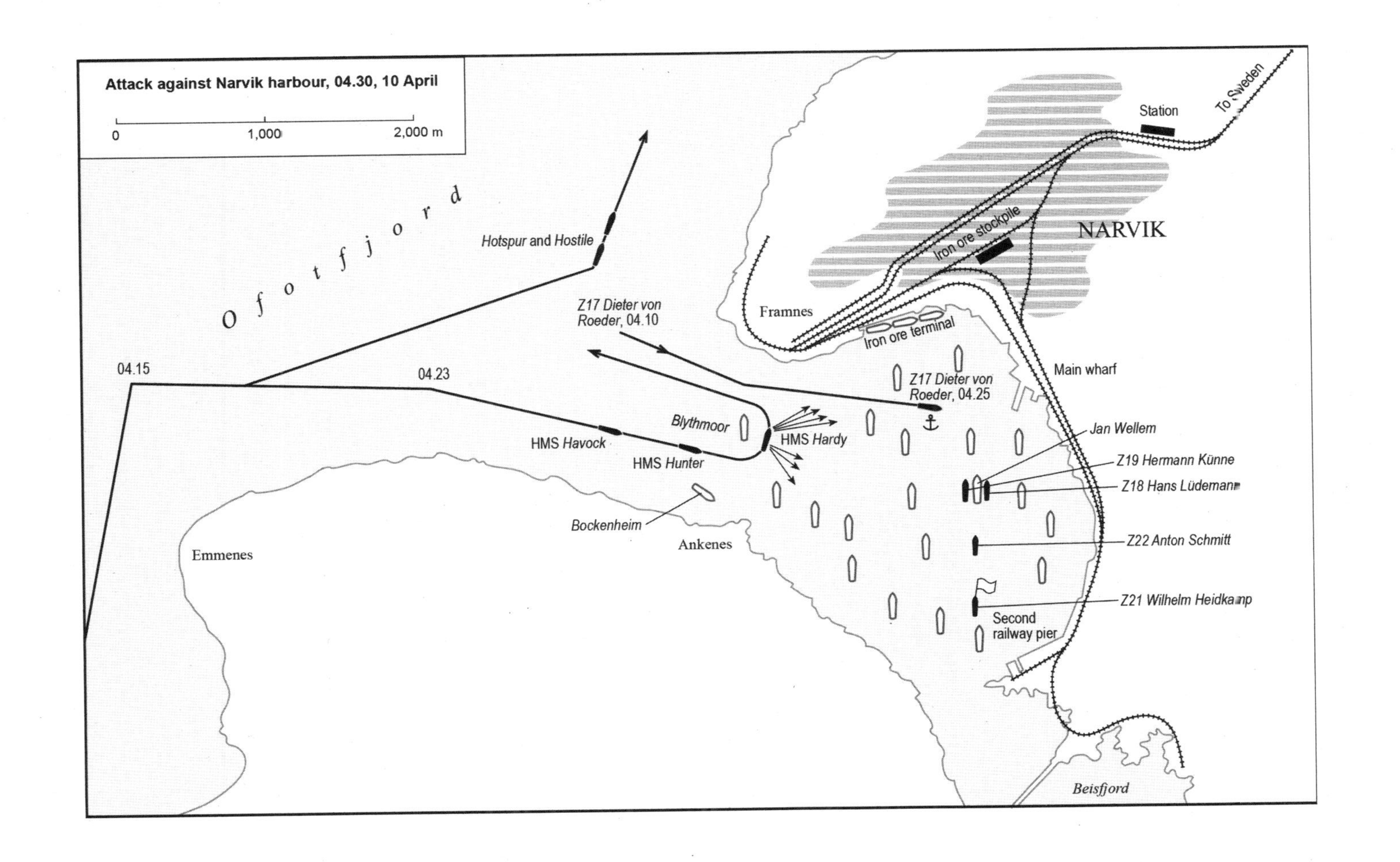
Attack against Narvik harbour, 04.30, 10 April
0
1,000
2,000 m
Ofotfjord
Hotspur and Hostile
04.15
04.23
Z17 Dieter von Roeder, 04.10
Framnes
Iron ore stockpile
NARVIK
Station
To Sweden
Iron ore terminal
Main wharf
Z17 Dieter von Roeder, 04.25
Blythmoor
HMS Hardy
HMS Havock
HMS Hunter
Bockenheim
Ankenes
Emmenes
Jan Wellem
Z19 Hermann Künne
Z22 Anton Schmitt
Second railway pier
Beisfjord

having qualms and refused to grant the captain's request. He wanted to avoid occupying the town by force and most definitely had no desire to slaughter an opponent that was as yet in no position to retaliate. 'It ran counter to his chivalrous nature as a soldier,' Erdmenger wrote.

But Hitler's friend and comrade-in-arms since the Nazi Party's early years, General Eduard Dietl, was of a different stamp altogether. In his capacity as Commander-in-Chief of the invasion force, he seized the initiative. *Schiessen*, he said. *Fire!*

Lieutenant Hans Rohr and his fellow mountain troops were gathered on the quarterdeck in full combat gear when the *Wilhelm Heidkamp*'s four port torpedoes were launched. 'I heard the splash and saw the four eels streaking through the water towards the ironclad,' he wrote in his memoirs. 'Before the Norwegians could fire a shot there was a violent explosion. It was like an earthquake! Spurts of flame shot up and a cloud of black smoke rose skywards. Seconds later the ship disappeared beneath the surface.'

On board the *Eidsvold* the cataclysm was immediate and complete. In the ironclad's rear turret Petty Officer Leidulf Holstad felt the ship heel over a little when the first torpedo struck. But when the next two hit the hull, it was as if the *Eidsvold* simply disintegrated. 'It was turmoil,' he said later. 'There was a great deal of noise and all I could see was smoke.'

Holstad had managed to fight his way past a maze of twisted metal and found himself on top of the turret when the *Eidsvold* capsized. 'I've no idea of how long I was underwater. When I surfaced, I could see the red-painted bottom of the stern some 20 to 30m away. I could hear frantic cries for help but couldn't see where they came from.'

Shortly after the *Eidsvold* went down, bow first. Holstad and Bandmaster Henry Backe managed to drag themselves onto a float drifting towards the shore; two other men survived in a dinghy, and Gerlach's pinnace rescued four more. It was a massacre, just as Bonte had feared. Only eight men survived the sinking, which was the greatest single tragedy suffered by Norway on 9 April 1940. Willoch, Jansen, Thorkelsen and the rest of the 175 men on board died with their ship.

The first ferryload of the Trøndelag Battalion's main force reached Narvik at about 02.00 that night. When the alarm was raised an hour and a half later, Colonel Sundlo had at his disposal some 300 men – under the command of the battalion commander, 58-year-old Major Sverre Spjeldnæs, in civilian life manager of an insurance company in Oslo. 'I drove over to the colonel, with whom was Major Spjeldnæs, the regiment's second-in-command, Sigurd Omdal, and a company commander, Arthur Bjørnson,' explained Captain Langlo, who had probably got to the regimental HQ sometime between 04.00 and 04.30 that same morning. 'The colonel told us news had been received of the presence of enemy warships in the fjord and issued his orders.'

With Captain Bjørnson in command and Langlo as guide, one of the newly arrived companies and an extra machine gun section were sent to reinforce the positions on Framnes Point. 'It was snowing extremely heavily and it was tough going,' said Langlo, who had still not reached the trench when, a few minutes before five, from somewhere just off the point, there was an ear-splitting bang. It was the *Eidsvold*, torpedoed and sinking. 'When we reached our positions north of Framnes Point, we could see a commotion in the water and hear men screaming and shouting.' It was a dreadful shock, and the officers didn't seem to know how to tackle it. To quote Langlo:

> I said to Bjørnson that we most certainly could *not* go down and see what it was all about. We had orders to occupy the position and we had to carry them out. For that reason I made my way back to the town's community centre, which was where I had been told to report to. On the way I met a soldier who was in shock and whom I directed to the hospital.

When Commodore Bonte first caught a glimpse of the *Eidsvold* through a break in the driving snow, he had ordered the rest of the landing force to continue deeper into the fjord. 'I carried on at 17 knots into the entrance to the harbour, the first of the flotilla to reach it,' wrote Lieutenant Commander Curt Rechel on board the *Bernd von Arnim*. In his wake followed the *Georg Thiele*, commanded by Rechel's rival, Max-Eckart Wolff. Drawn up on the destroyer's quarterdeck were Captain Salzer's mountain troops, fully equipped and ready to storm ashore. 'It was snowing and you couldn't see more than a hundred metres ahead. At times the snow was so thick that I could barely see the bow of my own ship.'

Without warning, dead ahead of the destroyer, the masts and superstructures of many steamers hove into view. 'I ordered full astern and brought the ship to a standstill. I was in Narvik harbour.' Some twenty-odd vessels lay at anchor in the roads and Rechel allowed the destroyer to drift slowly deeper into the harbour, with the *Georg Thiele* about 100m astern:

> The steamers' decks suddenly came alive! Between snow squalls I could make out British, German, Norwegian, Danish and Swedish flags. From some of the merchantmen there were cheers, from others shouts of *Heil Hitler!* and snatches of the German national anthem. Some of the sailors shouted over to us wanting to know if we were British while others hurriedly raised their anchors. Some even laid out chains.

Shortly afterwards, the port lookout saw the dim shape of the *Norge*. 'She kept flashing A A A in Morse, but I ignored her. I had something else to think about: the wharf I was supposed to berth at was nowhere to be seen.'

On board the *Norge*, Commodore Askim had cut the ship's mooring and moved her closer to the ore quay, from where he would have a clear field of fire, one that would enable him to cover the harbour entrance. He had just received a wireless message from the *Senja* informing him that they had sighted one of the German destroyers off Ramnes. Unfortunately, they wrongly identified it as a British cruiser.

'Once I was in the right position, I went below to get a scarf,' Askim wrote in his personal account of the incident. 'When I got back on deck and was handed the message from the *Senja*, I felt more cheerful. I said to one of the men on the bridge that the Good Lord hadn't deserted us after all. There were British ships in the fjord.' It was this error of identification that prompted Askim to hail the two German destroyers by signal lamp the moment they were seen, dark silhouettes against the mountains on the far side of the harbour. 'When I didn't get an answer, I gave the order to fire a live shell across their bows. Before it could be done, they disappeared in the snow, which was exceptionally thick.'

On board the *Bernd von Arnim*, binoculars were trained on the *Norge* as the German destroyer slowly made its way into the harbour in the hope of finding its appointed berth. In the event, it was not until, in a brief interval between snow showers, Rechel got a cross-bearing on the LKAB loading installations that he realised where he was:

> I made a 90 degree turn, and suddenly caught sight of the pier, a bare 80 metres away. The off-duty engine room watch had been lined up along the starboard rail to help if help were needed, and right behind them were crouched Salzer's troops, ready to leap ashore the moment we docked. It was then that I saw that the *Norge* was bringing both her heavy guns to bear on us. I immediately

gave the gunnery and torpedo officers permission to fire if the Norwegians did.

As the seconds ticked away, a taxi drew up on the quay, bringing with it Johannes Diesen, who was in charge of the telegraph office. A launch from the *Norge* was waiting for him. Diesen had an important message for Commodore Askim from his brother Henry Diesen, the admiral in command in Oslo. The admiral's message was short and to the point: 'German warships are to be fired on, British not.'

The Admiralty and government in the capital now knew who the invaders were and wished to make sure that Norwegians didn't open fire on their newly acquired British allies. 'I had promised to deliver the message in person,' wrote Johannes Diesen, who, somewhere between 04.30 and 05.00, had jumped into the waiting launch. 'The weather was awful, snow showers and a strong wind blowing. It wasn't long before the *Norge* loomed up in the murk. She had steam up and her guns had been swung into position.' Diesen handed his message to a deckhand and, as he did so, saw an alien destroyer approaching the pier a few hundred metres distant. 'As the launch drew away there were shouts from the *Norge* urging us to hurry. A moment later the guns blasted off. I saw flames belch from their muzzles and the force of the blast was so strong that I had to huddle down in the boat for cover.'

Without waiting for Diesen's telegram, Commodore Askim had let loose at the *Bernd von Arnim* with all the *Norge*'s 21cm and 15cm guns. 'By then the weather had improved a little, but it was still practically impossible to see anything through the viewfinders,' he wrote in his report. 'When I opened fire, the range was some 800 to 900 metres. Strangely, my navigator shouted, *No, no! They're not destroyers – they're only buildings on the quay!*'

From the *Bernd von Arnim*, Rechel observed that the *Norge*'s first salvo had fallen between 30 and 100m short. 'I immediately gave orders to return fire with every gun available – regardless of the fact that the *Norge* was partly masked by steamers. I completed the docking and saw the first of the troops leap ashore and take cover behind the concrete wall of the dock.'

Manoeuvring off the railhead, Lieutenant Commander Wolff in the *Georg Thiele* had joined the battle, and the *Norge* found herself under fire from two sides. 'I must confess that I felt a twinge of anxiety,' wrote Per Askim, who was standing on the bridge:

> I heard something whistling past. It was probably a shell striking and exploding forward, beneath the bridge. It was impossible to differentiate between explosions, there were so many. Once I saw a column of water rise up close to the quay. But I've no idea if it was a 21cm shell of ours exploding in the water or on board the destroyer.

The exchange lasted about ten minutes. The *Norge* fired five 21cm and eight 15cm shells without registering a single hit. Apart from the first salvo, which landed in the sea, they were all too high and fell on the mountainside east of the town. The old ironclad was superior in terms of firepower but its gunners were, at heart, peaceful civilians and totally unprepared for the brutal realities of modern warfare. To the onlookers, it seemed that the Norwegians didn't really want to hit their adversary for fear of killing someone. As Gunnery Officer Hans-Georg Buch aboard the German destroyer wrote: 'The lack of effect of our opponent's gunfire was incomprehensible to any gunner.'

Shortly before 05.00, Rechel put an end to the battle. He fired seven torpedoes at the *Norge* when it appeared for a few seconds between two steamships. The last two torpedoes struck the ironclad amidships. 'She turned over on her own axis and remained afloat for a short while, keel uppermost. When she went down, one of her propellers was still turning. One minute and it was all over.'

The ensuing moments were indescribable in their horror. With the engine room flooded, trapped as they were below deck, scores of young Norwegian men suffered agonising deaths.

'Out of sheer force of habit, I brought the engines to a stop,' Per Askim wrote. 'It didn't help, of course, as one of the torpedoes had gone right into the engine room, with disastrous results. I sounded the siren to summon assistance, then tried to make my way out of the wheelhouse by the port door.' But a searchlight had been wrenched from its mounting and blocked the exit:

> I went under where I was, on the bridge. Somehow or other the pressure of the water must have propelled me through the doorway – otherwise I would have been caught in there like a rat in a trap. When I reached the surface, the *Norge* was twenty-odd metres away, bottom-up. The propellers were still turning slowly, calling to mind an animal in its death throes.

Askim first grasped a length of planking, then a wooden bunk:

> A man black with oil and soot swam over and grabbed hold of the same bunk. I remember thinking that the least he could have done was to let his captain have the bunk to himself! He started shouting and wailing in mortal fear, prompting me to tell him to shut up and calm down. He either took offence at what I'd said or saw something better to cling to, as he swam off. That was the last I saw of him.

Askim didn't have the strength to swim and the current began to carry him further out into the harbour:

> In the end I could no longer see any ships or people. It was still dark. I've no idea of how long I lay there. All I remember is that I realised that I was beginning to lose consciousness and that I twice called for help. I recall thinking that my shouts sounded pitifully weak in the watery blackness. After that I remember nothing.

The murderous attack and explosions at 05.00 shook the little town and utterly demoralised its defenders. The main point of defence around the pillbox on Framnes Point was far from the landing area and had no effect on the outcome of the battle, which was precisely what the sceptics had feared. On the other hand, its occupants had a ringside view of the *Eidsvold*'s anchorage. Those still capable of action after the cold-blooded slaughter of their fellow countrymen spent the morning recovering the bodies that floated ashore.

The men entrenched around the pillbox at Fagernes were tactically better placed. They had an unobstructed view of the wharf where the destroyers berthed and had their fingers on their triggers when the *Bernd von Arnim*'s troops stormed ashore; the same was true of the men guarding the ore quay. But no one fired a shot when the Germans approached. They had seen with their own eyes the torpedoing of the *Norge* and heard the harrowing cries of the men in the water, many of whom were badly injured. Paralysed, they surrendered without thought of resistance. 'Of course, we hadn't a chance,' Colonel Sundlo wrote in his self-exculpatory post-war report of the incident. 'Although I gave the order to open fire, not a shot was fired by any of the land forces. The sinking of the two ironclads had taken the heart out of the men.'

When the flagship *Wilhelm Heidkamp* anchored up some 200m from the quay a little later, the situation devolved into what was little short of black comedy. General Dietl himself was in the first launch to reach land, together with his operations officer, Lieutenant Colonel Robert Bader, and Lieutenant Hans Rohr, both armed to the teeth. When the general saw a Norwegian officer on the quay, he immediately went over to him with outstretched hand and said: 'I salute the Norwegian Army!' But the officer concerned was a captain who had only recently risen from his bed and who had gone down to the quay simply to see what was happening. 'He didn't seem to have the faintest idea of what it was all about,' wrote Rohr, who, without further ado, commandeered a taxi that happened to be standing nearby. 'I seated myself beside the driver, machine pistol at the ready, while Dietl and Bader got into the back, along with two machine gunners. The German consul, Fritz Wussow, clung on, standing on the running board.'

On the railway bridge and in the square in the centre of the town, the troops recently landed from the *Bernd von Arnim* and *Georg Thiele* came face to face with the remnants of the Trøndelag Battalion, while the neighbouring streets were filled with curious civilians. The opposing forces had agreed on an informal truce, though Colonel Sundlo had threatened to open fire if the Germans didn't withdraw. 'There's no question of that!' retorted Dietl, who had insisted on paying the taxi driver before elbowing his way to the front of the assembled troops. Accompanied by Rohr as a self-appointed bodyguard, in his long overcoat and general's uniform with its scarlet and gold silk lapels, he cut an imposing figure as he strode to the fore. 'He had dressed up in his finest to make a good impression, in stark contrast to the rather drably clad Colonel Sundlo.'

It was a strange and tragic meeting between Hitler's old comrade-in-arms and his Norwegian admirer among the banks of snow lining the streets. Sundlo could have offered resistance and died a hero's death – had he succeeded in persuading the officers and men under his command to open fire. On the other hand, for years he had been proclaiming his support and admiration for the declared aim of Nazism: a united Europe under Hitler as a bulwark against Bolshevism. This was in effect the moment of truth. Why should he die for democracy and freedom when at heart he believed in the tyrannical regime that was Nazi Germany? And what could he say when Dietl reiterated Hitler's assurance that the Germans came in peace and urged him to avoid unnecessary bloodshed? Did he see through the lies or did he believe them?

'Colonel Sundlo saw things differently. The Norwegian soldiers he commanded were wandering about in bewilderment, regarding the foreign troops with amazement,' says the somewhat equivocally worded official history:

> To some extent they had gathered round the German troops for a closer look. The surrounding streets were full of civilians, men, women and children, who were watching it all unfold as though it were some kind of stage play. No one seemed to realise that it was war. Furthermore, dispersed among the crowds were German troops armed with hand grenades and making it clear by their whole demeanour that they knew exactly what they were about. One shot and a large number of innocent civilians would undoubtedly have paid with their lives.

It was a quarter past six when Colonel Sundlo finally made up his mind. He crossed over to Dietl and said: 'I surrender the town.'

In *The Privileged Nightmare*, Giles Romilly, who was an eyewitness to the confrontation, wrote:

> A sound sleeper, I was surprised when I woke to find that it was only twenty to five. Through half-drawn curtains I could see the usual dense unhurrying snowstorm and a leaden half-light, neither of night nor dawn. The window banged shut loudly – strangely, because there was no wind. The irregular, friendly rattle of the trains and hoppers was missing; the pall of silence seemed wrong. Then came two abominable, insulting bangs. Lifting the receiver of the room telephone I heard blurred sounds of distress and confusion and the voice of the hall clerk: Yes, yes, it is trouble in the harbour!

Romilly dressed hastily and hurried down to reception:

> On the landings, at the doors of bedrooms, were officers of the Norwegian garrison, in flowing nightshirts, in pyjamas of thickest flannel, buttoning shirts over hairy chests, fumbling with boots, buckling belts, some standing as though rooted, picking sleep off their eyelids. The hall, a mass of dressing-gowns and tousled heads, looked like a country-house party surprised by a fire.

The young British journalist followed in the wake of the people streaming out into the street, which was deep in snow, right down to the central square:

> Outside, soldiers were tumbling helter-skelter, rifles clutched anyhow, down the steep, slippery slope that led towards the harbour. The slope ran out into a straggling square, bounded on the right by the railway, sunk in a bridge-spanned cutting. On the left was a covered market. In the centre, to the right of the road, stood a small, lighthouse-shaped kiosk, and near it some trucks were parked. The heavy, whitish mist, leaving only a ragged, snow-drenched clearing between sky and land, made all beyond a region of mystery, now also of menace.

Romilly saw that some of the soldiers had climbed into lorries and propped their rifles up against the back of the drivers' cabs. Others had taken cover behind the kiosk, but most were standing in small groups in the square, totally unprotected:

> A sound cracked the almost palpable silence. There emerged, statically sudden, as if the sound had set it on the mist-screen, an oblong panel of forms kneeling on one knee, elbows supporting the weight of aimed guns, lines from knee to ground as close, straight and fixed as altar-rails. Minute against the endless front of the mist, this green-grey tableau suggested, in some sickening way, an appeal for forgiveness. Not more than thirty yards divided it from the Norwegians. Already all was too late. The Norwegian soldiers whispered together, and one of their number ran out of the ranks, pulling a white handkerchief from his pocket and waving it aloft. The tableau sprang to life.

At the Royal Hotel, Commodore Per Askim's wife Signe had been awakened by a loud noise, though she had no idea of what it was. 'At that moment the phone rang and a voice said: It's best you come down, Mrs Askim,' she wrote in her family memoirs. 'The vestibule was already overflowing with guests, all wanting to know what was going on. Did you hear the shooting? someone asked. Shooting, I thought, and remembered what my husband had said on the phone: If you hear gunfire this evening, it will be from us.'

Suddenly there was a commotion at the entrance to the hotel. 'In straggled a troop of unshaven soldiers, snow clinging to their uniforms. Dark-skinned and foreign-looking as they were, I took them for Frenchmen. But then they pointed their guns at us. They herded us together and uttered a sharp command – in German.' The soldiers, who were looking for the British consul, ushered the bewildered guests into the lounge. 'I crossed over to the window and looked out. It was still dark, the clouds hung low and it was snowing heavily. In the surrounding streets I could just make out a number of lorries packed tight with soldiers. It was the darkest and most terrifying morning imaginable.'

Sometime later, on her way up to her room, on the stairs Signe Askim ran into an army officer she knew. The *Norge* has gone down, he said. We don't know anything about the *Eidsvold*:

> My legs gave way beneath me and I fell to my knees on the stone staircase. The officer thought my husband was captain of the *Eidsvold*, otherwise he would have been more circumspect. Somehow I managed to pull myself together. Both my stockings had laddered from top to toe. I staggered into my room and sank down on the edge of the bed. I realised that there wasn't much hope. Never again would I see my beloved husband. The few words we'd exchanged the day before were the last I'd ever hear from him.

12

COUNTER-ATTACK

Narvik, Tuesday 9 April 08.00 to Wednesday 10 April 10.00

News of the German occupation of Narvik trickled piecemeal into the Admiralty all through the morning of 9 April, much of it garbled and difficult to interpret. This was because the Royal Navy, army and secret service representatives on the spot had been just as surprised by the swiftness and ruthlessness of the German attack as the Norwegians themselves and the foreign journalists.

'I was woken at about five o'clock in the morning by thunderous gunfire,' Intelligence Officer James Torrance wrote later. 'But when I peered out of my hotel room window, there was a thick blizzard. Nothing could be seen.' The young Scottish officer had arrived in Narvik in mufti a few days earlier to hire transport for the use of General Mackesy's troops when the British force landed. He had been assigned an office in the consulate, where 57-year-old Captain George Gibbs, assisted by Commander Geoffrey Vavasour, was acting as consul and naval control officer and regarded by most as the key representative of MI6 in the iron ore port.

Convinced that the 24th Guards Brigade was about to land, Torrance hastily dressed. 'I felt growing irritation that I hadn't received the advance notice by telegraph that I had been promised.' He woke Gibbs and Vavasour, who were sleeping in adjacent rooms at the Royal Hotel:

> We went down the street together, surely to meet our own forces. But when we reached the square, we suddenly found ourselves among German foot soldiers. We turned and blended in with the locals who were gathered behind a hopelessly confused and ill-prepared line of Norwegian soldiers in the open marketplace.

While Dietl's troops searched the consulate and their abandoned rooms at the Royal, the three British officers fled into the surrounding mountains. They sought refuge in a windswept barn far from all means of communication and watched with growing frustration as the town was soon fully in the hands of the Germans. 'The destroyers docked with their decks full of troops. Before the snow obscured our view once more, I counted at least five warships in port.'

At a stroke, the British intelligence unit had been rendered useless. There was an acute lack of reliable information, which explains the stream of slightly desperate signals that same morning. 'Narvik *must* be watched to prevent Germans landing,' insisted an urgent signal to the Commander-in-Chief of the Home Fleet at 08.45. But Admiral Forbes was far away to the south in the Norwegian Sea, so it was up to Captain Warburton-Lee to carry out the order. 'Send some destroyers up to Narvik to make certain no enemy troops land,' read another signal, despatched at 09.52. 'Norway is at war with Germany.'

It was only when the *Daily Express* containing Giles Romilly's eyewitness account appeared on the streets, and the Norwegian Broadcasting Corporation's newsflash from Oslo had been translated, that it dawned on the Chiefs-of-Staff and War Cabinet that it might already be too late. 'According to a broadcast from Oslo, a small German force has landed at Narvik,' read a cautiously worded message handed to the Cabinet's second emergency meeting at noon the same day.

But Churchill, who had started his day in his silk dressing gown in the Upper War Room some hours earlier, was still optimistic and refused to admit that he and his officers had erroneously directed the destroyer force *away* from the Vestfjord the previous day. 'The First Lord of the Admiralty said that the German transport which had reached Narvik must presumably have slipped past our patrol in the heavy weather prevailing at the time,' report the minutes. 'As regards the general situation in Scandinavia, he felt that we were in a far better position than we had been up to date. Our hands were now free, and we could apply our overwhelming sea power on the Norwegian coast.'

Bold words indeed, uttered as they were only a few hours after Churchill had assured his colleagues that the Royal Navy was on the alert; he convinced no one.

MESSAGE . OUT

SECRET. 0136/10 April.

To: Capt. D 2. Date 10.4.40.

Repeated F.O.C. B.C.S. 154.
C. in C. Home Fleet 862.

NAVAL CYPHER (A)

From Admiralty.

MOST IMMEDIATE.

Norwegian Coast Defence Vessels EIDVOLD and NORGE may be in German hands.

You alone can judge whether in these circumstances attack should be made. We shall support whatever decision you take.

0136/10

for 1st Sea Lord.

↑THE QUANDARY: Instead of telling him to wait for reinforcements, Churchill and his staff at the Admiralty placed responsibility for his next move on the shoulders of Captain Warburton-Lee. When Tranøy pilots informed the *Hardy*'s captain that the Germans had taken Narvik with a superior force, Warburton-Lee first conferred with his fellow commanders. He took the decision to attack after he had spent half an hour alone in his cabin, wrestling with his conscience. (Bernard Warburton-Lee's personal archive)

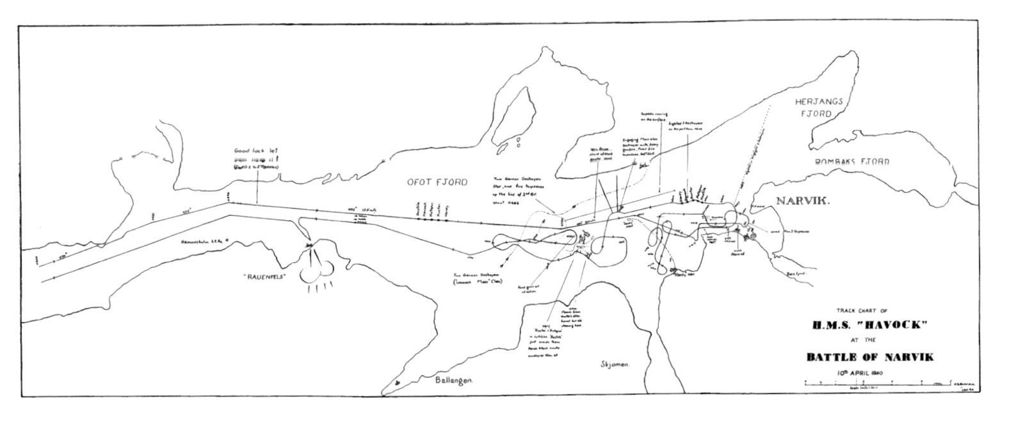

↑THE TRACK CHART: HMS *Havock*'s plot shows the British destroyer flotilla's manoeuvrings in the Ofot fjord and the course of the battle in Narvik harbour in the early morning of 10 April 1940. (National Archives, London)

←H-CLASS: HMS *Hunter* was a typical representative of Britain's H-Class destroyers built in 1936. She was lost in the Ofot fjord on 10 April after colliding with the *Hotspur*. Her captain, Lieutenant Lindsay de Villiers, and 107 men of her complement of 156 were lost with her. (Imperial War Museum)

←PUTTING THE BOOT IN: This unique photograph shows a German destroyer engaged in shelling the already burning *Hardy*, beached at Vidrek (shrouded in smoke). The destroyer concerned may have been the *Wolfgang Zenker*. The photograph was taken from the *Erich Giese*. (Bundesarchiv, Filmarchiv / Transit Film GmbH)

←UNDER FIRE: Exploding shells falling harmlessly into the sea close beside a German destroyer in the Ofot fjord. (Bundesarchiv, Filmarchiv / Transit Film GmbH)

↑SAVED: After the battle, the German destroyers *Wolfgang Zenker*, *Erich Giese* and *Erich Koellner* rescued some fifty or so of the 156 men on board the *Hunter*, but at least five of them died before reaching hospital in Narvik. (Bundesarchiv, Filmarchiv / Transit Film GmbH)

↗ABLAZE: A German destroyer on fire after the battles in the Ofot fjord. In all probability it is the *Georg Thiele*, which had lost her fire control equipment and had to call on the *Bernd von Arnim* for assistance. (Bernard Warburton-Lee's personal archive)

BLACK-OUT ZERO HOUR TO-NIGHT UNTIL 5.48 A.M. MOON RISES MOON SETS

Daily Express

No. 12,442 — Tuesday, April 9, 1940 — One Penny

Read IAN COSTER'S LIGHTER LONDON in the EVENING STANDARD

Norway darkens coast in fear of Nazi invasion

MIDNIGHT RAID ALARM IN BLACKED-OUT OSLO

All phones to Denmark cut off this morning

NAZI FLEET PUTS OUT FOR—?

FEARING an invasion by Germany, Norway last night announced that all lighthouses along 400 miles of coast, from the Swedish frontier to Bergen, would be put out and kept out.

This coastline is all south of the areas where the Allied fleet laid minefields yesterday to stop Nazi ships carrying ore from Narvik to Germany.

All radio and beam stations for airplanes in southern Norway were closed down last night.

OSLO WAS BLACKED OUT. AT MIDNIGHT AN AIR-RAID ALARM SOUNDED IN THE CAPITAL—WHY, IT WAS NOT REVEALED.

Simultaneously all telephone communication between Oslo and Copenhagen was cut off.

Threats to send an expeditionary force to Norway were uttered in Berlin by spokesmen for the German High Command late last night.

A message, relayed from Berlin through New York, said strong forces would be landed to establish naval, air and submarine bases.

The Nazis claimed that a landing would be justified "because the Allies have completely abolished Norway's neutrality."

'BRITAIN IS RESPONSIBLE'

Other messages from Berlin said that the Nazis, before landing men in Norway, would send an ultimatum demanding the instant clearing of the minefields.

Raging against Britain and France, Goering's newspaper, National Zeitung, said: "A decisive phase of the war has been reached. Britain is trying to extend the war to Scandinavia. She stands responsible before the world."

Authoritative reports from Paris said there was great activity on the airfields of north and west Germany.

THE ARMY ALONG GERMANY'S ENTIRE COASTLINE FROM THE NORTH SEA TO THE BALTIC HAS BEEN HEAVILY REINFORCED.

All these moves followed swiftly

This is where it all happened

Daily Express man on the spot reports—

Iron ore ships run for shelter

A Reuter message from Oslo early today says that the export of iron ore from the Norwegian port of Narvik was stopped yesterday afternoon.

From GILES ROMILLY,
Daily Express Staff Reporter
NARVIK, Monday.

CLOSELY following reports that the German fleet had approached the Norwegian coast it became known today that the British warships which had been standing off the Norwegian coast had moved out of sight.

On orders telephoned to Narvik by the Norwegian Admiralty this morning no ships lying in harbour have been allowed to sail.

Seven German iron ore ships were caught in Narvik harbour by the order. Five of them are still lying empty in the roads.

Two, the Martha Henrietta Fisser and the Neuenfels, of Bremen, were lying alongside the loading quay. The Martha Fisser, already loaded, was sunk down to her watermark, the Neuenfels was still empty.

92—if they all came

Daily Express Naval Reporter

On paper the German naval strength is:—

Battle cruisers	2
Pocket battleships	2
Aircraft carrier	1
Heavy cruisers	3
Light cruisers	4
Destroyers	30
Torpedo boats	42
Escort vessels	6
Minelayers	2

—Britain tells— Scandinavians

"LEAVE OUR MINES ALONE"

By GUY EDEN.

BRITAIN and France have given assurances to the Scandinavian countries that they will defend them from attack by Germany, but—

The British Navy will take vigorous action to prevent any country—including Norway—sweeping up the minefields laid by Britain off the Norwegian coast yesterday.

As seen in London, the present position, as it affects the Scandinavian countries, is this:—

They are being compelled, through fear of Germany, to supply large quantities of war materials to Germany, and to take a semi-hostile attitude to the Allies.

Britain and France have, therefore, been compelled to take action to protect their own interests, as well as those of the Scandinavian

HOW OUR NAVY SANK—

TRANSPORT, U-BOAT AND 2 TANKERS

Daily Express Correspondent
OSLO, Monday.

BRITAIN'S Navy followed up her mine-laying exploit off the Norwegian coast at dawn today by sinking this afternoon three German ships within two hours in the Skagerrak, the stretch of water between Denmark and Norway.

All the Nazis were sunk by submarines. One, the Rio de Janeiro, 5,261 tons, was either a troop transport or a submarine supply vessel.

She went down with the loss of about 150 lives. The crews of the other two ships were rescued.

INTERCEPTED

A fourth German ship, as well as a German U-boat, were also reported sunk by British action.

The Rio de Janeiro was the first ship to be sunk today. She was intercepted by a British submarine off Justoya Island, near Arendal on the south-east coast of Norway, at one o'clock this afternoon.

She refused to stop, and the submarine let loose some warning

→ BACK PAGE COL. THREE

IRA men strip strike at Dartmoor

Daily Express Correspondent
PRINCETOWN (Devon), Monday.

A "STRIP STRIKE" has been declared by the I.R.A. men in Dartmoor Prison who mutinied at Easter.

For ten days they have been sitting in cells with their clothes piled up on the beds. If they feel cold they drape themselves in a blanket, but they have central heating.

When they were called before visiting magistrates on Friday to be punished for the mutiny they refused to dress, and said they would wear nothing but blankets.

Canon J. M. Ryan, the Roman Catholic chaplain, had to be asked to reason with them. He visited each man in his cell and persuaded them all to put on their clothes.

But as soon as they had been awarded solitary confinement on bread and water they stripped again, and they are still "on strike."

B.E.F. bride vanishes

First time here

A pretty, fair-haired B.E.F. bride, thirty-two-year-old Mrs. Marcelline Denecker, who landed at a Channel port a week ago to join her N.C.O. husband, now back from France, has vanished—somewhere in England.

She cannot speak any English, and has no friends in this country.

The husband, Staff Quarter-

Scapa raided last night

AS dusk came last night German planes made another raid on Scapa Flow.

They did not cause any damage, and, said a joint Admiralty and Air Ministry statement: "It is certain that at least one enemy aircraft was brought down by our fighters."

At Stromness, in the Orkneys, the town council carried on talking about air-raid shelters while the raiders and fighters were heard overhead.

Provost Marwick thought the council behaved in the only fashion possible. "We already had arrears of business, and the position would have become worse if we had scuttled," he said.

The official German news agency claims that "several heavy units" were hit during the raid.

STOP PRESS

British and Nazi planes down in Norway

OSLO, Tuesday.—British plane made forced landing at ... south-western Norway, yesterday. Crew have been interned. A German plane is reported to have landed near Kristiansand with engine trouble.—British United Press.

NAZI POCKET WARSHIP OUT

COPENHAGEN, Tuesday. — One pocket battleship is believed to be among German war vessels which steamed northwards through Great Belt yesterday, says Copenhagen newspaper National Tidende.—British United Press.

↑HEADLINE COVERAGE: The front page of the *Daily Express* featuring Giles Romilly's last despatch from Narvik, phoned in on 8 April. The following day, he was arrested by the occupying Germans. (Facsimile of the *Daily Express*)

↑IN SAFETY: Men stream ashore from the beached and burning *Hardy* and make their way through the snow to Petra Christensen's farm at Vidrek, where they were given food and dry clothing. (Facsimile of the *London Illustrated News*)

↑THE OFOT FJORD: The engagement in the Ofot fjord in the morning of 10 April, as envisaged by an artist on the staff of the *London Illustrated News.* (Facsimile *London Illustrated News*)

↑PRE-CAPSIZE: Lieutenant Commander Hans Erdmenger managed to moor his badly damaged destroyer, the *Wilhelm Heidkamp*, to the Swedish merchantman *Oxelösund*. As can be seen, the destroyer's stern is already half submerged. The end came on 11 April, when Commodore Friedrich Bonte's flagship turned turtle and sank. On the right is the German ore carrier *Aachen*. (Erling Skjold's Collection)

↑WIDESPREAD DESTRUCTION: This photograph was taken in Narvik harbour in the morning of 10 April and gives a good idea of the destruction wrought by the British attack. Seven merchant ships and two German destroyers were destroyed and a number of other destroyers and ore carriers severely damaged. (Scanpix / akg-images)

A SHIPS' GRAVEYARD: Only the masts of the German ore carriers *Bockenheim* and *Altona* (left and centre respectively) are visible, while nothing but the bow of the *Hein Hoyer* and the stern of the British *Romanby* protrude above water. To the right is the Norwegian ore carrier *Cate B.* (Erling Skjold's Collection)

THE WRECKS: Burning and sinking wrecks in Narvik harbour following the British attack in the morning of 10 April 1940. Moored alongside the jetty in the foreground is the Norwegian guard ship *Michael Sars*, with her sister ship, *Senja*, on the other side. The destroyer is the *Diether von Roeder*, which was badly damaged by fire. (Bundesarchiv, Filmarchiv / Transit Film GmbH)

FIVE HITS: Five British shells penetrated the hull of the *Diether von Roeder*, causing serious fires in the engine room, fuel tanks and storerooms below deck. Welders from the *Jan Wellem* can be seen striving to make the destroyer seaworthy again. (Atle Wilmar's Collection)

A NORWEGIAN ORE CARRIER: The *Saphir* (7,100grt) slowly sinking off the steamship quay in Narvik after the British attack. Built in 1905, she was owned by the Edwin Endresen Shipping Company, Stavanger. (Bundesarchiv, Filmarchiv / Transit Film GmbH)

↑THE *RAUENFELS*: Heavily loaded with ammunition, the German supply ship *Rauenfels* (8,460grt) was sunk in Ballangen Bay by HMS *Havock*, which helped to isolate General Dietl's forces still further. (Erling Skjold's Collection)

↑MOUNTAIN TROOPS: Wet and shaken survivors from the sunken German destroyers were soon enrolled in naval detachments to defend Narvik against further British attacks. They were equipped with captured Norwegian small arms. (Bernard Warburton-Lee's personal archive)

↑↓RESCUED: In the course of Saturday evening and Sunday morning, 13–14 April, the *Hardy*'s survivors were taken to a nursing home in Ballangen and from there to the waiting *Ivanhoe*, a minelayer. The top photograph may be of Lieutenant Geoffrey Stanning, who had broken his ankle, being carefully hoisted on board from a pinnace. (Erling Skjold's Collection; Bernard Warburton-Lee's personal archive)

↑THE WRECK OF THE *HARDY*: The *Hardy* drifted clear of the beach at Vidrek and was carried by the tide deeper into the fjord to her last resting place off Einebærnes Point, where she finally turned over and remained lying on her side. (Erling Skjold's Collection)

↑SAFE IN THE SKJELL FJORD: The badly mauled *Hotspur* took refuge in the Skjell fjord on the outer rim of the Lofoten Islands. Later in April, after temporary repair, she was able to return to Scapa Flow. (Bernard Warburton-Lee's personal archive)

↑HONOURED: Commander Herbert Layman was awarded a DSO for his achievements as captain of the *Hotspur* in the attack on Narvik on 10 April. (Scanpix /TopFoto)

REPLACED BONTE: Fregattenkapitän Erich Bey, appointed flotilla commander after the death of Commodore Friedrich Bonte, was forced to turn back when, together with the flotilla's other two seaworthy destroyers, he tried to break out of the Ofot fjord in the evening of 10 April. (Source unknown)

BOARDED THE *RAUENFELS*: Lieutenant John Burfield boarded the German supply ship *Rauenfels* and found that her crew had set the ship ablaze and abandoned her. He had just got back to the *Havock* when the *Rauenfel*'s cargo of ammunition exploded. (Source unknown)

S. 1320b. **NAVAL MESSAGE.** Revised December, 1935.

For use in Signal Department only

Originators Instructions: (Indication of Priority, Intercept Group, etc.)

No. of Groups:

TO: Hotspur Hostile Havock Hunter

FROM: Captain D(2)

Write Across

5

Keep on engaging the enemy

10

15

=0555

20

THE FINAL SIGNAL: Captain Warburton-Lee's last order to the destroyer flotilla. Shortly afterwards the *Hardy*'s bridge was struck by two shells. (Bernard Warburton-Lee's personal archive)

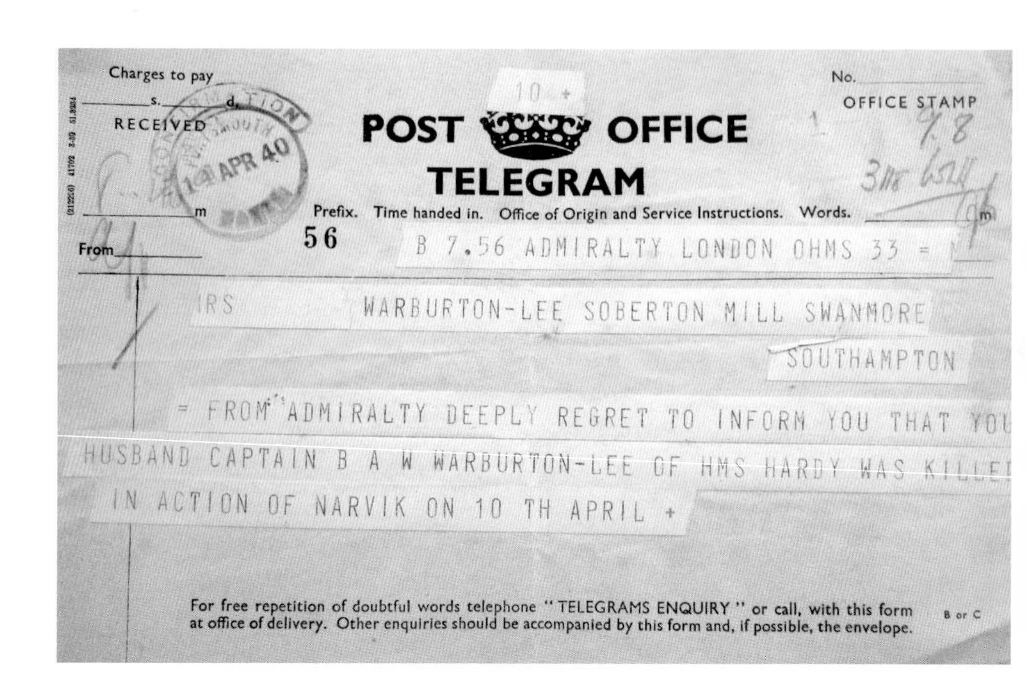

Charges to pay

s. d.

RECEIVED

No.

OFFICE STAMP

14 APR 40

POST OFFICE

TELEGRAM

Prefix. Time handed in. Office of Origin and Service Instructions. Words.

From

56 B 7.56 ADMIRALTY LONDON OHMS 33 =

MRS WARBURTON-LEE SOBERTON MILL SWANMORE SOUTHAMPTON

= FROM ADMIRALTY DEEPLY REGRET TO INFORM YOU THAT YOU
HUSBAND CAPTAIN B A W WARBURTON-LEE OF HMS HARDY WAS KILLE
IN ACTION OF NARVIK ON 10 TH APRIL +

For free repetition of doubtful words telephone "TELEGRAMS ENQUIRY" or call, with this form at office of delivery. Other enquiries should be accompanied by this form and, if possible, the envelope.

B or C

↑DREADED NEWS: The telegram that reached Soberton Mill on Sunday 14 April to inform Captain Warburton-Lee's wife of her husband's death. (Bernard Warburton-Lee's personal archive)

←LAST RESTING PLACE: Captain Bernard Warburton-Lee's grave in Ballangen. (Bernard Warburton-Lee's personal archive)

↑WILL THE BRITISH COME?: German soldiers and sailors in makeshift uniforms occupied positions around Narvik after Warburton-Lee's devastating attack. They feared a British landing was imminent. (Scan from Fritz-Otto Busch, *Narvik. Vom Heldenkampf deutscher Zerstörer*)

↑↓COMMANDEERED WEAPONS: The Germans took over sixty Colt machine guns (bottom), 6,000 rifles, 1.5 million rounds of ammunition and vast quantities of other military equipment from the stores at Elvegårdsmoen Camp. This unexpected haul was quickly portioned out and positioned around Narvik in anticipation of a British assault. (Scan from Fritz-Otto Busch, *Narvik. Vom Heldenkampf deutscher Zerstörer*; Scanpix / akg-images)

'No news from the Fleet – "wireless silence" – rather ominous,' Sir Alexander Cadogan wrote in his diary. 'Germans seem to have got into Narvik. How?!' General Edmund Ironside, Chief of the Imperial General Staff, was more direct: 'The Navy could not have prevented the Oslo landing,' he declared, 'but the Narvik one is inexcusable.'

On board HMS *Hardy*, far to the north, Warburton-Lee and his men were unaware of the discussions in London which soon would result in the order to attack the occupied town: 'Proceed Narvik and sink or harass enemy ships.'

Having given up pursuit of the *Scharnhorst* and *Gneisenau*, the destroyers decreased speed. 'It was a relief to turn round and have the wind coming from astern,' Lieutenant Stanning wrote. 'We were soaking wet and exhausted, since nobody had had a proper night's sleep in almost a week.' When Warburton-Lee's Maltese cook, Carmelo Aquilina, took a breakfast of hardboiled eggs, sandwiches and coffee up onto the bridge, the wind had dropped. 'We saw Skomvær approaching on the port bow and felt quite content, in spite of the cold. *Renown* continued the chase, and we knew that the enemy had at least been dealt *some* damage.' Leslie Smale commented: 'The Captain and Gunnery Officer were full of praise for the way the men had behaved, and the ship was full of talk of what was the most exciting moments of most of our lives.'

In Narvik, the situation was rapidly deteriorating.

'Narvik's capture was an incredibly quick action, lasting half an hour,' Harold Callender cabled to the *New York Times*. 'In another half hour the Germans had established headquarters at the Royal Hotel and had sent the first forces to the hills to prepare for the defense of the town.'

Callender had been roused from his sleep by the explosions and had immediately made his way down to the harbour. He arrived in time to meet the first German soldiers as they entered the marketplace and to witness Colonel Sundlo's abject surrender of the Norwegian garrison:

> It was the end of much more than two Norwegian warships, some British merchant vessels and perhaps 300 lives – all destroyed in the space of ten minutes. It was also the end of a shaky neutrality that the Scandinavian countries had tried to preserve out of fear of Germany, and of all Nordic independence, at least for the time being.

While many Norwegians claimed that the German troops had staggered ashore exhausted and near-prostrate from seasickness, Callender had a completely different impression:

> I encountered smartly erect army officers in grey uniforms and naval officers in shining blue and gold, as if they were on a cruise holiday. The young Austrians sitting in the hotel lobby loaded down with weapons, the piles of steel helmets in the railway station's waiting room, and the lean, well-proportioned officer giving orders to the Norwegian stationmaster were all symbols of Germany's ability to project power 125 miles north of the Arctic Circle.

In virtue of his British citizenship and standing as Churchill's nephew, Romilly was arrested; as Americans, Callender and Rhodes were able to cross into nearby Sweden on one of the few trains that were allowed to leave Narvik that afternoon. 'I'll never forget the scenes that took place at that railway station on 9 April,' Callender wrote. 'The soldiers revealed a complete ruthlessness and a kind of jovial and self-confident efficiency that scared the Norwegians stiff as they waited to flee to Sweden. The Germans were young. They clearly thought that the world belonged to them.'

The military camp at Elvegårdsmoen, 20km north of Narvik, also fell without a shot being fired. Some 600 mountain troops, commanded by Oberst Alois Windisch, had gone ashore from three destroyers to march on the snow-banked road to the camp, which lay some few kilometres further inland. The battalion commander, Lieutenant Colonel Wolf Hagemann, and his second-in-command personally overpowered two guards and moved straight onto the parade ground. 'In between the large wooden buildings we could see some soldiers strolling nonchalantly about,' Windisch wrote. 'They were in the middle of their morning ablutions and were only partly dressed.'

After a brief period of negotiation and a phone call to Oberst Konrad Sundlo, the remaining 375 soldiers and civilian workers in the camp surrendered the barracks and stores to Windisch, who was surprised to find that he had acquired control of the equipment of an entire Norwegian regiment, a battalion of engineers and a medical company: 6,000 rifles and carbines, 600 pistols and revolvers, more than 150 Madsen machine guns with twin magazines, sixty Colt machine guns, 300 spare magazines and 1.5 million rounds of ammunition, along with a wide range of accoutrements and equipment, medical supplies, provisions, skis, sledges and some thirty horses. 'It gradually turned into a brisk but quite sunny day,' wrote Windisch, who was delighted with this unexpected haul. 'At around ten o'clock I was able to telephone our Operations Officer, Lieutenant Colonel Bader, and give him our first situation report.'

That the Germans were able to take the camp so easily was primarily the responsibility of General Carl Gustav Fleischer; but, weather-bound as he was in Vadsø, far to the north in eastern Finnmark, there was little the divisional commander could do. The telephone link was still open, however, and in his frustration he vented his wrath on Oberst Sundlo, whom he accused of high treason for having surrendered Narvik without a fight. 'At 06.30 or thereabouts Major Spjeldnæs received a phone call from General Fleischer ordering him to arrest Sundlo and expel the Germans from the town,' says the official account of the incident.

It would have been difficult, if not impossible, to arrest a man who was already in enemy hands, however, and it would have been no easy task to offer resistance in a small town that had already been occupied – certainly not for troops who were both outnumbered and, to a great extent, had already been disarmed and were generally demoralised. Instead, on receipt of Fleischer's order, Spjeldnæs and a fellow officer, Major Omdal, gathered what troops they could find and marched them out of the town, rifles over their shoulders. A bewildered German sentry shouted 'Halt!' but Spjeldnæs merely saluted and said in a reassuring voice, 'Doch wir marschieren. Guten Morgen' ('We're marching on, no matter what. Good morning'); unhindered, they then continued on their way. Thanks to this officer's audacity and quick thinking, 180 Norwegian soldiers evaded German captivity – on a day which, for the army at large, was destined to be a day of ignominy.

On board HMS *Hardy* in the entrance to the Vestfjord, Captain Warburton-Lee was preparing his counter-attack with his customary resoluteness. 'There was extremely little intelligence on what sort of forces had reached the town,' Stanning wrote. 'But if it was troops from one or two ships, the task looked distinctly straightforward.' But Warburton-Lee was a man who never left anything to chance. Shortly after lunch, Stanning was summoned to the captain's cabin:

> He said that he was thinking of paying a visit to the pilot station at Tranøy to investigate whether the pilots had any more exact information. I was burning

to ask if I could carry out the task, but before I could do so, he asked: 'Which boat are you going to use?'

Meanwhile, at the Royal Hotel, Signe Askim was undergoing one of the most harrowing experiences of her life. As she wrote in her family memoirs:

> I began feverishly packing suitcases, all the lovely dresses of which I was so proud, the silver fox furs from Tromsø and all sorts of odds and ends. I was in a daze. Sometimes I gave in to tears, but not often. I knew from experience that people don't do that in moments of real crisis.
>
> Later that morning there was a knock at the door and Dr Waaler came in.
>
> 'Have you heard the news?' he asked.
>
> 'Yes. I know the *Norge*'s gone down.'
>
> 'No, I don't mean that,' he said. 'Your husband's alive! Get yourself up to the hospital and you can see him.'
>
> 'He's alive, you mean he's alive!' I exclaimed, and threw my arms around him.
>
> 'Yes, off you go. Hurry up! They'll be expecting you, I'm sure.'
>
> I shall never forget the warmth in his eyes, which were filled with tears.
>
> I didn't hesitate! I put on my coat and, hat in hand, raced down the stairs, past a group of Germans in the foyer and out of the door. The weather had cleared up, there were only a few light snowflakes in the air, and the sun was breaking through as I stumbled along in my slippery ski boots. I must have passed quite a number of Germans, but none of them took any notice of me. There was only one thought in my mind – that my husband was alive and that I was going to see him again!

On seeing the *Norge* capsize and sink, the merchant ships in the harbour immediately lowered lifeboats and hastened to the rescue, as did the *Bernd von Armin*, which had just torpedoed her. Despite their good intentions, they were unable to prevent the tragedy that ensued. Of a complement of 191, 101 men lost their lives, most of them youngsters from northern Norway and the southern county of Vestfold. The merchant seamen managed to save eighty-one exhausted officers and ratings from the ice-cold water, and the *Bernd von Armin*'s pinnace picked up a further nine, among them an unconscious Per Askim, who was given first aid on board the destroyer before being taken to hospital by ambulance.

Narvik Hospital occupied a commanding position high above the town, and Signe found the last stretch tough going in the slush. She remembers taking off her heavy fur coat and draping it over her arm, as it was too hot on top of her ski suit. When she reached the hospital, it was to find the corridor packed with wounded and bedraggled men:

> I found myself surrounded by people I knew and loved. How many men I embraced and how many embraced me in return, I have no idea. Tears streamed down my cheeks and every time I saw someone I knew, I exclaimed, 'Oh, I'm so glad! Thank God you're alive too!' Some of the men were all bandaged up, and one of them, his head swathed in bandages, came over to me and said, 'I'm from the *Norge* as well.' I gave him a hug too.

There were stretchers everywhere, and here and there Signe saw many German uniforms. A young Norwegian beckoned her over. 'We managed to do something after all,' he said. The doors of the ward were open and Signe could see that all the beds were full. Eventually, the second-in-command of the *Norge*, Captain Sandved, took her arm and led her over to one of the open doors:

> 'The Captain's here,' he said. I took out my handkerchief, wiped my tear-stained cheeks and went in. There were two beds occupied by men I didn't know and another one surrounded by a tall screen. I took a cautious look behind it, and there was my husband, deathly pale and with his face all cuts and bruises. His eyes were closed. I hardly dared to breathe. Was he dead after all? Slowly he opened his eyes. I stepped closer. He gazed at me intently and his lips moved in an attempt to speak. I sat down beside him on the bed and laid my cheek against his. 'What did they manage to do ashore?' he asked, his voice barely audible. 'Nothing,' I answered. 'There was nothing they *could* do.'

Signe moistened a towel:

> I bathed the cuts on his face, which were still bleeding. He was still black with soot – and my falling tears made him blacker still. His mouth was a rigid line and I could hardly make out what he was trying to tell me. Finally he mumbled, 'Can you believe that I'm still alive?'
>
> 'You're going to do a lot more yet,' I answered. Unable to hold back any longer, I laid my head on the pillow and wept unashamedly – both with joy at finding him alive and in sorrow because of all the dreadful things that had happened.

HMS *Hardy* and the rest of the flotilla hove to off Tranøy Island at about 16.00. 'We landed on the nearest point and ordered the motorboat to continue to the jetty we could see inside the bay itself,' wrote Stanning, who took ashore with him a signalman and Torpedo Officer George Heppel:

> We climbed over stones covered with seaweed, and slipped onto our knees in the ice-cold water. In the distance, the locals were pouring onto the pier, maybe as many as twenty or thirty of them. The people moved without any apparent concern, which I took as a sign that the fishing station had not been occupied by the Germans.

Among the people who gathered round the three British sailors and the pilots were the assistant lighthouse keeper Erling Andreassen and his 13-year-old son Torbjørn. 'All day Monday and throughout the night into Tuesday 9 April, a fresh to strong wind had been blowing, interspersed with flurries of snow,' recalled Torbjørn Andreassen in an article he wrote some years later entitled 'Childhood Years at Tranøy Lighthouse':

> My father went on duty at two o'clock that night to relieve the other keeper, Noer. At about half past three, in the grey light of dawn, he came and woke my mother and me and beckoned us over to the kitchen window to see something quite extraordinary. Just disappearing into a snow shower was a warship heading up the fjord towards Narvik. My father told us that there had been more ships heading into the fjord at high speed.

They had seen Commodore Bonte's destroyers. They weren't at all sure of how many there had been and their poor command of English made communication difficult. 'I rolled out the chart, but then I realised that in my haste I had grabbed one showing the Vestfjord in large scale,' Stanning wrote:

> Instead we drew a map in the snow of Narvik and the surrounding area. One man said that he had seen a submarine entering the fjord and that he was sure that the channel was mined. A young boy told us that he had seen six destroyers, not five as the older man claimed. They asked if we were intending to attack Narvik. I gave them a fairly vague answer. They pointed at the *Hardy* and said that the German destroyers were larger. If we were really planning to strike, then we should get more ships.

The discussion took some time, and Stanning ordered the signalman to give Warburton-Lee a provisional summing-up. 'A sailor with two flags walked out onto the edge of the pier and semaphored a message out to the destroyer waiting beyond the light,' wrote Olav Elsbak, who would later be elected mayor. Eleven years old at the time, he had gone down to the pier with his father, a staunch patriot also named Olav. 'It was an impressive sight for an eleven-year-old who had just learned the alphabet – and a lesson for life.'

Stanning was never quite able to free himself from the thought that he might have misunderstood what the Norwegians were trying to tell him. 'There was clearly some disagreement about how many destroyers they had seen. But it never occurred to us that they might have been meaning to tell us that five *plus* six destroyers had entered the fjord. If we had realised that, we might have acted differently.'

Meanwhile, back in London, Prime Minister Neville Chamberlain had given the House of Commons an initial account of the night's dramatic events in Denmark and Norway: unconditional surrender in Copenhagen and landings in the face of sporadic resistance in Norway's principal ports. 'His Majesty's Government have at once assured the Norwegian Government that, in view of the German invasion of their country, His Majesty's Government have decided forthwith to extend their full aid to Norway; and have intimated that they will fight the war in full association with them,' he said, though his main concern appeared to be to emphasise that the Germans had launched their invasion *before* Britain had violated Norwegian territorial waters:

> The information which is now coming to hand clearly indicates that the invasion was not only planned, but was already under way, before the mines were laid in Norwegian waters. I have no doubt that this further and rash act of aggression will rebound to Germany's disadvantage, and contribute to her ultimate defeat.

With regard to ongoing British military operations, the prime minister was decidedly vague: 'Powerful units of the Navy are at sea. Hon. Members will realise that it would not be in the public interest to give details at this stage as to any operations in which they are now engaged.'

Sound though this evaluation of the situation undoubtedly was, it nonetheless helped to camouflage the heated discussions taking place behind the scenes about *where* a counter-attack should be concentrated. In private, both the Royal Navy and Churchill, in his capacity as First Lord of the Admiralty, came in for severe criticism, and, as the day wore on, senior army officers began to show signs of increasing frustration. According to John Colville, even General Hastings Ismay, normally the most loyal of officers, was near to exploding: 'During the Cabinet "Pug" Ismay came out and said that as far as he could see the Cabinet were proposing to do the only thing that could lose us the war: namely *not* to take vigorous action.' Ismay's immediate superior, General Edmund Ironside, was equally aggravated: 'The War Cabinet was the most dreadful exhibition of loose talk. You cannot make war by referring everything to Committees and sitting wobbling and havering.'

In the War Office, Major General Richard Dewing had been at work since 04.00. As Director of Operations, he doubted the wisdom of giving priority to Narvik and was disappointed by the Chiefs of Staff's lack of resolution. 'Ineffective meeting of COS at 6.30,' he wrote in his diary. 'Newall, who was chairman, had no grip, and no one had constructive proposals, though clearly plans prepared for landings against little or no opposition could not be implemented now that the Germans are in possession.' He ordered his staff to draw up plans for an attack on Trondheim as a possible alternative to Narvik.

Following his discussions with the flotilla's staff officers and his lonely struggle with his conscience in the privacy of his cabin,[5] Captain Warburton-Lee dictated his decision to Stanning. 'I went immediately to encrypt a telegram to the Admiralty containing the new intelligence Heppel and I had acquired.' The historic wireless signal with its carefully considered wording went out at 17.51: 'Norwegians report Germans holding Narvik in force. Six destroyers and one submarine. Channel possibly mined. Intend attacking at dawn high water.'

The use of the word 'intend' was unusual. As Captain Peter Dickens wrote in his eminent study of the battle, *Narvik*, 'The naval meaning of "intend" when used by a junior officer to a senior, is that the act will be carried out unless otherwise ordered ... That is official naval usage; naval custom exhorts, "Never propose when you can intend, and never, never ask for guidance."' Warburton-Lee did not know that the battlecruisers *Renown* and *Repulse*,

5 See Prologue.

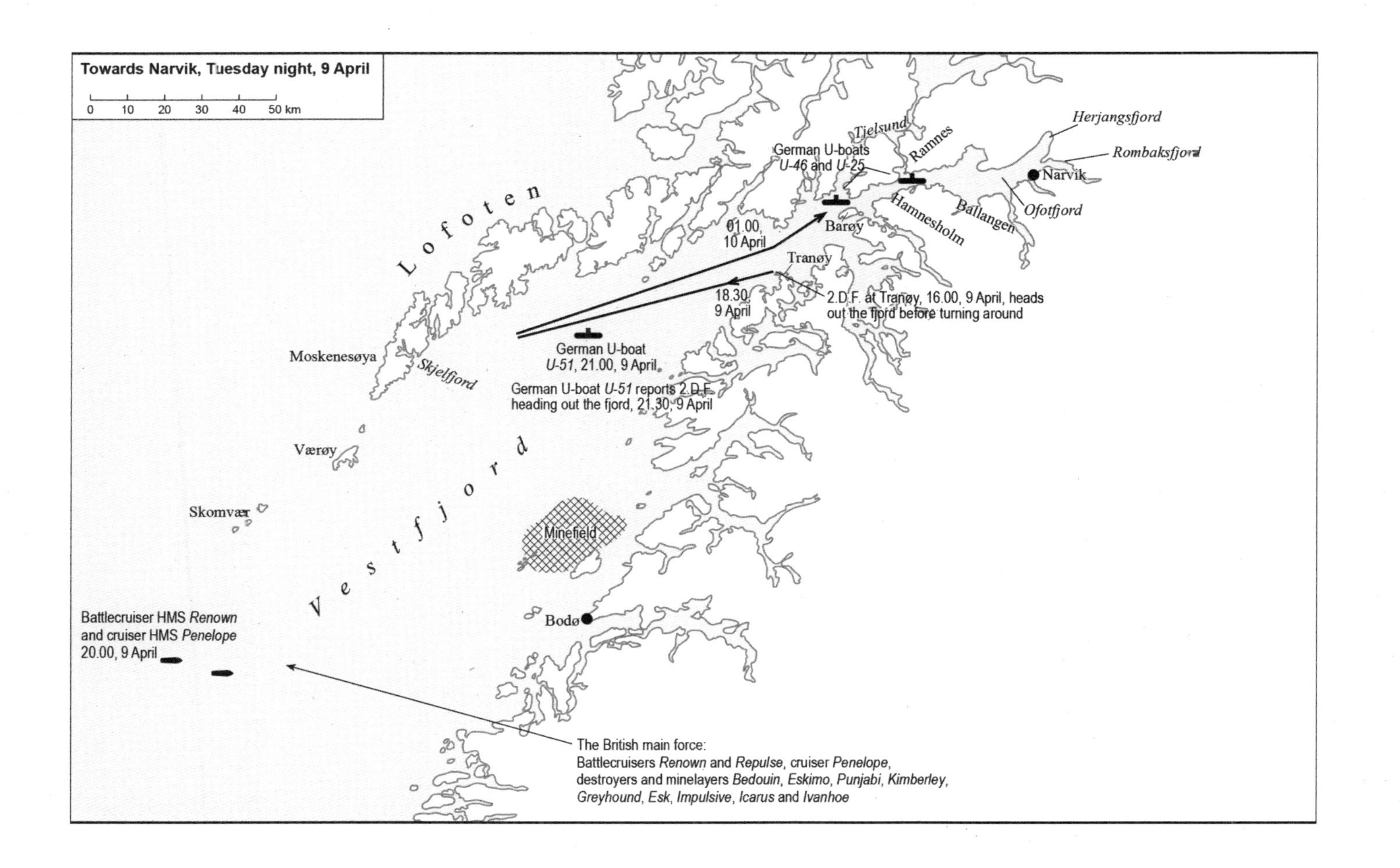
Towards Narvik, Tuesday night, 9 April
0
10
20
30
40
50 km
Herjangsfjord
Rombaksfjord
Narvik
Ofotfjord
Ballangen
Hamnesholm
Ramnes
Tjelsund
German U-boats
U-46 and U-25
Barøy
01.00,
10 April
Tranøy
18.30,
9 April
2.D.F. at Tranøy, 16.00, 9 April, heads
out the fjord before turning around
Lofoten
German U-boat
U-51, 21.00, 9 April
Moskenesøya
Skjelfjord
German U-boat U-51 reports 2.D.F.
heading out the fjord, 21.30, 9 April
Værøy
Vestfjord
Skomvær
Minefield
Bodø
Battlecruiser HMS Renown
and cruiser HMS Penelope
20.00, 9 April
The British main force:
Battlecruisers Renown and Repulse, cruiser Penelope,
destroyers and minelayers Bedouin, Eskimo, Punjabi, Kimberley,
Greyhound, Esk, Impulsive, Icarus and Ivanhoe

the light cruiser *Penelope* and ten destroyers were off Lofoten Point and could reach Narvik well before dawn the next day. In consequence, he had himself assumed responsibility and elected to attack superior German forces on his own, thereby acting in the most heroic traditions of the Royal Navy. It was now up to the Admiralty to decide whether he should continue or await reinforcements. 'Warburton-Lee was a man of integrity, honour and ambition,' Dickens wrote:

> He was a dedicated man, intensely professional, and although an excellent games-player, somewhat aloof and single-minded. Would it have been possible for him to add a paragraph 'Request reinforcements if available'? Or might a subconscious conflict between integrity and ambition have whispered that the commander of such reinforcements might be senior to him and either purloin his glory or bungle the operation? Or that the least hint of uncertainty in his tone might cause his seniors to doubt his competence and to cancel the project. *No!* The only concession he could make to his well-grounded fears was to allow his seniors time to take the proper action. He must have hoped beyond hope that they would.

While the *Hardy* and the rest of the flotilla set course out of the fjord to wait for nightfall and to deceive any enemy observers, in Narvik, German Flotilla Commander Friedrich Bonte was also wrestling with his conscience. 'When I reported to him about the sinking of the *Norge*, he rose to his feet and grabbed me by the shoulders,' wrote Lieutenant Commander Curt Rechel in the *Bernd von Arnim*'s war diary. '"I'm very grateful to you for leaving it to them to fire the first shot," he said. "I was forced to sink the other one before it was able to defend itself."'

Forty-three years old, Bonte had entered the Imperial Navy in 1914 and had been present as a young midshipman on board the SMS *Seydlitz* at the Battle of Jutland when the battlecruiser was struck by twenty-one shells and a torpedo. In the course of the next twenty-five years he had risen through the ranks in the destroyer and torpedo arms to become, in the autumn of 1939, the Kriegsmarine's first Commander of Destroyers – not by ingratiating himself with the Nazi Party's high-ups, but by virtue of his ability and experience. Bonte was a professional naval officer to his fingertips and his anti-Nazi views were well known among his close friends.

When, that same morning, he had hesitated to give the order to torpedo the *Eidsvold*, General Dietl, a committed, hard-boiled Nazi, had intervened and virtually taken over command and the Flotilla Commander had neither the courage nor strength of will to protest. The ensuing massacre had so shaken Bonte that he had still not completely recovered several hours later. 'He was still profoundly affected by the sinking of the *Eidsvold*,' Rechel reported. 'In his chivalrous world it was distressing to think that the ship had been torpedoed without having offered any resistance.'

Many other officers were of the same opinion. 'The sinking of these two coastal defence vessels was a great tragedy,' opined Karl-Theodor Raeder, a junior officer on board the *Erich Giese*. 'It was an extra heavy psychological burden on the occupying forces. We created many widows that day, and many people lost sons and brothers. Antipathy towards us grew correspondingly.'

Grand Admiral Raeder had had a number of heated discussions with Hitler and still insisted that the destroyers should return to Germany immediately on completion of their task, to avoid being caught in the narrow confines of the fjord, which could quickly be transformed into a death-trap. But the coastal defences at Ramnes had proved to be non-existent, and the ships carrying reserve artillery had still not reached Narvik. Accordingly, in his discussions with Dietl, Bonte had decided to allow two destroyers to stay behind to provide firepower for the infantry. The remaining eight were to break out of the Vestfjord, join the *Scharnhorst* and *Gneisenau* in the Norwegian Sea, slip past the British Home Fleet and return to Wilhelmshaven.

'The *Georg Thiele* and *Erich Giese* were allotted a supporting role,' Rechel wrote. 'Both had sustained damage to their engines, so they couldn't have undertaken a fast return home in any case.' Another problem was that the reserve tanker *Kattegat* had not reached Narvik on schedule. Without exception, the destroyers were almost completely out of fuel and were compelled to refuel from the whale factory ship *Jan Wellem*, which still had 8,500 tonnes of oil on board. But the *Jan Wellem*'s pumping capacity left much to be desired, so that only two destroyers could be refuelled at a time, one on each side. 'It proceeded very slowly,' wrote Hans Erdmenger on board the flagship *Wilhelm Heidkamp*, the first to moor alongside the *Jan Wellem*. 'It was eight hours before our tanks were full.'

While the operations officer, Robert Bader, Lieutenant Albert Bach and the rest of the staff took taxis from the pier to the Royal Hotel, where the Germans had commandeered rooms, General Dietl, accompanied by his adjutant, Captain Kurt Herrmann, was here, there and everywhere. 'Positions in the centre of the town and on the outskirts had been selected in advance and assigned to various units,' Herrmann wrote. 'The battalion and company commanders quickly issued the orders needed to ensure that defences were set up without delay.'

In the course of the morning all strategic buildings were occupied and instructions given for cooperation with the civil authorities. Motor vehicles and horses were requisitioned and anti-aircraft guns taken over and relocated. Even the monetary system came under German control with the issue of a scrip, known as *Reichskassenscheine*, which was introduced as local currency at the rate of 1.67 to the krone. 'After a few hours the German organisational machinery was running like clockwork,' Herrmann noted.

The well-stocked stores at Elvegårdsmoen proved an unexpected windfall for the occupying forces. But there was more to come. Stockpiled in Reserve Store No. 17 in the Market Hall the Germans discovered enough provisions to last 1,000 men for four weeks, while on board the *Jan Wellem* there were more than 8,000 cases of tinned food and other comestibles. 'We'd be fine for the next few weeks, even if the supply ships failed to turn up.'

That very first morning the German currency printing press aroused inflationary concerns as the troops went on a spending spree. To quote the official history of the Norwegian state railways, 'The Germans' purchases and requisitions with new *Reichskassenscheine* made heavy inroads into the banks' cash holdings and shops' stocks – and emptied the shelves of the state-owned Wine and Spirits Monopoly.'

At 09.30 Warburton-Lee's destroyers turned about and set course for Narvik. In the absence of orders to the contrary from his superiors, the Flotilla Commander had no alternative but to mount the counter-attack with the forces at his disposal, the *Hardy*, *Hotspur*, *Havock*, *Hunter* and *Hostile*.

'I had barely managed to get some hot food into me when the Captain sent for me again,' Stanning wrote:

> Poor Wash was still worried about what we would encounter at Narvik, and he wondered terribly what the Admiralty would think about the risk and the fact that he had postponed the operation. I said that the whole crew would be desperately disappointed if the attack was not carried out. That was the truth, because I'd come from the mess and I could sense the mood on board.

The captain and his short-sighted secretary, who was constantly polishing his glasses, had grown to be close friends in the months they had spent together at sea. Their chat in the captain's cabin helped to alleviate Warburton-Lee's anxiety, and they went up onto the bridge together. 'The landscape was in twilight, it was cold and clear. In the stillness, we could see the snow-clad mountains rising up on both sides from the surface of the sea. The sight filled us with awe, while at the same time making the whole affair seem totally surreal.'

In Narvik, wireless traffic monitored by the Germans told them that the Royal Navy was gathering significant forces off Lofoten Point, and the *U-51*, commanded by Lieutenant Dietrich Knorr, had observed Warburton-Lee's destroyers in the outer reaches of the Vestfjord, proceeding westwards, *out* of the fjord. There were two more U-boats deeper inside the fjord and with the *Hermann Künne* they established a defensive line between the harbour channel and the small community of Bogen. Commodore Friedrich Bonte, who was still suffering from remorse at the cold-blooded sinking of the *Eidsvold*, despatched an additional three destroyers to Herjangen and two more to Ballangen, retaining the remaining five in Narvik, partly for patrol duties and partly to continue refuelling from the *Jan Wellem*. 'Bonte expected trouble, but he underestimated the risk,' Karl-Theodor Raeder wrote. 'He was quite simply unable to imagine that British destroyers would penetrate right into Narvik harbour without warning.'

With security measures in place, Bonte retired for some much-needed sleep in the Flotilla Commander's cabin on board the *Wilhelm Heidkamp*, which was anchored deep inside the harbour, behind the line of merchant ships that had been taken as prizes. Most of the off-duty officers and ratings also turned in. 'I was worn out after the rigours of our time at sea and put on my pyjamas,' Raeder wrote. 'But the Artillery Officer came in and demanded to know if I was mad. I oughtn't to take off my clothes in case the alarm went. So I got dressed again, tumbled into bed and slept the sleep of the dead.'

Ashore, Lieutenant Albert Bach and his fellow staff officers had had a long and tiring day. They had dined well at the Royal Hotel, then quickly gone up to their rooms. 'I was worn out and fell asleep immediately,' Bach wrote. 'I was happy and grateful at having survived the voyage and once again being able to go to sleep in a warm hotel bed.' General Dietl, too, was finally able to close his bedroom door shortly after midnight. He had to be up early; the first conference with his battalion commanders to discuss the situation was scheduled for 08.00. But now there was only one thing on his mind: sleep.

It was the same in London. The 9 April had been an exceptionally wearying day, packed as it was with hastily convened meetings from early morning to late at night. It was past midnight when Churchill finally got to bed. 'I was very worried about Winston,' wrote his private secretary, Eric Seal. 'Churchill was knocked out, and I had to manoeuvre him to bed.'

A little earlier, in consultation with his staff, the First Lord had composed an answer to Warburton-Lee's signal from the Vestfjord, which had been received some hours earlier. It read: 'Norwegian coast defence ships *Eidsvold* and *Norge* may be in German hands. You alone can judge whether in these circumstances attack should be made. We shall support whatever decision you take.'

Deep down, Warburton-Lee had probably been hoping for reinforcements. Instead, the Admiralty had elected to leave it all to him. Now there was no escape: he had to go through with what he had begun.

The destroyer *Anton Schmitt* had relieved the *Hermann Künne* on patrol outside Narvik at midnight, and had in turn been relieved at 03.00 by the *Dieter von Roeder* under Lieutenant Commander Erich Holtorf. However, the order issued to Holtorf was hesitantly worded and merely directed the destroyer to keep watch on the harbour entrance until first light. The 39-year-old skipper chose to interpret the order literally and broke off patrol at 04.00, when the first gleam of light appeared on the horizon. He had no wish to be left holding the baby, as his main concern was to refuel as quickly as possible in case the order was given to return to Germany. 'Anchored up in the harbour as instructed,' he noted in the war diary at 04.25. 'Visibility highly variable, 100 to 1,000 metres. Snow showers. Expect to start refuelling from the *Jan Wellem* within next half hour.'

Meanwhile, hugging the southern shore of the fjord a few nautical miles to the west, Warburton-Lee's destroyers were making their slow approach. The call to action stations had been sounded shortly after midnight. All guns were manned and groups of men, twenty-five-strong, were lined up on the decks of the five destroyers, ready to retake the town should opportunity offer. 'Until now we had not seen any signs of civilisation of any sort, and no Germans at all,' Stanning wrote. 'The whole situation was so extraordinary that some men asked Heppel and me if we had misunderstood everything that the pilots had said at Tranøy. Maybe there were only a handful of Germans in Narvik after all? That gave us hope for the landing.'

In a brief break between snow showers the lookouts caught a glimpse of a wharf to starboard, together with a fishing boat, and on the opposite side the outline of Framnes Point. Ahead of them they could just make out the masts of the blacked-out fleet of ore ships, ghostly in the half-light. The 2nd Destroyer Flotilla had reached Narvik harbour undetected. The air was electric. 'I suddenly remembered that it was my birthday,' wrote Stanning, who was born in 1912 and had thus just turned 28. 'I think Wash would have sent for a bottle of champagne if we had not just arrived.'

The British 6,000-tonner *Blythmoor*, owned by the Runciman Line of Glasgow, was lying at anchor at the outermost point of the approach. From the *Hardy*'s bridge, officers and men could see a solitary watchman tramping to and fro. 'Should we call over to him and ask where the Germans are?' Stanning asked. 'No,' Warburton-Lee replied. 'We don't want to wake up the whole town.'

The Flotilla Commander had despatched *Hotspur* and *Hostile* to Framnes Point to reconnoitre the fjord to the north while *Hunter* and *Havock* followed in *Hardy*'s wake. In the next nerve-racking minutes he allowed the flagship to drift past the *Blythmoor* until the full width of the harbour basin suddenly opened up before them. 'The silence was eerie. We felt that somebody *had* to wake up if we raised our voices.' Seconds later there was a low call from one of the lookouts: 'There they are!'

It was just gone half-past four. Less than 1,500m away, between the merchant ships, loomed the dark grey shapes of the *Anton Schmitt* and *Wilhelm Heidkamp*. There was no sign of life. 'Incredible,' Torpedo Officer Heppel muttered. 'I've never seen such an enticing target!' Warburton-Lee didn't hesitate: 'Then let's get going,' he said.

On board the *Wilhelm Heidkamp*, Lieutenant Commander Erdmenger was woken by a distant shout. It transpired that someone had heard a shot, but there was nothing to be seen. 'The men were alerted by the clamour of the alarm bells,' he noted. But it was too late. A few seconds later, one of the *Hardy*'s torpedoes tore through the steel plating of the hull and exploded in the aft magazine. A series of violent explosions followed, causing widespread damage. The stern broke away and the three 15-tonne guns were wrenched from their mountings and tossed aside like matchsticks; one landed on the foredeck.

'Thousands of rounds of ammunition exploded in the air, making for one enormous firework,' wrote Stanning, who stood watching the dramatic spectacle with a mixture of shock and awe. 'The result far exceeded our expectations. But at the same time, we could not help thinking with horror about the loss of human life that we had caused.' It seemed that nemesis had caught up with the high-ranking German officers who had so cold-bloodedly slaughtered the *Eidsvold*'s young sailors. Flotilla Commander Friedrich Bonte and his First Staff Officer Rudolf Heyke were both killed outright, and the man who had fired the signal pistol, Second Staff Officer Heinrich Gerlach, was severely wounded. Below deck, carnage reigned. In a matter of minutes, eighty-one men died and dozens more were injured. 'The ship was shrouded in suffocating smoke and sinking fast,' Erdmenger wrote.

Warburton-Lee had increased speed to 20 knots and brought the destroyer about on the inner side of the *Blythmoor*. All her guns opened up and a further three torpedoes were fired – to no avail, as they all struck the quays in the north-east corner of the harbour. But the *Hunter* had followed in the *Hardy*'s wake and Lieutenant Lindsay de Villiers was quick to emulate his commander. He fired no fewer than eight torpedoes at the ships anchored deep in the harbour.

On board the *Anton Schmitt*, 44-year-old Lieutenant Fritz Böhme was rudely roused from his sleep when one of the *Hunter*'s torpedoes detonated in the engine room. 'We were anchored a little astern of the *Jan Wellem*, awaiting our turn to refuel,' Böhme wrote many years later. 'I hadn't had any sleep for forty-eight hours and had more or less collapsed onto my bunk at three that night, fully clothed and wearing my life jacket. In my subconscious state I was dimly aware of a commotion a long way off, but what actually woke me was the rocking of my own ship.'

Böhme sprang over to the door of his cabin, only to find it jammed by the force of the explosion. After a struggle he managed to wrench it open and climb out onto the deck on the starboard side. 'The gunners had all manned their guns but nothing could be seen in the fog and swirling snow. All was confusion and a lot of the men thought we were being attacked from the air.'

The destroyer was already starting to heel over. Böhme just had time to race round the quarterdeck and over to the port side when there was a second explosion. 'I was thrown overboard. When I came to my senses I was floating in my life jacket, surrounded by pieces of wreckage and a number of other survivors, close alongside the sinking *Anton Schmitt*, which had broken in two.'

It was a torpedo from the third and last destroyer of the first wave of attackers, the *Havock*, that had finished off the *Anton Schmitt*. Lieutenant

Commander Rafe Courage had rounded the *Blythmoor* some fifteen minutes after the *Hardy*, fired three torpedoes and withdrawn under heavy fire from every quarter.

Inside the harbour, chaos reigned. The destroyer *Hermann Künne*, moored to the port side of the *Jan Wellem*, had taken on some 200 tonnes of oil when the silence of the night was abruptly rent by a succession of violent explosions. Heavy with sleep, Lieutenant Commander Friedrich Kothe hurried out onto the open bridge without quite realising what had happened. 'I saw numerous hits on the ships in the harbour,' he wrote in the war diary. 'Several of them were blown apart by explosions, while others were on fire and enveloping the surroundings in black smoke. It took several minutes for me to grasp that the shells were coming from light forces somewhere in the harbour entrance.'

The moorings and hoses were swiftly cut and Kothe ordered full astern to distance himself from the doomed *Jan Wellem*. As he backed away, the *Anton Schmitt* was struck by the *Havock*'s torpedo. 'I was about 40 metres away when it detonated. The pressure wave shook the hull violently, the turbines seized, the lights went out and we were left without any means of communication.' Nine men were killed by the explosion. When the *Anton Schmitt*'s stern turned over, her after mast became entangled with the now stationary *Hermann Künne*. The men were near to panic: more than twenty of them jumped overboard before discipline was restored and they could be hauled back on board.

Kothe himself was not unaffected by what was happening for at 05.15 he ordered the ship to be readied for scuttling. It was only some minutes later, after conferring with the chief engineer, that he learned that the damage was repairable. 'I was informed that we would have our steam back within some fifteen to twenty minutes, and at 05.45 I was able to order slow ahead on one turbine.'

On the top three floors of the Royal Hotel, the German officers had also been awakened by the explosions. Lieutenant Albert Bach hastened over to the window, from where he could see a red glow against the low clouds. 'Then I heard General Dietl's voice in the corridor outside my room,' he wrote in his memoirs. 'When I opened the door, he immediately ordered me to get down to the harbour and find out what was going on.' Bach dressed hurriedly and rushed out into the street. It had been snowing all night. Coming towards him was a crowd of wounded and traumatised men who had just been dragged from the sea; all of them were soaked in oil and blood. 'Some of the explosions sounded like heavy bombs going off, others were more like the bursts of light shells. I also heard the muffled and frightening sound of steam escaping from boilers, a sure sign that ships were on the verge of sinking.'

The first attack by the British destroyers had been carried out with deadly precision in less than twenty minutes. Most of the damage inflicted was to destroyers and merchant ships, but driving snow and thick smoke from burning oil made it difficult to assess the full scale of the destruction. The *Hostile* and *Hotspur* still had an almost full supply of torpedoes and ammunition aboard. 'We circled in front of the harbour entry and fired our guns towards the enemy's muzzle flashes,' Stanning wrote:

> We stayed as close to the harbour entrance as we dared in order to prevent any of them from getting out. There was a good deal of steel in the air so most of us thought it would be quite smart to put on our steel helmets. After a while I saw that most of the men had put them away.

The *Hostile* and *Hotspur* fired torpedoes into the harbour during this second attack and scored hits on several merchantmen, but it was almost impossible to judge the results. 'The Germans were firing blindly out of the harbour, and we were firing blindly into the harbour. The whole thing was almost comical as we were only about half a mile from each other, yet were unable to see anything at all.'

For the Germans, taken unawares as they were, the situation was far more dramatic. On board the ill-starred *Dieter von Roeder*, which had terminated its spell of guard duty too early, and was now lying at anchor close to the harbour entrance, shells seemed to be coming from every direction. 'Shortly after the alarm sounded, we took two hits in the oil tank of Boiler Room No. 2,' wrote Erich Holtorf in the ship's war diary. 'A fierce fire broke out, there was a lot of smoke and flames were coming out of the gash in the hull.' Nine men were killed when a third shell exploded on the main deck and started new fires, and another four lost their lives when one of the gun turrets was hit and put out of action. Electric power was cut off, and because of the heat and smoke in the forepart of the ship, it was impossible to cut the anchor chain. 'The ship was blazing like a torch. Although the remaining guns were still firing away for all they were worth, I feared the ship was in danger of sinking, so I gave the order to fire all eight torpedoes into the harbour mouth.'

Just after 05.00 the *Dieter von Roeder* and *Hans Lüdemann*, the latter of which had barely managed to extricate itself from the *Jan Wellem*, together fired no fewer than twelve torpedoes out into the fjord. The torpedoes' approaching tracks were sighted by lookouts on the British destroyers, which immediately altered course to the south-east – right into their path. They were all able to steer clear, with the exception of the *Havock*, whose captain, Lieutenant Commander Rafe Courage, crouched down beside the binnacle and said, 'Sorry, lads. There's no more I can do. Here it comes!'

But Courage, a member of the well-known brewing family and a great bear of a man who was very popular with his men, was wrong. While the officers and lookouts held their breath, the torpedo passed harmlessly beneath the ship. 'I think it was a signalman who dared to peer over the other side and saw the torpedo track continue,' wrote Lieutenant John Burfield. 'We all gave a sigh of relief. We had been given an enormous moral boost. From then on we believed we were invincible.'

On board the *Hardy*, Flotilla Commander Warburton-Lee was relieved. He had taken a chance and completed the attack without loss to his own ships. 'Lieutenant Commander Mansell came up to the bridge and said that we had a small hole in the aft funnel. That was the only one,' Stanning reported. 'We felt very pleased and elated.'

While the flotilla steered westwards, away from Narvik, Warburton-Lee convened a new meeting of his staff; but when he proposed making their getaway while the going was good, his fellow officers objected. 'All the guns seemed to have gone silent at the end of the second attack,' Stanning wrote. 'It was entirely possible that all opposition had been silenced. If the opposition had been neutralised, it would be ridiculous to call off the operation. We should at least check more closely how strong the enemy was and give as complete a report as possible.' Warburton-Lee allowed himself to be persuaded. At about 05.30, he turned the flotilla about and set a course for the ships still burning in the harbour. The troops scheduled for the landing, some 125 in all, assembled on the decks of the five destroyers. Word was passed along from man to man: 'We've shot the enemy to pieces. If we go in now, we'll be staying!'

In Narvik, General Dietl had reacted long before he received Albert Bach's report. At 05.00 Lieutenant Hans Rohr's elite troops had been roused from their sleep, lined up in the school playground and marched at the double to take up defensive positions around the harbour, ammunition transported on sledges drawn by horses the Germans had commandeered.

'The darkness, dense fog and driving snow made visibility difficult, but on several ships out in the harbour fierce fires were raging,' wrote Rohr, who lost no time in setting up his machine guns and mortars. 'The smoke was choking and stank to high heaven. The fearsome thunder of exploding British shells and torpedoes mingled with the sound of our own ships' guns. Even after an hour we still didn't know the outcome of the battle.'

When, for a third time, Warburton-Lee's destroyers headed in towards Narvik on that dramatic Wednesday morning of 10 April, the clouds were starting to lift. After a time it stopped snowing to reveal a scene of untold devastation. Two German destroyers were complete write-offs, two others were badly damaged and seven merchant vessels had been sunk or were still going down.

'It was not easy to discern exactly what was what, but the destruction was formidable,' Stanning wrote. 'We were steaming straight across the harbour entrance when Wash suddenly saw what looked like a cruiser and two destroyers coming out of the Rombaksfjord. They were clearly enemy ships. We opened fire on each other simultaneously.'

All thought of a landing was instantly abandoned. At 05.51 the *Hardy* sent the following signal: 'One cruiser, three destroyers off Narvik. Am withdrawing to westward.'

For some unaccountable reason, nearly an hour elapsed before the alarm was sounded on board the German destroyers anchored in the neighbouring fjords. 'Message to Duty Officer: Sound of gunfire from the direction of Narvik,' Lieutenant Commander Karl Smidt on board the *Erich Giese* wrote in the ship's war diary at 05.30. The destroyer was lying at anchor off Bjerkvik, less than fifteen minutes' steaming away from Narvik. Shortly afterwards a signal was received in clear reading: 'British attacking Narvik!'

Tall and cool-headed, Smidt was an unusual type for an officer. He came from a family of Free Church theologians in the Frisian Islands and, thanks to his Bible studies, was well versed in Latin, Greek, French and English and also had a working knowledge of Hebrew. Like Bonte, he was opposed to the Nazi Party, but his duty as a naval officer came first. Along with the *Erich Koellner* and *Wolfgang Zenker*, the *Erich Giese* weighed anchor. With its five quick-firing 12.7cm single-mounted guns, eight torpedoes and a wide range of lighter weapons, the *Erich Giese* was a formidable adversary; at that crucial moment, however, the destroyer was handicapped by a shortage of fuel. 'Lack of fuel meant that we were only able to fire two boilers,' Smidt noted in the war diary.

Tucked inside another arm of the fjord, known as Ballangen, were two smaller and older destroyers, the *Georg Thiele* and *Bernd von Arnim*. Having been the first to enter Narvik harbour, they had also been the first to refuel – after the flagship, the *Wilhelm Heidkamp*. 'We slipped our cable immediately on receipt of the signal and informed the *Georg Thiele*,' wrote Curt Rechel in the war diary. Having undergone their baptism of fire against the *Glowworm* only forty-eight hours earlier, the men were on their toes. 'As soon as we were underway I gave the order for action stations. We were sailing some 1,000m astern of the *Georg Thiele*. When we reached the Ofot fjord, I saw approaching behind a smoke screen a flotilla of British destroyers.'

The presence of five additional destroyers, all armed with 12.7cm guns and a full complement of torpedoes, came as a nasty surprise to the flotilla staff. What they had feared when off Tranøy Island was now a reality. There was little Captain Warburton-Lee could do, apart from increase speed to 30 knots:

> Wash ordered the signal to withdraw (red Very light) and 30 knots; Clark protested that we were hitting them and wanted to stay and have a crack at them. But just at that moment two more ships appeared ahead and Cross said 'Birmingham'. They certainly looked like our own cruisers and as they were some distance away it was hard to tell; the distance was actually about four miles, I should think. I looked at them through glasses and caught sight of hoods on the funnels and knew they were not Birmingham whatever else they were. We had *Jane's Fighting Ships* on the bridge so I looked up in that, found they were large German destroyers and convinced Wash. It looked as if we were in a tight corner.

Thirty-year-old Lieutenant Commander Max-Eckart Wolff opened fire at a range of 4,500m. Crossing in front of the fleeing British destroyers, the *Georg Thiele* and *Bernd von Arnim* had a perfect field of fire. Each shell was 57cm long, weighed 28kg and was capable of inflicting death and terror on most opponents. 'The effect was devastating,' says the war diary. 'The *Hardy* immediately took several hits.'

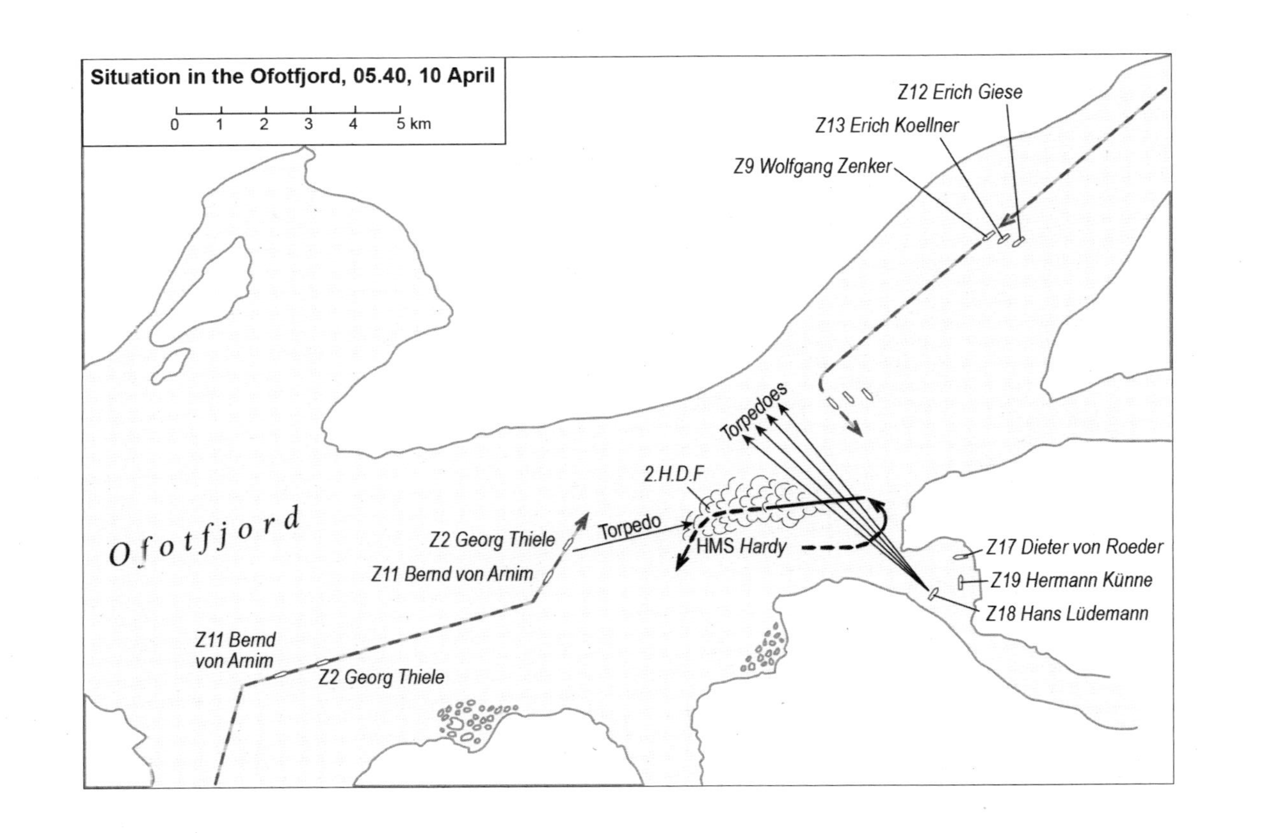
Situation in the Ofotfjord, 05.40, 10 April
0 1 2 3 4 5 km
Z12 Erich Giese
Z13 Erich Koellner
Z9 Wolfgang Zenker
Torpedoes
2.H.D.F
Torpedo
HMS Hardy
Z17 Dieter von Roeder
Z19 Hermann Künne
Z18 Hans Lüdemann
Ofotfjord
Z2 Georg Thiele
Z11 Bernd von Arnim
Z11 Bernd
von Arnim
Z2 Georg Thiele

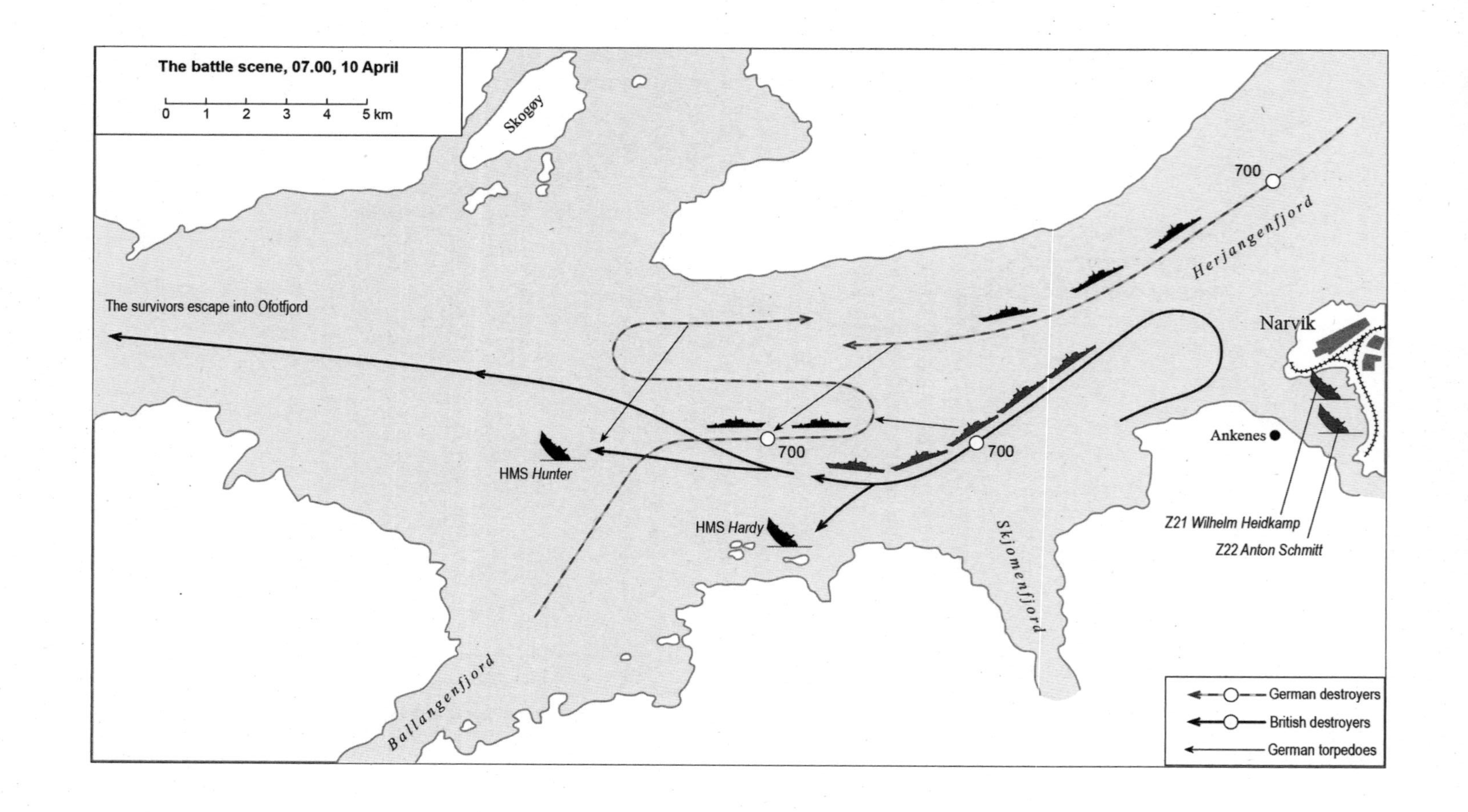
The battle scene, 07.00, 10 April
0
1
2
3
4
5 km
Skogøy
700
Herjangenfjord
The survivors escape into Ofotfjord
Narvik
Ankenes
700
700
HMS Hunter
HMS Hardy
Skjomenfjord
Z21 Wilhelm Heidkamp
Z22 Anton Schmitt
Ballangenfjord
German destroyers
British destroyers
German torpedoes

The destroyers closed at a combined speed of more than 60 knots. In a matter of minutes a collision would be unavoidable. Warburton-Lee's hour had come. He had entered Narvik harbour and inflicted grave damage on the enemy. To his surprise, the Germans had large forces in reserve, ships that were bigger and more heavily armed than his own. But Warburton-Lee was not a man given to despair. Seemingly unperturbed, at 05.55 he made what proved to be his last signal: 'Continue to engage the enemy.'

A moment later several shells struck the *Hardy*'s superstructure. 'I had been wounded in the face and gone aft to clean the cuts and stop the blood,' wrote George Heppel, who even at the best of times tended to be more accident-prone than the rest of the ship's company. Shortly afterwards he was knocked off his feet by another, more powerful, explosion. 'At least two shells struck the bridge and the wheelhouse below it at the same time. A seaman reported that everyone had been killed. I assumed that the ship was no longer under control, so I ran aft to prepare the emergency control.'

But on the bridge his friend Stanning was slowly coming to, despite severe pains in his back and left foot:

> The first shell exploded in the wheelhouse, killing the helmsman and everyone nearby. The deck-plates buckled up violently, and I was thrown into the air like a rag doll, at the very moment when the second shell exploded on the bridge itself. I do not know exactly what happened, but I landed with a crash on the compass, breaking all the bones in my left ankle.

The rain of splinters had transformed the *Hardy*'s bridge into a slaughterhouse. Clark and Cross, both of whom were badly wounded, lay crumpled on the deck. The gifted Edward Clark, studiously inclined and a lover of the music of Bach, was rarely to be seen without a book by Marcel Proust protruding from his pocket. Twenty-nine years of age, he was newly married and had a 1-month-old son. Charles Cross was younger. He had won awards for his innovative achievements as a wireless operator, most recently while serving as an assistant fleet wireless operator with the Home Fleet. He too was newly married, but, unlike Clark, had no children. Now both were gone, their lives snuffed out in an instant before they had a chance to take cover.

A short distance away lay Warburton-Lee. Although he was still alive, blood was pouring from gaping wounds in his face and chest. Sprawled on a ledge, deathly pale and seemingly lifeless, was navigator Russell Gordon-Smith. Stanning recalled, 'The destroyer made a sharp turn towards port and I saw that we were going to run aground if nothing was done.' He limped over to the ladder and slid down into the wheelhouse, where the carnage was equally bad:

> There was a piece of the wheel left, and I could see out through the centre window where the iron housing had been torn apart. There were body parts everywhere, and the stench of cordite was intense. I was in shock and felt terribly alone, as if I were the only one on board who was alive.

He managed to get the destroyer back on course towards the south-west and was hugging the coast at high speed when his personal assistant, Leslie Smale, appeared, threading his way through the wreckage. 'It was a huge relief to see Smale, whom I knew I could trust. I handed him the wheel while I climbed up onto the bridge to get an overview of the situation.'

The *Hardy*'s forward quarter had been badly damaged, and the gun was out of action. A few hundred metres to starboard, the *Georg Thiele* and *Bernd von Arnim* were still raining shells down onto the flagship:

> Our capacity to continue fighting was extremely limited, and I thought for a moment of trying to ram them. But then another salvo smashed into the engine room. Great clouds of smoke and steam poured out and the destroyer lost speed. I felt sure that nobody in the turbine or boiler rooms could have survived. Now we had to save as many of those who were left as possible. I decided to beach the *Hardy*.

Heppel came over, and after a brief exchange of views the two officers steered the stricken destroyer towards the rocky shore some 200m from the small community of Vidrek.

'We slipped in so gently and calmly that we hardly felt the ship run aground,' Stanning wrote. 'However it soon became lively on board. I was absolutely flabbergasted by the number of men who poured onto the deck and quite shocked when they suddenly began leaving the ship. I was afraid I would be left alone to deal with the code books and everything else that had to be destroyed.'

With the aid of First Officer Mansell and a number of petty officers, Stanning managed to restore a semblance of order. The code books and various items of secret equipment were destroyed and dumped overboard, and Warburton-Lee, who was still losing blood, was strapped to a stretcher and floated ashore.

The ship's doctor, the appropriately named Arthur Wound, who himself had a jagged piece of shrapnel lodged beneath his shoulder blade, ministered to the captain as best he could. But it was too late. The Flotilla Commander breathed his last among the snow-covered rocks of the foreshore below Vidrek. He was 44 years old. The Royal Navy had lost one of its finest and most gallant officers.

The *Hardy*'s aft gun had remained in action throughout, with only occasional return fire from the Germans. 'I remember seeing several shells hit the beach not far from our men going ashore who were in a thin black stream up the snow. When a shell hit the aft funnel, killing several of the waiting seamen, I realised it was time to give up.'

Stanning and Heppel were among the last to leave the burning *Hardy*. 'I slid out into the water and felt solid ground under my feet after a swim of 50 yards. I would not have got any further without help. My ankle hurt terribly and was swollen like a football when I took off my boot.' Miraculously, of the 175 men on board, 154 survived. Most of them sought refuge at a small farm, the property of Petra Christensen. Many of the local men were away fishing off the Lofoten Islands, but the women and children who were left brought food and dry clothing for the shipwrecked men.

'It was pandemonium in the house, which was full of men stinking of sweat, cordite and wet clothes,' Stanning wrote. 'In the two bedrooms on the first floor, the seamen put on clothes and bedclothes that belonged to the mother and daughter, who cut up curtains, blankets and mats to wrap up the most frostbitten men. All the available food was laid out, and there was bread and butter for all the men.'

An hour after beaching, a solitary figure was seen pacing the *Hardy*'s quarterdeck. It was the navigator, Lieutenant Commander Gordon-Smith, who, having been wounded in the head, had regained consciousness and was now wandering aimlessly about on the burning ship. Accompanied by two seamen, Heppel returned to the wreck, took off Gordon-Smith and placed explosive charges in the captain's cabin:

> We put 10 kilos of TNT behind the two steel safes and covered them with a couple of armchairs. Then we bid our last farewell to the beautiful cabin with

> its beige carpet, silverware and mahogany furniture. Our hope was to blow out the safes through the sides of the ship.

Meanwhile, out in the fjord a running battle was being fought between the five heavy German destroyers and the remaining four British ships, which were steaming westwards, line astern, at a speed of 30 knots. The range was short, and the *Georg Thiele*, *Bernd von Arnim*, *Hotspur* and *Hunter* all suffered severe damage. From the few surviving accounts it appears that the *Hunter* had been hit in the engine room and had lost both speed and steering.

'There was a terrible amount of smoke everywhere,' wrote Commander Herbert Layman on board the *Hotspur*, last in line of the destroyers. 'Straight in front of us *Hunter* suddenly swerved off to one side and stopped dead. She had been hit badly, and the flames were shooting out of her funnel. I immediately ordered the helmsman and the engine room to take an emergency manoeuvre, but nothing happened. A shell had exploded in the superstructure, destroying all our communications.'

A collision was unavoidable. Aghast, Layman could only watch helplessly as, a few seconds later, the destroyer's bow clove deep into the starboard side of the *Hunter*'s hull amidships. 'I saw *Hotspur* coming towards us at great speed,' wrote Lieutenant Harold Stuart-Menteth. 'She hit us at an angle of 45 degrees, right next to me.' In the collision, the torpedo davit fell onto Stuart-Menteth, leaving him pinned beneath it with a fractured left foot.

The *Hunter*'s hull had been pierced by several shells, the rudder and control system were unserviceable and the starboard turbine had broken down. The collision caused the destroyer to list badly and water flooded in through the gaping holes in her hull. 'The captain, Lindsay de Villiers, knew that it was over and calmly gave the order to abandon ship. He remained standing at attention on the bridge.'

The *Georg Thiele* and *Bernd von Arnim* were still pouring shells into the two disabled ships, and Herbert Layman had great difficulty in making his way aft from the bridge to the engine room hatch. 'I shouted down to the engine room that they had to switch from full ahead to full astern,' he wrote, and had to wait for another ten nerve-racking minutes before the *Hotspur* managed to tear herself away from the sinking *Hunter*:

> I began a slow retreat to the west. The aft gun was intact, and Lieutenant Leopold Tillie had maintained fire alone. I could not see whether he was

> hitting them. But I was concerned for the ship and found comfort in seeing that he was able to shoot back at all.

It was just past 06.00 and an hour and a half's intense fighting was drawing to a close. Deeper inside the fjord, the *Erich Giese*, *Werner Zenker* and *Erich Koeller* were in danger of running out of fuel. The *Georg Thiele* was on fire and had to ask for assistance from the *Bernd von Arnim*. 'Damage to the engine room forced me to proceed at reduced speed,' wrote Max-Eckart Wolff in the war diary. 'I resolved to break off pursuit.'

In the meantime, the *Hunter* had gone down. Of her complement of 156 men, only forty-eight were saved by the German destroyers and taken as prisoners of war to Narvik. Among them was Lieutenant Stuart-Menteth, who had been freed from beneath the davit by a courageous seaman, Norman Stewart.

To their relief, when the *Hostile*, *Havock* and the badly mauled *Hotspur* passed Tranøy Island about 07.00 that morning, they sighted in the distance the cruiser *Penelope*, accompanied by several destroyers. On board the *Hostile*, Commander John Wright immediately despatched the following signal: 'Returning with *Hotspur* and *Havock*. *Hunter* sunk Vest fiord. *Hardy* ashore. Five to six large German destroyers in Narvik.'

The first round was over; but the battle for Narvik had barely begun.

EPILOGUE

Spurred on by the First Lord of the Admiralty, with his unshakeable confidence in ultimate victory, the House of Commons celebrated the First Battle of Narvik as a triumph.

'Herr Hitler has committed a grave strategic error in spreading the war so far to the North,' Churchill declared before a packed House on Thursday 11 April. 'That cursed corridor', by which he meant the 800 nautical mile-long coastal channel inside Norwegian territorial waters, had been 'closed for ever', and Hitler's invasion of Scandinavia was 'as great a strategic and political error as that which was committed by Napoleon, when he invaded Spain'. His allusion to the Peninsular War, which eventually led to the French emperor's downfall, was greeted with uproarious applause.

'We are greatly advantaged by what has occurred,' Churchill claimed, and pointed out that since Monday 8 April the Kriegsmarine had lost four cruisers, a significant number of destroyers and U-boats, as well as sixteen merchant vessels, mostly thanks to Warburton-Lee and his flotilla. The hope was 'to take unceasing toll' on the remaining ships. 'We are not going to allow the enemy to supply their armies across these waters with impunity.'

Even the Admiralty's Pilate-like signal to Warburton-Lee on 9 April was made to appear as an example of wise leadership. 'To the Narvik epic of the five destroyers who sailed into the superior forces he added one flashing insight on the navy's indomitable courage,' wrote the *Daily Express*. 'The Admiralty was so conscious that the assault was hazardous that they left the decision to the captain of the flotilla on the spot.' Churchill added just one sentence – to dramatic effect: 'Captain Warburton-Lee attacked.'

In the course of Wednesday evening, the *Hardy*'s survivors were evacuated to a nursing home at Ballangen. Two days later they were taken off by British destroyers, and towards the end of the week the Admiralty received the first eyewitness accounts of the battle.

For Elizabeth Warburton-Lee Sunday 14 April was an agonising day. She had long hoped for the best, but the telegram she received from the Admiralty in London left no room for doubt: 'Deeply regret to inform you that your husband Captain B.A.W. Warburton-Lee of HMS *Hardy* was killed in action off Narvik on 10th April.' In a follow-up letter the next day Churchill wrote:

> The engagement was of his own conception and in view of the great risks involved he was given full discretion by their Lordships to attack or refrain from attack. His decision, immediately taken, led directly to the subsequent destruction of the enemy and may well prove to be of major importance in the progress of the war.

Comforting words, but they did nothing to alter the fact that after her husband's death Elizabeth Warburton-Lee's life was never the same. In the words of her grandson John, who, many years later, was to take over the family home, Broad Oaks in Wales, 'My grandmother was heartbroken from grief. I think she never really recovered from the loss of her husband.' Captain Warburton-Lee's last letter to his wife was dated 5 April. It reached her in the middle of the month, long after his death. 'Darling,' he had written from Sullom Voe a few hours before putting to sea, 'I've been telling you repeatedly that you won't hear from me for a bit – I think now that it is really so.' That he was pressed for time was apparent from his handwriting:

> Today we had a really lovely day. We had a paperchase and ran up the local mountain – which was lovely – after it was over! Lewis went to explore the local metropolis today but didn't find much – not even fish, which was funny ... Will you please order me a dozen 2lb pots of Cooper's marmalade to be delivered to Greening and addressed to me. Goodnight, darling one. I love you.

Simple words, penned by a man full of optimism, zest for life and faith in the future. It was heartbreaking for his widow to know that she would never see him or hear from him again.

But life had to go on. In the Royal Navy a captain's wife is more than a wife: she is also an anchor, a source of security for the ship's company and their dependants. When the Admiralty released its list of casualties, Warburton-Lee's widow immediately set about writing personal letters of condolence to each and every one of the bereaved. The answers she received reveal how the war disrupted the lives of families the length and breadth of Britain – and, in time, all over the world.

'It was very kind of you to write to me in your sorrow as well as mine,' wrote a young mother from St Ives, who continued:

> The blow was bitter but we have one consolation, they died heroes. I have been very ill since as I made an idol of my boy, so you can understand what it meant to me, he was such a dear good boy and I shall miss him in many ways. I have 2 little ones left, one 10 and the other 3 and my husband is serving being a pensioner recalled so you see the Navy is in the blood. Only time can soften the blow. It seems so hard when you think we shall never see them again. The Navy has done well. I hope we shall crush this monster who has created such misery and loss ... They tell me I cannot claim a pension as my son did not make an allotment, he used to send his money to help for the little brothers and I suppose that any pay that was due I shall get in due course. Thank you again for your letter and for any advice you could give me.

A widow wrote from Nottingham in much the same vein:

> I cannot say how I thank you for thinking about me when I know you are sharing the same sorrow but we have the comfort of knowing they did their best for the world's freedom, and we must be proud to know the *Hardy* was led by a proud and good Captain for my husband spoke so highly of him when he was home on leave in January ... But there is one thing I would like you to do for me is if you can get to know what was my husband's fate as they wrote 'Missing believed to be drowned' and that is all I can get to know and the waiting for further news of him is near driving me mad. So if you can get to know further for me I should be so pleased.

Another bereaved mother wrote from Wales:

> Both of us have received a great loss. We however have the consolation that they died with honour and their work well done. My son was only 18 years. I have another one in the Air Force. He is twenty-one. I also have two other sons who have registered for service, one being twenty-three and the other twenty-five. I wonder if you could please tell me if they have buried them on land or sea. I would like to know, my son being the first one to be killed in action in

> this village. No one can tell me anything about it. He was the only sailor boy that has ever been here. He was in the Navy nine months. My other son is in the Air Force two years. He is out in France. I have another son sixteen and a daughter twelve. Life seems rather difficult at times but it seems that we must bear up as well as we can.

As by a miracle, a Lancaster mother's grief was abruptly turned to joy:

> I must tell you that my sorrow lasted one week. My son was reported *Killed in Action* at Narvik in that sharp little battle in which your husband led the *Hardy* and her small 'sisters'. I got news about his death on the Monday morning following the battle and mourned him dead until Saturday the same week then they sent me news that he was coming on leave, so just fancy how I felt when he arrived home on Sunday morning … He has told me everything possible about the fight and how your late husband met his death and my son has nothing but praise for him for he has been with him quite a long time. He brought your husband's photograph from some London book and I framed it and put it alongside my son and I shall always take care of it for he was a very gallant man to do what he did for his country and people.

As details of Captain Warburton-Lee's death emerged, letters of condolence poured in from hundreds of people who had known and admired him and from many others who were strangers: fellow officers and friends, people from all walks of life, among them the royal family, who wrote from Buckingham Palace, and the Admiralty.

The 2nd Destroyer Flotilla's battle against overwhelming odds was made the subject of a radio play by the BBC and Warburton-Lee's name became known and honoured throughout the Allied world as a result of the wide coverage given to the battle by the free press. 'All of us would have followed him anywhere, as indeed we did when he led us into Narvik,' wrote Commander Herbert Layman, who had managed to save his ship, the *Hotspur*, against all odds following her entanglement with the *Hunter* and subsequent engagement with the German destroyers:

> Having found out exactly what we were up against he weighed up the whole situation carefully and it was no rash or hasty decision he made when he informed the Admiralty that he was going to attack. He took the entire responsibility on his shoulders, and, with amazing skill, took us through

> 50 miles of snowstorms right into the inner harbour of Narvik. His sheer audacity took the Germans completely by surprise and one of their destroyers was sunk before being able to open fire. Later, when we were outnumbered and in a tight corner the last signal he ever made (and how typical of him!) was 'Keep on engaging the enemy.' The results of the raid have not yet been perfectly assessed but when history is written it will find an honoured place.

Layman concluded by saying:

> In my official report I have attempted, in plain unvarnished language, to do full justice to all this, so that the service shall have it all properly on record. But I know quite well that absolutely nothing can make any better the tremendous loss you have suffered. We, too, have lost our leader and know how difficult it will be to attempt to replace him. Few would have dared to do what he did.

It wasn't merely a primitive kind of hero worship or propaganda at a low point in the war when the Nazis seemed, as they claimed, to be 'victorious on every front'. Bernard Warburton-Lee was a profoundly human hero with whom one and all could identify; in his struggle with his conscience, beset by doubt and uncertainty, he had made no effort to hide his feelings. His final – and fateful – decision was reached only after due deliberation and executed with courage, verve and resolution, actions and attributes recognised and revered by all. His life and untimely death struck a chord in the hearts of people everywhere. As his chronicler and former secretary Lieutenant Geoffrey Stanning wrote in an obituary notice in *The Times*:

> Much has been written of his final exploit at Narvik, of which, I think, the episode most creditable to him was his decision on the day before to attack at dawn the next day. There is no space here to tell of the pros and cons which had to be weighed, but I can remember with intense sympathy the agonizing half-hour of doubt he spent before making the final momentous decision. My deep sympathy for Mrs. Warburton-Lee and Philip is only equalled by my pride at having been privileged to serve such a very fine officer and gentleman, an inspiration and high example to all who served under him.

When, in June 1940, Captain Warburton-Lee was awarded the first Victoria Cross of the war, it was universally agreed that it was richly deserved.

In occupied Narvik the local authorities did all they could to alleviate their people's suffering. Subsequent to the horrifying sinking of the *Eidsvold* and *Norge*, some 2,000 people had fled across the mountains and fjords to take refuge in neighbouring villages, and after the first British attack hundreds more followed in their wake.

'It was impossible to organise a planned evacuation,' wrote Mayor Theodor Broch, who proved himself a born leader in the ensuing turmoil – bold, enterprising and patriotic to the core. 'There was no panic, it wasn't that, it was simply that people set off with no clear idea of where they were going.'

Meanwhile, those who remained had to be provided with food, medicines and other necessities of life – in agreement with the Germans. All communication with the outside world had been cut off, all vacant premises requisitioned and the local hospital was full to bursting with dead and wounded men. Along with the Swedish-owned iron ore mining company LKAB, all industrial undertakings had closed down, and among the populace the mood varied from hope to apathy to despair. Would the Allies come to the rescue? What would happen if their intervention resulted in street-by-street fighting?

'The days were a nightmare of feverish activity and hard work,' Broch wrote. 'For a time it seemed hopeless to try to restore order from the chaos created by the new situation. However, some of us set ourselves up in the council offices and began to issue and distribute orders.' Guards were posted outside the building and young boys pressed into service as runners to go from door to door with improvised instructions. 'We didn't have much time for reflection. Norway was at war. Here in the north of the country there'd never been a cannon fired against a human target. But now we were about to experience the horrors of war as they really were.'

In the meantime, General Eduard Dietl and Friedrich Bonte's replacement as Flotilla Commander, Commodore Erich Bey, were desperately trying to make good the damage resulting from the British attack. The *Anton Schmitt* had blown up and sunk in a matter of minutes. With great effort Lieutenant Commander Hans Erdmenger had succeeded in bringing the *Wilhelm Heidkamp* alongside the Swedish ore carrier *Oxeløsund*, despite the fact that the whole of the destroyer's stern was underwater. With the aid of the surviving members of the crew, substantial quantities of ammunition and provisions, together with some of the destroyer's 37mm guns, were salvaged and transported ashore. However, despite all her captain's efforts, on the morning of Thursday 11 April Bonte's flagship turned turtle and sank.

As the forepart of the *Dieter von Roeder* was completely burnt out, to avoid losing his ship altogether, Lieutenant Commander Erich Holtorf warped the destroyer to the steamship quay, where it was destined to remain, a near-useless wreck; only the two forward 12.7cm guns were undamaged and capable of warding off further attacks.

Both the *Georg Thiele* and *Bernd von Arnim* had sustained hits in the final stage of the bloody battle in the Ofot fjord, and several of the other destroyers had been damaged to a greater or lesser extent. When, late in the evening of 10 April, Commodore Bey made a last desperate attempt to join the *Scharnhorst* and *Gneisenau* in the Norwegian Sea, only two of the ten destroyers in his flotilla, the *Werner Zenker* and *Erich Giese*, were able to take part. In the event, it proved not to matter: on the horizon, off Tranøy Island, observers could see several ships. The British Home Fleet had arrived. The Vestfjord was effectively closed and Bey had no option but to turn about and make his way back to Narvik.

Seven of the iron ore carriers anchored in Narvik harbour had gone to the bottom and several of the remainder had been badly damaged. Of greater concern to Dietl and Bey, however, was that none of the three merchant ships bringing much-needed guns, ammunition and other heavy equipment had arrived. The *Alster*, *Rauenfels* and *Bärenfels* had left Hamburg as early as 3 April, but nothing had since been heard from either the *Alster* or the *Bärenfels*.

As chance would have it, the *Rauenfels* had reached Ballangen just as the battle in the Ofot fjord had come to an end. When the *Havock*, *Hostile* and *Hotspur*, which by then were on their way out of the fjord, sighted the 11,000-tonner, she was brought to a stop by two shells which penetrated her hull. On boarding her, Lieutenant John Burfield from the *Havock* was surprised to see the German crew rowing furiously towards the shore.

'We eyed the plumes of smoke coming out of her holds with some suspicion. As well we might: she carried ammunition. We pulled back to *Havock* a bloody sight faster than the Germans, in time to get peppered with ironmongery as she went up.' Burfield and the prize crew reached the *Havock* just before the air was rent by a violent explosion. Pieces of wreckage rained down all over the fjord and an enormous column of smoke rose high into the air.

'Are you all right?' the *Hostile*'s captain, Commander J.P. Wright, signalled his sister ship.

'Only just,' was the answer. 'Merchant ship contained all reserve ammunition for Narvik, and I blew her up.'

'Well done,' Wright replied.

The loss of the *Rauenfels* was a severe setback for Dietl and Bey, who realised that they would have to hold onto Narvik without any heavy artillery to back them up. It promised to be a tough job for the 2,000 Alpine troops Dietl had under his command, even with the aid of the survivors from the *Anton Schmitt*, *Wilhelm Heidkamp* and *Dieter von Roeder*, who had been formed into a separate naval force, 500 strong, armed with captured Norwegian rifles and machine guns. 'We took over the one existing Norwegian field gun and 120 rounds of ammunition, the pillboxes and machine guns,' wrote Lieutenant Hans Rohr. 'We felt sure that we would be able to repulse a landing if the British returned.'

In the Commons, Churchill spoke of the sinking of the *Rauenfels* as a new and significant victory in the battle for Narvik. 'I am all for propaganda and publicity, but the best propaganda is results, and I must say that these are coming to hand in no unsatisfactory manner,' he declared to loud cheers:

> On the way back the two destroyers, who were escorting their wounded comrade out of the Fjord, unpursued by the enemy, who had received an equal battering, got the *Rauenfels*, full of reserve ammunition with which, I suppose, it was intended to turn Narvik into a kind of Sebastopol or Gibraltar.

Without going into detail as to exactly what he meant, he added: 'The ship was blown up, and we must regard that as simplifying the task which obviously might be among those which lie ahead of us.'

One of the tasks he had in mind was a large-scale counter-attack to be launched against the Nazi German troops ensconced in Narvik. This was to be carried out by the Royal Navy and the 24th Guards Brigade under the command of the highly regarded Scottish Major General Pierse Mackesy, who, on Thursday 11 April, had just got to Scapa Flow – at about the same time as Churchill was speaking before Parliament.

The impending attack was one Churchill had been pressing for for more than six months and for which he still had great hopes as a possible turning point in the war. A few days later everything seemed to have gone wrong, and a furious Churchill signalled his representative on the spot, Admiral of the Fleet, the Earl of Cork and Orrery: 'If this officer appears to spread a bad spirit through higher ranks of land forces, do not hesitate to relieve him or put him under arrest.'

What was it that had gone so disastrously awry? Why wasn't Narvik re-taken? Who bore responsibility and why had one of the army's foremost generals so suddenly fallen into disfavour? Had Captain Warburton-Lee's sacrifice been in vain after all?

APPENDIX

THE NORWEGIAN PLANS FOR THE DEFENCE OF NARVIK: A RETROSPECTIVE REVIEW

By General (Retd) Sverre Diesen, Norway's Former Chief of Defence and Commander Land Forces North Norway

Alf R. Jacobsen's account of Nazi Germany's attack on Narvik casts an interesting light on the dissension among Norwegian commanders in the weeks leading up to the attack, and the controversy that arose over how the town could best be defended. The Commander of the 6th Division and Land Forces North Norway, Major General Carl Gustav Fleischer, wished to defend the town with units positioned, quite literally, on the shoreline, supported by six pillboxes with machine guns – pillboxes that were still under construction when the invasion came. The local commander, the CO of the 15th Infantry Regiment, Colonel Konrad Sundlo, on the other hand, maintained that a forward static defence force would be incapable of repelling a determined invader. He wanted to pull back his one battalion from the town itself and deploy it as an uncommitted counter-strike force, once it became clear where the invaders would land and which direction they would take. However, since Fleischer was his direct superior, in the event it was Fleischer's, plan – or, rather, something closely resembling it – which was adopted in the chaos that characterised the early hours of 9 April.

Today, seventy-five years after the German attack, it may be of interest to reflect upon the two officers' assessments of the classic problem of defending a coastline: forward defence on the shore or a counter-strike from further inland once the attacker shows his hand. Following the campaign in 1940, events led to history judging the two officers very differently. Thanks to his subsequent skilful handling of the operations in the mountains around Narvik and recapture of the town in May, General Fleischer emerged as an officer of international standing – the first commander in the Second World War to force the Germans to retreat. Colonel Sundlo, however, who, even before the war, was widely recognised as being pro-German and a Nazi sympathiser, was not only held responsible for the Germans' easy conquest of Narvik but, after the war, was also found guilty of betraying his country during the occupation, when he was both a high-ranking officer in the Rikshird (the military arm of Quisling's party) and a Nazi-appointed regional commissioner. Viewed in this light, it would seem obvious whose assessment was right in the run-up to the attack: the widely recognised commander and national hero, or the Nazi collaborator and traitor. Nevertheless, it is both appropriate and important to ask whether it really is as simple as that.

Following mid-nineteenth-century advances in weapons technology, the defences of Norway's principal ports were moved from the old fortresses directly overlooking the ports to locations further out in the narrow fjords and inlets commanding their approaches. Oslo's defences were relocated to a cluster of islets in the middle of the extremely narrow Drøbak Sound, some 35km south of the capital and 90km from the mouth of the Oslo fjord. Bergen's defences were moved to the Kors fjord, while Trondheim was to be defended by new coastal forts on either side of the mouth of the fjord of the same name. These defences consisted of coastal artillery, with heavy calibre guns, torpedo batteries and minefields, complemented by mobile units of torpedo boats or other naval vessels. Conceptually, enemy forces attempting to land were to be repelled or annihilated while still on board their transports. In the case of Narvik, it was planned to establish a coastal artillery fort in the Ofoten fjord, where the narrow Ramsund Sound links it with the Vågs fjord. But, as will have become apparent from the reading of this book, these plans came to naught. Defence cuts in the interwar years meant that although the guns were purchased and moved to a location near the actual site, they were never installed in their emplacements.

Both Fleischer and Sundlo were well aware of Narvik's strategic importance and understood that the lack of proper defences at the entrance to the roads and harbour was a serious handicap. Dissension arose, however, when the two men met to decide how best to defend the town with land forces alone. Should it be defended from forward positions on the shore or ought their forces to be held further back, for use in a counter-attack once the invader had committed his forces? In favour of the former alternative, in principle, was the fact that the enemy could then be engaged at his most vulnerable, with his troops either crowded together on the deck of a transport or crammed into landing craft, from which they would have limited opportunities to return fire. The weak point of this option was that the defenders would be badly exposed if the attackers were supported by warships. The naval gunners would then be able to observe and bombard defences on the shore almost with impunity. Moreover, if the invader had a choice of several landing areas, the defenders would have to spread their resources so thinly that they would be too weak to repel the main thrust when and where it came, whereas the rest of the troops, dispersed in different locations, would be rendered ineffective. The reverse was true of the inland alternative. In that case, the defending forces could have been kept concentrated 'on the reverse slope', invisible to any supporting warships, until it was clear where the landing would be made. On the other hand, it would require careful timing if the attackers were to be thrown back into the sea. A counter-move would have to be launched before the attackers had secured a foothold and prepared defensive positions. To sum up, there is no definite answer as to which is the better course of action. This has to be decided on a case-by-case basis, depending on the circumstances.

How, then, did these factors affect the issue at Narvik? It is true that General Fleischer, who favoured a forward line of defence, was quite certain of where a landing would take place. Narvik's strategic significance was closely linked to the military importance of its iron ore exports, which meant that it would be imperative for the Germans to gain control of both the port and the railway on which the ore was transported from the mines in Sweden. This presupposes that, because of the limitations imposed by the narrowness of the Narvik Peninsula and the deep fjords on either side – Rombaken in the north and Beisfjorden in the south – the landing would be directed at the town itself, along with the harbour area.

But as the invader would in all probability be one of the great European powers, the forces would have to be transported to northern Norway by sea, in or protected by warships. In that case, a complete lack of suitable artillery or other heavy weapons would make defence on the shoreline a hazardous undertaking indeed with nothing but rifles, machine guns and mortars. Even if a forward defensive force had at its disposal field artillery, it would still be poorly equipped to do battle with naval vessels out at sea, owing to the defending gunners' minimal training for that, and also a lack of suitable ammunition. It would also be impossible to give battle from within the harbour area without causing extensive destruction to surrounding buildings and harm to the civilian population. Narvik was a small town of mainly wooden houses, which would have been set alight by tracers and exploding shells.

Consequently it is difficult to see how General Fleischer's plan could have succeeded under the circumstances – at least, without heavy loss of life among both soldiers and civilians. Had a similar situation arisen today, a prerequisite would be the evacuation of the population, the razing in advance of key areas (which in Narvik's case would have meant burning down most of the wooden buildings) and the establishment of defensive positions in the ruins, once they had cooled down. This is borne out by experience gained later in the Second World War during battles for large cities and built-up areas. However, in the case of Narvik this would have required timely political approval, something which, at the time, was quite inconceivable. Nor is it very likely that the knowledge and mentality required for this kind of ruthless warfare was present in the not particularly warlike Norwegian officer corps in 1940.

At first glance, therefore, it would appear that Colonel Sundlo's preference for an initial deployment of the troops under his command further to the rear had much to recommend it. However, this too had its flaws. Providing the defenders knew for certain where the main landing would be, a position further inland would count for little when it came to economising with the available troops. And had a Norwegian counter-attack been launched, it would inevitably have brought the attacking units into the sights of the German gunners on the destroyers out in the roads.

Another important point is that this would have resulted in street-to-street and house-to-house fighting in the town itself between the well-equipped and well-trained German infantrymen and Norwegian soldiers who had only recently been called up to safeguard the country's neutrality, and whose sole military training and experience consisted of a few weeks' basic training at the regimental depot the previous summer.

Admittedly, the German mountain troops were not particularly suited for fighting in built-up areas either. But with their superior general training, equipment and discipline, they were light years ahead of their Norwegian opponents, who, in addition to being virtually untrained, had neither sub-machine guns, hand grenades nor other weapons required for this kind of close-quarter combat.

To sum up, neither of the two alternatives looks much better than the other on paper. The question is, however, whether Colonel Sundlo's plan to defend the town from the rear was preferable, primarily because it would have preserved the defending battalion for subsequent operations. If so, the Norwegian command would have had a significant force available for the defence of the railway. Instead, the troops in Narvik were completely demoralised and allowed themselves to be taken prisoner without firing a shot – not only for reasons that have already been mentioned, but also because of the all-enveloping darkness and driving snow, which made observation and accurate firing virtually impossible.

Moreover, the unprepared Norwegian units were more or less paralysed by the inferno unfolding in front of them. Fires, explosions, the cries of wounded and dying sailors from the two ironclads – all the horrors of modern war played out before officers and men who were neither physically nor mentally prepared for it. The consequence was that, apart from the 100 or so men who brazenly marched out of the town under the noses of the German sentries, no one escaped capture. The remainder found themselves prisoners of the Germans when the forward defence line on the shore proved totally ineffective. As a result, the invaders were soon able to secure the entire length of the railway line, right up to the Swedish border at Bjørnfjell.

Only hours after the landing, therefore, Narvik was under the domination of self-assured German mountain troops who had taken over all important points in the town, while the Norwegian soldiers stood idly by and watched them, a large number of curious civilians doing the same. In view of these circumstances, Colonel Sundlo can hardly be blamed for surrendering the town as he did. The surrender was in many ways a consequence of Fleischer's plan – a plan which failed to take into consideration either the Norwegian troops' deplorable lack of training or the implications for the town and its population of turning it into a battlefield. In actual fact, the plan had required far more experienced and more battle-hardened soldiers than the hastily mobilised Norwegian reserve units, officered by part-timers who had never heard a shot fired in anger. Not surprisingly, therefore, the court which found Colonel Sundlo guilty of treason for his actions later in the war acquitted him for the surrender of Narvik in the early hours of 9 April.

The salient point is, therefore, whether the forces defending Narvik should have been deployed further to the rear along the railway line initially, and *whether there was any reason to try to counter-attack at all.* It must be borne in mind that an important premise for the Norwegian plan was that the Germans' whole strategic objective was to gain control of the iron ore outlet. But the ore traffic could have been halted just as well by taking control of the rest of the Ofoten railway from a position closer to the Swedish border. To achieve their strategic objective, the Germans would then have been forced to attack along the railway line in the precipitous mountains east of Narvik. There, the terrain would have greatly favoured the otherwise poorly trained Norwegian soldiers, who could have made use of their native skills, which would have put them on a par with, or even given them an advantage over, their German adversaries when it came to two crucial things: individually, they were all very proficient skiers and excellent shots. Not, it should be noted, thanks to any aspect of their pathetic military training, but because, in those days, cross-country skiing and shooting were an integral part of growing up in the Norwegian countryside. They were, as one German officer would later write in his memoirs of the campaign, 'hervorragende Schützen und Skiläufer', first-class shots and skiers. These qualities would have counted for nothing in the streets of Narvik, but would prove themselves to be of inestimable value later in the campaign, in the mountain strongholds around the town.

Another point is that the German destroyers would not have been anywhere near as effective supporting an inland advance as they were overcoming the defences in Narvik, even had they managed to enter the narrow confines of Rombaken, the innermost arm of the Ofoten fjord. After a while the attackers would probably have had to resort to indirect fire, directed by observers ashore on the mountain plateau, relying on visual observation of the fall of shot and then relaying corrections back to the ships by wireless. This would have required procedures and equipment which the German Navy did not possess at the time.

In planning for the defence of Narvik, in other words, we [Norway] ought to have opted for defence in depth. Then we could have taken advantage of the fact that the requirements imposed on the attacker by the terrain as well as by the very purpose of the attack would eventually force him to fight over ground and under circumstances more favourable to us than to him.

On the assumption that an invasion would have to be mounted from far away, meaning that the troops taking part would have to be transported on ships, the invader also had two other strategic considerations to contend with. Firstly, the attacking force had to be limited, at least in the opening phase, because of the constraints on shipping. Secondly, in 1940 no continental power was capable of supplying and reinforcing an expeditionary force in northern Norway by sea because of Britain's naval superiority and domination of both the North Sea and the Norwegian Sea. Norway's entire security policy – to the extent that Foreign Minister Koht's and the Nygaardsvold government's feeble vacillations deserve to be called 'policy' – was based on the fact that they relied on Britain, and Britain's naval supremacy in the waters surrounding us.

With this in mind, we should have permitted ourselves to concentrate on local, tactical measures to defend Narvik. The Royal Navy would, as subsequent events were to prove, make short work of an attack from Germany or any other hostile power. Even if the attacker succeeded in gaining a foothold at the outset, we could have allowed the wild and trackless areas bordering the Ofoten railway to swallow up and whittle away his limited forces, employing our own modest forces to do what they were best equipped to do – to wear him down by making full use of their superior shooting and skiing skills in open country, waiting for the invader to collapse due to lack of supplies and reinforcements. But this is very far from how Norwegian officers were thinking in 1940, born as they were in another century and inculcated, both tactically and strategically, with entirely different ideas.

Later in the campaign, towards the end of May 1940, Narvik was recaptured by Norwegian and Allied forces. Fortunately, this was achieved without having to fight for every house and every street, as would have been necessary had the town been strongly defended. The Germans were forced to give it up because of the way the campaign developed in the surrounding areas, both in the Ankenes Mountains south of the Beis fjord and in the mountains north and east of the town. This underscores the fact that the strategic effect of a military campaign does not necessarily presuppose a tactical thrust directed straight at the point of strategic importance.

It should also be noted that, when the same problem surfaced in the minds of Norway's military planners after the war, the original plan for a coastal artillery fort at the entrance to the Ofoten fjord was realised with the construction of Nes fort in Lødingen, as well as a torpedo battery on the southern side of the fjord. But that is another story.

NOTES

Prologue

p. 13 '*At about six this evening* ...' See the last of Giles Romilly's despatches from Narvik in the *Daily Express* of 9 April 1940. For more information on the Romilly brothers, see their Wikipedia biography and Giles's book *The Privileged Nightmare*.

p. 14 '*Press report states* ...' Quoted from Peter Dickens's study *Narvik* (p. 42). See also Dickens's Narvik archive no. 90/36 in the Imperial War Museum, London, which contains copies of most of the wireless signals, together with documents and correspondence of considerable interest. The Admiralty's war diary is in ADM 223/126 in the National Archives (NA), London.

p. 14 '*The pilots operated* ...' Quoted from *Tranøy losstasjons historie* (*The History of Tranøy Pilot Station*) by Hjalmar Varde. I wish to thank Steinar Samuelsen, a Lødingen pilot, who obtained this material for me. See also Olav Elsbak Jr's article 'Handelsbetjenten og bonden' in *Årbok for Hamarøy 2008* (*Hamarøy Year Book 2008*). Olav Elsbak also provided information in a letter to me dated 28 September 2011. I am indebted to him for this material and for his reminiscences.

p. 16 '*Captain Warburton-Lee was in two minds* ...' The principal chronicler of Warburton-Lee's last days and life on board HMS *Hardy* is the destroyer's paymaster, Lieutenant Geoffrey Stanning, who was also the Flotilla Commander's secretary and confidant. There are several versions of Stanning's testimony. His official report is dated 18 April 1940 and is in ADM 199/473, NA. He amplified his account in lengthy interviews with and

letters to Peter Dickens in 1972–73. The original documents are in IWM 90/36/2 and 3. The main source is, however, Stanning's highly personal and detailed report to Warburton-Lee's widow Elizabeth, which he probably wrote in the summer of 1940 and which is to be found in Warburton-Lee's private papers in the family home, Broad Oaks, Flintshire. Taken together, Stanning's reports, letters and statements are a source of prime importance to an understanding of the run-up to the encounter in the Vestfjord and subsequent events there, up to and including 10 April 1940. This material will hereinafter be referred to as 'Stanning's Reports'. These occurrences are also dealt with in Lieutenant George Heppel's report of 24 April 1940 (ADM 199/473) and in his interviews with Dickens in 1972–73, a copy of which is in IWM 90/36, hereinafter referred to as 'Heppel's Report').
p. 17 '*That fateful spring day* ...' For more on the Lofoten fishery, see various articles in the *Lofotposten* 8 March to 12 April 1940.

1 Narvik the Focal Point – For the Third Time Running

p. 23 '*Although inwardly seething* ...' There is an enormous amount of literature relating to the period from the outbreak of war in September 1939 to the invasion of Norway in April 1940, a period which is still a source of bitter controversy, not least in Norway itself. I would refer the reader to the Bibliography at the end of this book, but will especially draw attention to the following: Martin Gilbert's Churchill biography *Finest Hour*; Churchill's own account in Volume II of his history of the war, *The Twilight War 1939–1940*; William Shirer's *The Collapse of the Third Republic*; John Collville's *The Fringes of Power*; Edward Spears's *Assignment to Catastrophe*; R.J. Minney's *The Private Papers of Hore-Belisha*; Stephen Roskill's *The War at Sea* (Vol. I) and *Churchill and the Admirals*; John Harvey's *The Diplomatic Diaries of Oliver Harvey 1937–40*; James Leasor's *War at the Top*; Alex Danchev and Daniel Todman's *Field Marshal Lord Allenbrooke: War Diaries 1939–1945*; Roderick Macleod's *Time*

Unguarded: The Ironside Diaries 1937–1940; John Kennedy's *The Business of War*; and Andrew Roberts's *The Holy Fox: The Life of Lord Halifax* and Robert Self's *Neville Chamberlain: A Biography*. I have also read countless diaries and documents from the same period in the NA, the Liddell Hart Centre for Military Archives, King's College, London, and the Churchill Archives, Cambridge, all of which are fundamental to this book.

p. 24 '*The Cabinet brought forth …*' Ironside, pp. 235ff.

p. 24 '*except a twitch …*' See Self, pp. 5ff.

p. 25 '*The Germans have …*' Ironside's diary 12 August 1939, pp. 59ff.

p. 26 '*The manager greeted the guests …*' Marchant's article in the *Daily Express* of 28 March 1940.

p. 27 '*Although Prime Minister Reynaud …*' See Spears, p. 103.

p. 27 '*Reynaud's and Daladier's scheming mistresses …*' See Spears' description, pp. 96ff. The Comtesse de Portes was among the group of insiders called *La Porte à Côté* (The Side Door), while the Marquise de Crussol, who came from a family whose wealth stemmed from tinned sardines, was known as '*la Sardine qui s'est crue Sole*' ('the Sardine who thought herself a Sole'). The chaotic state of the country's politics notwithstanding, the French people clearly retained their sense of humour. See also Shirer, pp. 484ff.

p. 27 '*In the streets of Paris …*' Shirer, pp. 514ff.

p. 28 '*I found the atmosphere heavy …*' Spears, p. 22.

p. 28 '*Monsieur Reynaud has issued …*' Ironside, pp. 234ff. See also Gilbert, pp. 197ff.

p. 29 '*The main source of discord …*' See Ironside, p. 236 and Shirer, pp. 545ff.

p. 31 '*Little Reynaud sat there …*' Ironside, p. 237.

2 'Iron and war are inextricably interlinked'

p. 32 '*Rails of the heaviest calibre …*' See Rickman, pp. 111ff. Rickman also worked for Section D of Britain's Secret Service which, in 1938, had been instructed to prepare for sabotage operations directed against the Swedish iron ore export terminals in Luleå and Oxelösund. His travels and account thereof were a part of these preparations. Rickman was arrested on 19 April 1940 after having, that same winter, made several unsuccessful attempts to blow up loading facilities in Oxelösund with 220kg of dynamite smuggled into Stockholm in a British diplomatic bag. One of his helpers was a Norwegian advertising agent, Helmer Bonnevie, whom I interviewed in 1985. Rickman was sentenced to eight years' imprisonment, one of the most savage sentences handed down to a spy on Swedish soil in the course of the Second World War. Bonnevie was later apprehended by the Gestapo and sentenced to two years' hard labour in Germany. See my book *Muldvarpene* (*The Moles*), pp. 148f.

p. 34 '*The thunderous noises ...*' See Callender's report in the *New York Times*, 2 April 1940. Different sources quote different figures for ore exports to Nazi Germany, but there can be little doubt that they amounted to some 8 to 10 million tonnes annually up to the outbreak of war. Discussions have been heated on the ore's importance to the German war effort. In my opinion, Churchill was correct in claiming that the ore was crucial to Hitler's ability to wage war – and that protection of the ore fields and shipping lanes was the main reason for his invasion of Norway and Denmark. For a modern understanding of Nazi Germany's overstretched economy and shortage of raw materials, see Adam Tooze's study, *The Wages of Destruction*.

p. 35 '*Shipments continued to increase ...*' See Broch, pp. 79ff. Broch's book, a blend of reminiscences and propaganda, was first published during the war in Britain and the United States under the title of *The Mountains Wait*. It radiates the author's enthusiasm and joy in storytelling. I am grateful to Supreme Court Judge Lars Oftedal Broch, who placed his late stepfather's private archives at my disposal.

3 'Equal to a first-class victory in the field …'

p. 38 '*It must be understood* …' Churchill's memo of 23 September 1939 to the War Cabinet, ADM 205/2, NA. See also his memoirs and Gilbert, pp. 34ff.
p. 39 '*These sinkings, Churchill felt* …' Gilbert, p. 104.
p. 39 '*In a broad-based memorandum* …' See Churchill, p. 119 and Gilbert, pp. 105ff.
p. 40 '*He showed me the original* …' See Showell, pp. 63ff and Hans Fr. Dahl's Quisling biography, pp. 30ff.
p. 41 '*The offensive through Narvik* …' See Ironside, p. 188. The literature surrounding the Allies' deliberations from December 1939 to April 1940 is overwhelming and the discerning reader will see that I have made a clean cut and concentrated on Narvik. The Allied plans developed in stages and provided for landings in Stavanger, Bergen and Trondheim, in addition to the operations directed at Narvik and Kiruna/Luleå with a force of more than 100,000 men. For a concise description, see Haarr, pp. 25ff. A comprehensive account of the Norwegian and Swedish response is contained in Odd-Bjørn Fure's *Mellomkrigstid* (*Interwar Years*), pp. 311ff. See also Koht, pp. 123ff. Countless documents of vital importance to an understanding of this period are also to be found in the private papers of Major General Pierse Mackesy who, towards the end of January 1940, was appointed Commander-in-Chief of Operations in Scandinavia. I am grateful to the late Piers Mackesy, Fellow of Pembroke College, Oxford and a distinguished military historian, who kindly made his father's papers available to me when I visited him at his home in Scotland in 2011. Another important source is General John Kennedy, who was appointed Mackesy's chief of staff in February 1940. His views are set out in his memoirs, *The Business of War*, pp. 46ff, which in turn are based on his diaries, which are now in the Liddell Hart Archives in King's College, London.
p. 42 '*It is now decided* …' Colville, pp. 60f.
p. 42 '*To try to get up* …' Ironside, p. 225.
p. 43 '*In no uncertain terms* …' Jodl's diary is held in the collection Nachlass Jodl, N 69/10, Bundesarchiv-Militärarchiv (BA-MA),

Freiburg. Also of great importance to the account are the unpublished memoirs of Lieutenant Albert Bach, which were completed in Graz, Austria, in 1983 with the title *Meine Teilnahme am Norwegen-feldzug: Am Unternehmen Narvik*. In Berlin in March 1940, Bach, who was aide-de-camp on General Dietl's staff, drew up the detailed plan for the attack on Narvik with the operations officer of the 3rd Mountain Division, Lieutenant Colonel Robert Bader. In consequence, Bach must be regarded as having been a key witness to the events of this dramatic period in the history of the war. Bach went on to fight throughout the rest of the war, in the Balkans and on the Eastern Front, and was taken prisoner by the Russians in 1945, by which time he had risen to the rank of colonel. He was released in 1948 and from 1956 he served as an officer in the Austrian Bundesheer. He was appointed General of Infantry in 1969, but resigned three years later in protest at the direction taken by Austria's defence policy. In all likelihood his memoirs were written after his retirement. A copy of them is in the War History Museum in Narvik. I wish to thank the museum's curator, Ulf Eirik Torgersen, who provided me with this invaluable material.

p. 44 '*We had a dreadful Cabinet* ...' Ironside, p. 227.

p. 44 '*It is hard to believe* ...' Quoted from various documents in Mackesy's private papers. Most of them appear to have been written between the summer of 1940 and the winter of 1941, i.e. a relatively short time after the events they portray.

p. 45 '*Churchill's disappointment knew no bounds* ...' See Gilbert, pp. 189f.

4 Hitler's Fateful Decision

p. 46 '*The peace treaty signed in Moscow* ...' Nachlass Jodl, N 69/10, BA-MA, Freiburg.

p. 46 '*We have to admit* ...' Bach, pp. 47ff.

p. 48 '*He liked to put off* ...' See Linge's memoirs, *With Hitler to the End*, pp. 133f. This is one of the better books written by people in Hitler's inner circle and republished in recent years. See also Volume 4 of *Die Tagebücher von Joseph Goebbels: Sämtliche Fragmente* (pp. 89ff) for the period 1 January–8 July 1940, and the English translation of Halder's diary for the relevant period, in the Liddell Hart Centre, King's College. It is also an illuminating experience to read William Shirer's recently republished *Berlin Diary*, pp. 305ff, and the collected scripts of his CBS radio broadcasts, *This is Berlin*, pp. 231ff, which vividly capture the prevailing atmosphere in the German capital that fateful Easter in 1940. Hitler's decision is to be found in Showell, pp. 87ff.

5 Ominous Rumours

p. 53 '*Although guardedly worded* ...'Virtually all the world's media covered the meeting of the War Council. The quotations are from the newspapers referred to in the text for 28 March 1940 and in the days that followed.
p. 55 '*This action would give us* ...' Phillips' memo is in ADM 116/4471, NA, London. The same applies to the intelligence report from Stockholm. For relations between Churchill and Phillips, see Roskill's *Churchill and the Admirals*, pp. 198ff. Pound's comments are in the same book, p. 125.
p. 56 '*In the course of Friday 29 March* ...'The dates are from Ironside's diary, p. 238.
p. 56 '*The alarm was sounded* ...' Bickford's report *Operation Wilfred* in ADM 199/474, NA. Interview with Thomas Chilton in IWM Sound Archive, no. 27345.
p. 57 '*Part of the 2nd D.F.* ...' Stanning's reports (ADM 199/473, NA) and other documents from the 1920s and 1930s in Warburton-Lee's private papers, Broad Oaks, which, among other things, contain a complete collection of the captain's letters to his wife Elizabeth. See also Williams, pp. 323ff.
p. 57 '*Warburton-Lee was* ...'This depiction is based on letters and documents in Warburton-Lee's private archives and the following interviews in the Imperial War Museum's Sound Archive: Charles

Parham, HMS *Hostile* (IWM 10719); Maurice Cutler, *Havock* (IWM 11328); Alfred Surridge, *Havock* (IWM 11455); Marshal Soult, *Hunter* (IWM 12297); Harry Jenkins, *Havock* (IWM 10490); Charles Cheshire, *Hardy* (IWM 16304); Frederick Mason, *Hardy* (IWM 10747); Douglas Bourton, *Hardy* (IWM 10746); Cyril Cope, *Hardy* (IWM 11586); Leslie Smale, *Hardy* (IWM 11094); John Dodds, *Havock* (IWM 13148); Frederick Kemp, *Havock* (IWM 10503); Alan Martin, *Hostile* (IWM 10696); Stanley Robinson, *Hardy* (IWM 11286); Arthur Townsend, *Hotspur* (IWM 10590); James Brown, *Havock* (IWM 10504); William Pulford, *Hardy* (IWM 10610).

p. 61 '*Very late at night* ...' All from General Mackesy's private papers in Scotland, which, among other things, contain a copy of his service record. Of particular importance is his Narvik report, *A brief account of the Narvik expedition in 1940*, which he compiled between June 1940 and March 1941, working from drafts, supplementary papers and comments from officers who served under him.

p. 62 '*At the Foreign Office* ...' Cadogan's diary, p. 266.

p. 63 '*I personally believe* ...' Colban is quoted from the findings of the *Undersøkelseskommisjon av 1945 [Investigative Commission of 1945]*, Recommendation I, Appendix 3, p. 259.

p. 63 '*Sweden's prime minister, Per Albin Hansson* ...' See Isaksson's biography of Hansson, *Per Albin*, pp. 441ff.

p. 64 '*In Narvik, too* ...' This portrayal of Colonel Sundlo is based on documents produced and evidence given in the proceedings against him after the war. A shorthand record is in the archives of the Military Investigative Commission of 1946, Box 2515, Riksarkivet (National Archives), Oslo. The letters are quoted from Lars Borgersrud's groundbreaking study of the National Unity Party's influence on the Norwegian officer corps, *Vi er jo et militært parti* (*We are, after all, a military party*), pp. 131 and 288. I have slightly modified some of Sundlo's rather colourful language. Sundlo published his own version in the Nasjonal Samling's own periodical, *Folk og land*, in 1962–64 under the title *Narvik 1940. Byen med kanonen* (*Narvik 1940: The Town with the Cannon*). The officers quoted in this chapter were witnesses in court.

p. 66 '*We kept bombarding* ...' Lindbäck-Larsen, p. 28.

p. 67 '*We drove all that Saturday ...*' Commodore Per Askim's (1881–1963) personal report, *Kampen om Narvik april 1940* (*The Battle for Narvik April 1940*), was completed in London in July 1940 and is more comprehensive than the published version. While working on it, Askim kept a detailed diary which, in the 1950s, he expanded into a book of memoirs for his family. Under the title of *Fars erindringer* (*Father's Reminiscences*), it spanned the period from his childhood in Moss before the turn of the century to his return from exile in May 1945. He first married Anne Marie Hanssen from Horten, who died in 1935 at the age of 55. After two years as a widower, he married Anne Marie's younger sister, Signe, who, after the war, wrote her own account of their wartime experiences, *Fra Narvik til Washington*. Together, this unpublished material constitutes an extremely valuable source for anyone wishing to know what happened in Narvik during and after the sinking of the two ironclads. I wish to thank Dr Ole Petter Børmer who, on behalf of the family, allowed me to use this material.

6 The Calm Before the Storm

p. 69 '*It seems rather hard ...*' Churchill's speech is from the *New York Times* of 31 March 1940. See also Gilbert, pp. 201f. It was Churchill's broadcasts that gloomy winter and spring that, more than anything else, confirmed his paramount position among the Allied leaders. In the field, one reverse followed another, and Hitler's war machine appeared to be invincible. Confronting it was Churchill, who, in speech after speech and in immortal prose, denounced Nazi barbarism and unwaveringly – and seemingly without a shred of doubt – proclaimed his faith in ultimate victory. The psychological effect was overwhelming and his speeches probably did much to ensure that defeatism never gained the upper hand in political circles. Some of his most inspiring speeches are available on a CD released by the Imperial War Museum as *Churchill's Famous Speeches*.
p. 71 '*Churchill has delivered nothing ...*' See Goebbels diaries in Fröhlich, p. 93. Von Rundstedt is quoted from Liddell Hart, p. 37.

p. 72 '*The commanders of all the detachments* ...'The conference in the Reich Chancellery on 1 April has been reconstructed on the basis of Bach's memoirs, Pohlmann's unpublished account *Norwegen 1940* and Paul Klatt's book *3. Gebirgs-division 1939–45* (pp. 24f).
p. 74 '*These pillboxes were extremely* ...' Nitter Hauge's evidence at the trial of Konrad Sundlo, MUK 46, Box 2515, Riksarkivet, Oslo. Besides this, there is practically no information available on the appearance and location of these pillboxes, possibly because after the war there was little interest in turning the spotlight on this particular aspect of Narvik's defences. For example, I have been unable to find a single photograph of these controversial pillboxes.
p. 75 '*The officers did their best* ...'This is based on Per Askim's report and reminiscences.
p. 78 '*Glad to find* ...' See Cadogan diaries, pp. 266f, and Colville, p. 71.

7 No to Royal Marine, Yes to Wilfred

p. 79 '*I was called to the telephone* ...' Spears, p. 96.
p. 80 '*The Führer decides* ...' Nachlass Jodl, N 69/10, BA-MA, Freiburg.
p. 80 '*With disaster fast approaching* ...' For more on Koht and the Norwegian government's vacillations, see my books *Krysseren Blücher* and *Kongens nei*, together with the report of the *Undersøkelseskommisjon*, Appendix 3.
p. 81 '*The general failure to comprehend* ...' Neither Fleischer nor Lindbäck-Larsen, both of whom distinguished themselves in the campaign on their return to the battle zone by air from eastern Finnmark on the night between 11 and 12 April, ever gave a proper explanation of why they accorded priority to manoeuvres in Varanger instead of hastening to Narvik, considering the tense situation obtaining there in the first week of April. On Friday 5 and Saturday 6 April, the Inspector-General of Infantry, Colonel Otto Ruge, was engaged in a round of inspection at Elvegårdsmoen and, in all probability, also in Narvik. None the less, to the best of my

knowledge, Ruge's findings were never made public. He got back to Terningmoen Camp at Elverum on Tuesday 9 April – just in time to take part in the fighting at Midtskogen that same evening.
p. 82 '*All of us naval personnel* ...' See Signe Askim's memoirs, p. 2.
p. 82 '*Despite his misgivings* ...' See Isaksson, p. 442. For more on Forshell and the warnings from Berlin, see Jacobsen, *Krysseren Blücher*, pp. 40ff.
p. 83 '*At two in the morning* ...' See Ryeng's article, 'De fem trojanske hestene [The Five Trojan Horses]', published in Narvik 1998. See also Nachlass Jodl, N 69/10, BA-MA, Freiburg.
p. 84 '*Along Germany's winter life-line* ...' All of the quotations that follow are from Romilly's and Callender's despatches in the *Daily Express* and *New York Times* of 5 April and the days immediately following. With the exception of his despatch of 9 April, I have been unable to trace Peter Rhodes's articles, which were distributed by UPI. Rhodes was later suspected of having been a Soviet agent, but rejected all allegations when confronted by the FBI. See the FBI Silvermaster File and John Earl Haynes and Harvey Klehr's study *Venona: Decoding Soviet Espionage in America* (1999).
p. 86 '*Shortly after leaving Scapa* ...' See Stanning's reports (ADM 199/473, NA) and Warburton-Lee's letters in his papers. The ship's movements are also documented in the *Home Fleet War Diary*, ADM 199/361, NA, London.
p. 88 '*At Bedale Hall* ...' All quotations are from Mackesy's private papers, Ironside's diary (p. 238) and Major General Richard Dewing's handwritten diary for 4 April in the Liddell Hart Centre, King's College, London. See also Gilbert, pp. 200f.
p. 89 '*Churchill and Spears* ...' See Spears, pp. 97ff, Cadogan's diaries p. 268, and Colville's diaries, pp. 78ff.

8 The Invasion Fleet Puts to Sea

p. 93 '*The flotilla left Sullom Voe* ...' See Bickford's report in ADM 199/474, NA. Brown, see note to p. 57, Stanning's reports and Warburton-Lee's collected letters.

p. 94 '*In the Vestfjord* ...' In the period preceding the outbreak of war, the *Lofotposten* ran a series of articles on the Lofoten fishery – until it was abruptly brought to an end by the invasion. Under the trade agreement between Norway and Germany, in the winter of 1940 provision was made for delivery of 50,000 tonnes of fish, some of which was to be packed in ice and shipped to Germany, the remainder despatched to a new filleting plant, Frostfilet, in Trondheim.
p. 95 '*In Narvik, at the head of the fjord* ...' See Romilly's and Callender's despatches of 6 and 8 April 1940 and Askim's report.
p. 97 '*Saturday morning the weather was glorious* ...' This is based on Dietl, pp. 39f, and Albert Bach's unpublished memoirs.
p. 99 '*On the neighbouring destroyer* ...' See Laugs, pp. 26f.
p. 99 '*Only an hour earlier* ...' Information derived from Mackesy's private papers and Colonel William Fraser's unpublished memoirs *Norwegian Adventure*, in the Liddell Hart Centre, King's College. See also Erskine, pp. 26f, and Fitzgerald, pp. 7ff. Major General Dewing's diary entry was made on 19 April; the original is in the Liddell Hart archives.

9 Race to the North

p. 102 '*The ship forged steadily ahead* ...' See Albert Bach's memoirs. Other references to Bach are from Barthou.
p. 102 '*The golden orb of the sun* ...' Colonel Hans Rohr of the Austrian Bundeswehr, who was highly decorated for his war service, completed his unpublished memoirs, *Tagebuch eines Gebirgjägers im II. Weltkrig vom 28.8.1939–2.10.1945*, in 1987 and deposited a copy in the War Museum in Narvik. Rohr and his company effectively acted as Dietl's personal bodyguard. He accompanied the general from the quay to the marketplace and was present when Colonel Sundlo surrendered the town without offering resistance. In consequence, Rohr must be regarded as a key witness to the landing and subsequent capitulation. Information on Bonte and Erdmenger is from Dietl, pp. 46f and the *Wilhelm Heidkamp* war diary, RM 94/99, BA-MA, Freiburg.

p. 104 '*The signal reached the Admiralty …*' The dramatic events of 7–9 April 1940 and the part played in them by Churchill have been the subject of considerable discussion, some of it quite heated, especially among British authors and historians. Captain Stephen Roskill, who served at the Admiralty throughout the war, was the first to criticise in public the First Lord's interference in operational matters. He did so in 1954 in the first volume of the official history, *War at Sea 1939–45* and in the years that followed he further developed his arguments in, among other writings, his insightful and highly entertaining book *Churchill and His Admirals*. There can be little doubt that the First Lord's highly personal engagement in the Narvik campaign had a considerable and, to some extent, fateful effect on its outcome. The description of the War Room and working routines are from Gilbert, pp. 158ff, along with the many reminiscences published by Churchill's closest associates, among them General Leslie Hollis/James Leasor's *War at the Top*. A vivid impression of Churchill's personality and astonishing achievements may also be gained from two more recent books, Andrew Roberts's *Masters and Commanders* (2008) and Max Hastings's *Finest Years* (2009). Fleet movements and times are derived from the many war diaries that are available, most notably those of the Admiralty and Home Fleet in, respectively, ADM 223/126 and ADM 199/361, NA, together with the reports of admirals Forbes and Whitworth. Extracts from the war diaries of some of the other units involved can be found on www.naval-history.net. Unless otherwise stated in the text, all quotations are from these sources.
p. 106 '*The Admiralty's attention was still …*' See Roskill, *The War at Sea*, pp. 158ff.
p. 106 '*Rather an uninteresting day …*' As duty officer at the Admiralty, Captain Ralph Edwards was a close witness to the events leading up to 9 April. His diary was first brought to public notice by Roskill in *Churchill and His Admirals*, pp. 92ff and pp. 233ff. I have since obtained copies of the originals, both the handwritten and the typewritten versions, from the Roskill archives at the Churchill Document Centre, Cambridge, Boxes 4/75 and 4/76. Wherever possible, I have relied on the handwritten notes, which appear to have been jotted down on an office pad at more or less the same time as the events in question.

p. 108 '*We steered towards the position* ...' See Whitworth's report in ADM 199/474 and Stanning's reports. Both enlarged upon their views in 1950 or thereabouts in correspondence with Roskill.
p. 108 '*In Scotland, Major General Mackesy* ...' See the Mackesy papers.
p. 109 '*The approaching British bombers* ...' See Bach's memoirs and the *Scharnhorst* war diary in RM 92/5178, BA-MA.
p. 109 '*Back at the Admiralty* ...' Sources as per note on p. 104.
p. 110 '*What happened was a complete fiasco* ...' See Roskill, *The War at Sea*, pp. 159f, and Edwards's diaries.
p. 111 '*Expecting disaster* ...' See Romilly, p. 4.
p. 111 '*The crews of the German cruisers* ...' See the *Wilhelm Heidkamp* war diary in RM 94/99 and Bach's and Rohr's reminiscences.

10 The Mining of the Vestfjord

p. 112 '*The mining of* ...' Bickford's and Stanning's reports.
p. 113 '*On board the Norwegian Navy's guard ship* ...' See archive of the 3rd Naval Defence District, Box 192, FKA, Riksarkivet, Oslo and Steen, pp. 44ff.
p. 113 '*During the night* ...'This account of the German force's dramatic voyage north is largely based on the war diaries of the ships involved in BA-MA, Freiburg, Germany: *Georg Thiele* (RM 94/45), *Wolfgang Zenker* (RM 94/72), *Bernd von Arnim* (RM 94/78), *Erich Koellner* (RM 94/80), *Dieter von Roeder* (RM 94/93), *Hans Lüdemann* (RM 94/94, *Hermann Künne* (RM 994/95), *Wilhelm Heidkamp* (RM 94/99) and *Anton Schmitt* (RM 94/100), together with Bach's and Rohr's reminiscences. All of the original war diaries were lost in the fighting around Narvik, with the exception of that kept by Erich Holtorf on board the *Dieter von Roeder*. The loss of these diaries notwithstanding, it may be assumed that the reconstructions, which were undertaken a few weeks after the battle, afford a realistic picture of what happened. I have also had reference to the war diary of the 3rd Mountain Division, which Per Erik Olsen, editor of the magazine *Militærhistorie*, most kindly placed at my disposal.
p. 114 '*I immediately rang* ...' See Koht, p. 213 and Per Askim's report and reminiscences.

p. 117 '*Then, dead ahead …*' See Laugs, p. 36 and the war diaries of the *Hans Lüdemann* and *Bernd von Arnim*. Rechel made no attempt to hide his fury with Friedrichs, and he was backed by Bonte's successor as Flotilla Commander, Commodore Erich Bey who, in his *Stellungnahme* of 15 July 1940, criticised Friedrichs's handling of the *Hans Lüdemann* both before and after the destroyer's arrival in Narvik. See RM 94/94, pp. 126ff. It is interesting to note that it was the captain of the *Hipper*, Commodore Hellmuth Heye who, after the war, via the Red Cross, drew the attention of the British authorities to Roope's gallant action against a vastly superior opponent. His testimony, which was substantiated by survivors, led to Lieutenant Commander Roope being awarded a posthumous VC in 1945.

p. 119 '*At the Admiralty …*' Sources as per note to p. 104; see also Stanning's and Heppel's reports.

p. 121 '*Winston is back from France*' See Ironside, p. 248 and the minutes of the War Cabinet meeting in CAB 656, NA, the *Undersøkelseskommisjon*, Vol. I, Appendix 3, pp. 176f and Askim's reminiscences.

p. 123 '*The town itself today …*' Romilly's last despatch to the *Daily Express* on 9 April and *Fjellene venter*, p. 107.

p. 124 '*I dressed quickly …*' Signe Askim's reminiscences, pp. 3f.

p. 125 '*The First Lord who at last …*' Colville, p. 76 and Fraser *Norwegian Adventure*, Liddell Hart archives.

p. 126 '*acutely uncomfortable …*' Stanning's report and Whitworth's *Report of Proceedings* of 29 April 1940, ADM 199/474. In the letters Forbes and Whitworth exchanged with Roskill after the war, both were critical of their own actions and of Churchill's persistent interference. As Whitworth wrote of the days after 9 April on board the *Renown*: '[They were] the four most miserably unhappy days of the whole of my service …' Roskill archives, at the Churchill Document Centre, Cambridge, Boxes 4/75 and 4/76.

p. 127 '*We steered a course …*' See the *Wilhelm Heidkamp* war diary and note to p. 113.

11 The Sinking of the Ironclads

p. 131 '*I had spent the whole night* ...' See Stanning's report in Warburton-Lee's private papers, the *Scharnhorst* and *Gneisenau* war diaries in RM 92/5178 and 92/5245 and analogous documents in ADM 199/379 and 199/474, NA, London.
p. 132 '*In the deeper reaches* ...' See note to p. 113.
p. 134 '*The weather was pretty thick* ...' Reports in Box 492, FKA, Riksarkivet, Oslo and Askim's reminiscences.
p. 135 '*Round about midday* ...' See Lindbäck-Larsen, p. 33 and his testimony at the trial of Konrad Sundlo.
p. 137 '*Despite the acrimonious exchange* ...' *Daily Express*, 9 April 1940.
p. 138 '*Suddenly we saw the outline* ...' See the *Wilhelm Heidkamp* war diary, Gerlach's entries in the Flotilla Commander's war diary, RM 54/2, and statements of *Eidsvold* survivors in interviews and interrogations, Box 492, FKA. I wish to thank Ingrid Willoch, who kindly made available this information about her grandfather.
p. 139 '*Bonte was a torpedo officer* ...' Peter Dickens both corresponded with and interviewed a number of the German officers who took part in the battle for Narvik, among them Max-Eckart Wolff, Curt Rechel, Fritz Böhme, Karl Smidt, Herbert Friedrichs and Karl-Theodor Raeder. The letters and transcripts of the interviews are in Dickens's archives (IWM 90/36); they contribute much towards an understanding of the personalities involved. Following their denazification, Wolff, Smidt and Gerlach all ended their military careers with the rank of admiral, and in the 1960s they played prominent roles in NATO and the West German Bundesmarine. Gerlach, for example, was Commander-in-Chief of the West German Navy but, as far as I have been able to ascertain, never wrote anything about his two visits to the *Eidsvold*, apart from the entries he made in Flotilla Commander Bonte's war diary on his return to Germany in the summer of 1940 (RM 54/2). Although the other officers' views on Hitler and Nazism are not known, Smidt is believed to have been anti-Nazi from 1935 onwards for he was a member of the Evangelical Confessional Church, which

worked against the system from within. See Alfred de Zaya's article 'Kart Ernst Smidt' in *Ostfriesische Landschaft* (2007). For more on Gerlach, see *Der Spiegel*, no. 14/57.

p. 141 '*Some few kilometres distant* ...' During and after the war, Sundlo was lumped together with such outright traitors as Jonas Lie (a Norwegian SS and police officer), Karl Marthinsen (an exceptionally callous Norwegian police officer and leader of Quisling's *Hird*) and other notorious traitors on account of his having surrendered Narvik without a fight, his pro-Nazi leanings pre-war and his treasonous conduct as a prominent bureaucrat in Quisling's administration throughout the rest of the war. It is extremely difficult to form an objective judgement of what really happened in Narvik on the night of 9–10 April. One reason for this is that some of his subordinates were similarly arraigned, while others appear to have taken advantage of the confusion to blame their own failings on Sundlo. From the testimonies of the Norwegian officers alone, therefore, it is impossible to reconstruct with any degree of accuracy what actually occurred prior to and during the capitulation, but Romilly's and Callender's on-the-spot reports provide a useful corrective. Accordingly, I believe that my version is as close to reality as it is possible to get. The quotations are taken from police interrogations and the testimony of witnesses in the Sundlo trial.

p. 142 '*The ironclads suddenly increased speed* ...' See note to p. 113.

p. 146 '*As the seconds* ...' Johannes Diesen's testimony in the Sundlo trial.

p. 147 '*The lack of effect* ...' Buch's report in the *Bernd von Arnim* war diary, RM 94/78.

p. 150 '*Colonel Sundlo saw things differently* ...' See Steen, p. 96.

p. 150 '*A sound sleeper* ...' See Romilly, p. 5.

12 Counter-attack

p. 153 '*I was woken* ...' See Torrance's report of 1 June 1940, WO 373/5, NA, London.

p. 154 '*The First Lord of the Admiralty said* ...' See the minutes of the Cabinet Meeting in CAB 65/6, NA. Also Ironside, p. 250 and Cadogan, p. 268.
p. 156 '*In between the large wooden buildings* ...' See Colonel Windisch's unpublished memoirs, pp. 16ff. Narvik museum.
p. 158 '*I began feverishly packing* ...' Signe Askim's memoirs, pp. 8ff.
p. 160 '*All day Monday* ...' Torbjørn Andreassen's article in *Årbok for Hamarøy 2000*, Olav Elsbak's statement and Stanning's reports.
p. 161 '*His Majesty's Government have at once assured* ...' Quoted from the *Daily Express* of 10 April 1940.
p. 162 '*During the Cabinet "Pug" Ismay came out* ...' See Colville, p. 75, Ironside, p. 249, and Dewing's diary.
p. 162 '*I went immediately to encrypt* ...' See Stanning's reports, Dickens, p. 46, and Roskill, *Churchill and the Admirals*, p. 100.
p. 163 '*When I reported to him* ...' See *Bernd von Arnim* war diary in RM 94/78 and information contained in Dickens's private papers, IWM.
p. 164 '*Positions in the centre of the town* ...' See Dietl, p. 71 and notes to pp. 13 and 112; also Gilbert, p. 223.
p. 167 '*The destroyer Anton Schmitt* ...' See the war diaries of the three destroyers involved in RM 94/93, RM 94/95 and RM 94/100. Korvettenkapitän Holtorf on board the *Dieter von Roeder*, which broke off its patrol at the first faint light of dawn, was the only one to save his original war diary. Entries in the diary confirm that the captain had acted in accordance with the orders he had been given, which undoubtedly saved him from a court martial.
p. 167 '*Until now we had not seen any signs of civilisation* ...' No doubt surrounds the overall effect of the British attack on the ships in Narvik harbour, but there is a great deal of uncertainty attaching to the details and times. My depiction of the action is based on the accounts of key witnesses Stanning and Heppel and the written descriptions of, and interviews with, Herbert Lyman, Cyril Cope, John Burfield and two other officers, Millns and Little, in Dickens's private archives (IWM 90/36). More information is to be found in the official reports of Layman and Wright in ADM 199/379, NA, and in the interviews referred to in the note to p. 57. Unless otherwise stated, all quotations are from these sources, which

together provide the basis of the mosaic that makes up the rest of this chapter. For German sources, see the note to p. 113.
p. 178 '*I saw Hotspur coming towards us ...*' Little information is available on what occurred on board the *Hunter*, but Stuart-Menteth provides brief explanations, see Warburton-Lee's private papers and Dickens's archives.

Epilogue

p. 180 '*Herr Hitler has committed ...*' All quotations in what follows are from Churchill's speech in the House of Commons as reported in the *Daily Express* on Friday 12 April 1940. Other material is from reports in ADM 199/474 and Warburton-Lee's and Mackesy's private papers.

BIBLIOGRAPHY

Adams, Jack, *The Doomed Expedition* (London, 1989).

Barnett, Corelli, *Engage the Enemy More Closely* (London, 1990).

Barthou, Peter, *Der 'Obeerstenparagraph' im Bundesheer* (Vienna, 2007).

Bekker, Cajus, *Verdammte See: Ein Kriegstagebuch der Deutschen Marine* (Oldenburg, 1971).

Below, Nikolaus von, *At Hitler's Side: The Memoirs of Hitler's Luftwaffe Adjutant 1937–1945* (Barnsley, 2010).

Bennett, Gill, *Churchill's Man of Mystery* (Abingdon, 2009).

Bjørnsen, Bjørn, *Narvik* (Oslo, 1980).

Boehm, Hermann, *Norge mellom England og Tyskland* (Oslo, 1957).

Bonatz, Heinz, *Seekrieg im Äther* (Herford, 1981).

Borgersrud, Lars, *Konspirasjon og kapitulasjon. Nytt lys på forsvarshistorien fra 1814 til 1940* (Oslo, 2000).

——, *Vi er jo et militært parti* (Oslo, 2010).

Broch Theodor, *The Mountains Wait* (St Paul, 1942). Published in Norwegian as *Fjellene venter* (Oslo, 1946).

Brodhurst, Robin, *Churchill's Anchor* (Barnsley, 2000).

Busch, Fritz Otto, *Narvik: Von Heldenkampf deutscher Zerstörer* (Berlin, 1940).

Cadogan, Alexander, *The Diaries of Alexander Cadogan 1938–1945*, ed. David Dilks (New York, 1972).

Churchill, Winston, *The Second World War*. Vols I and II (London, 1948/49).

Claasen, Adam, *Hitler's Northern War: The Luftwaffe's Ill-Fated Campaign 1940–45* (Lawrence, 2001).

Colville, John, *The Fringes of Power: Downing Street Diaries 1939–1945* (London, 1985).

Corrigan, Gordon, *Blood, Sweat and Arrogance and the Myths of Churchill's War* (London, 2006).

Dahl, Hans Fredrik, *'Dette er London.' NRK i krig 1940–1945* (Oslo, 1978).

——, *Vidkun Quisling, en fører for fall* (Oslo, 1992).

Danchev, Alex and Todman, Daniel, *Field Marshal Lord Alanbrooke: War Diaries 1939–1945* (London, 2002).

Derry, T.K., *The Campaign in Norway* (London, 1952).

Dickens, Peter, *Narvik* (Annapolis, 1974).

Dietl, Gerda-Luise and Herrmann, Kurt, *General Dietl: Das Leben eines Soldaten* (Munich, 1951).

Erikson, Lars et al., *Beredskap i väst: Sveriges militära beredskap och västgrensen 1940–1945* (Stockholm, 1991).

Erskine, David, *The Scots Guards 1919–1955* (London, 1956).

Fantur, Werner, *Narvik: Sieg des Glaubens* (Berlin, 1941).

Fitzgerald, Desmond, *A History of the Irish Guards in the Second World War* (London, 1986).

Fjeld, Odd T. (ed.), *Klar til strid – kystartilleriet gjennom århundrene* (Oslo, 1999).

Fritz, Martin, *German Steel and Swedish Iron Ore* (Gothenburg, 1974).

Fröhlich, Elke, *Die Tagebücher von Joseph Goebbels, sämtliche Fragmente 1. Januar–8. Juli 1940*.Vol. 4 (Stuttgart, 1997).

Fure, Odd-Bjørn, *Mellomkrigstid* (Oslo, 1996).

Furre, Berge, *Norsk historie 1905–1940* (Oslo, 1971).

Gilbert, Martin, *Finest Hour: Winston S. Churchill 1939–1941* (London, 1983).

Haarr, Geirr H., *The German Invasion of Norway* (Barnsley, 2009).

Hambro, Johan, *C.J. Hambro – liv og drøm* (Oslo, 1984).

Harriman, Florence, *Mission to the North* (New York, 1941).

Hartmann, Sverre, *Spillet om Norge* (Oslo, 1958).

Harvey, John, *The Diplomatic Diaries of Oliver Harvey 1937–40* (London, 1970).

Hase, Georg, *Die Kriegsmarine erobert Norwegen Fjorde* (Leipzig, 1940).

Hastings, Max, *Finest Years* (London, 2009).

Haynes, John Earl and Klehr, Harvey, *Venona: Decoding Soviet Espionage in America* (New Haven, CT, 1999).

Heysig, Günther, *Propagandatruppen der Deutschen Kriegsmarine* (Hamburg, 1964).

Hickman, Tom, *Churchill's Bodyguard* (London, 2005).

Hinsley, F.H., *British Intelligence in the Second World War* (London, 1979–90).

Hobson, Rolf and Kristiansen, Tom, *Norsk forsvarshistorie*, Vol. 3 (Bergen, 2001).

Hollis, Leslie, *One Marine's Tale* (London, 1946).

Hovland, Torkel, *Fleischer* (Oslo, 2005).

Hubatsch, Walther, *Weserübung: Die Deutsche Besetzung von Danemark und Norwegen 1940* (Göttingen, 1960).

Irving, David, *Hitler und seine Feldherren* (Berlin, 1975).

Isaksson, Anders, *Per Albin* (Stockholm, 2002).

Ismay, Lord, *The Memoirs of Lord Ismay* (London, 1960).

Jacobsen, Alf R., *Muldvarpene* (Oslo, 1986).

——, *Svartkammeret* (Oslo, 1987).

——, *Scharnhorst* (Oslo, 2001).

——, *Forlis* (Oslo, 2002).

——, *Nikkel, jern og blod* (Oslo, 2004).

——, *Krysseren Blücher* (Oslo, 2010).

——, *Kongens nei* (Oslo, 2011).

Jervell, Sverre, *Scener fra en ambasssades liv: Berlin 1905–2000* (Oslo, 2002).

Joakimsen, Oddmund, *Narvik 1940: Nazi-Tysklands første tilbakeslag under 2. Verdenskrig* (Narvik, 2010).

Kaltenegger, Roland, *General Dietl: Der Held von Narvik* (Munich, 1990).

——, *Krieg am Eismeer: Gebirgsjäger im Kampf um Narvik, Murmansk und die Murmanbahn* (Graz, 1999).

Keegan, John, *Churchill's Generals* (London, 1991).

Kennedy, John, *The Business of War* (London, 1997).

Kersaudy, Françoise, *Norway 1940* (London, 1990).

Kjølsen, Fritz Hammer, *Opptakten til den 9. April 1940* (Copenhagen, 1945).

——, *Mitt livs logbook: En søoffisers og diplomats erindringer før og efter 9. April 1940* (Copenhagen, 1957).

Klatt, Paul, *3. Gebirgs-Division 1939–1945* (Bad Nauheim, 1958).

Koht, Halvdan, *For fred og fridom i krigstid 1939–1940* (Oslo, 1957).

Kotze, Hildegard, *Heeresadjutant bei Hitler 1938–1943: Aufzeichnungen des Majors Engel* (Stuttgart, 1974).
Kräutler, Mathias, *Es war ein Edelweiss* (Graz, 1962).
Kungliga Utrikesdepartememtet, *Förspelet til det tyske angreppet på Danmark och Norge den 9. April 1940* (Stockholm, 1947).
Laugs, Hermann, *Kampf um der Erzbahn* (Berlin, 1941).
Leasor, James, *War at the Top* (Kelly Bray, 2001).
Liddell Hart, Basil H., *The German Generals Talk* (London, 1948).
——, *History of the Second World War* (London, 1970).
Lindbäck-Larsen, Odd, *Veien til katastrofen* [The Road to Disaster] (Oslo, 1973).
Linge, Heinz, *With Hitler to the End* (Barnsley, 2009).
Lossberg, Bernhard von, *Im Wehrmachtführungsstab* (Hamburg, 1950).
Lundberg, Lennart, *Krigsmalmens offer* (Danderyd, 1993).
Lunde, Henrik, *Hitler's Pre-Emptive War* (Newbury, 2009).
Macintyre, Donald, *Narvik* (London, 1959).
Macleod, Roderick, *Time Unguarded: The Ironside Diaries 1937–1940* (New York, 1962).
Mann, Chris and Jörgensen, Christer, *Hitler's Arctic War* (New York, 2002).
Megargee, Geoffrey, *Inside Hitler's High Command* (Lawrence, 2000).
Milward, Alan S., *The Fascist Economy of Norway* (Oxford, 1972).
Minney, R.J., *The Private Papers of Hore-Belisha* (London, 1960).
Moran, Lord, *Churchill at War 1940–1945* (London, 2002).
Mountevans, Lord, *Adventurous Life* (London, 1946).
Nevakivi, Jukka, *The Appeal That Was Never Made: The Allies, Scandinavia and the Finnish Winter War 1939–1940* (London, 1976).
Nicholson, Nigel, *The Harold Nicholson Diaries 1907–1964* (London, 2005).
Ørvik, Nils, *Sikkerhetspolitikken 1920–1939*. Vols I and II (Oslo, 1960–61).
Paulsen, Helge (ed.), *1940: Fra nøytral til okkupert* (Oslo, 1969).
Peck, John, *Dublin from Downing Street* (Dublin, 1978).
Raeder, Gudrun, *De uunnværlige flinke* (Oslo, 1975).
Read, Anthony, *The Devil's Disciples* (London, 2004).
Reynaud, Paul, *In the Thick of the Fight* (New York, 1955).

Rhys-Jones, Graham, *Churchill and the Norway Campaign* (Barnsley, 2008).

Rickman, Alfred, *Swedish Iron Ore* (London, 1939).

Roberts, Andrew, *The Holy Fox: The Life of Lord Halifax* (London, 1991).

——, *Masters and Commanders* (London, 2008).

Rohwer, J. and Hümmelchen, G., *Chronology of the War at Sea* (London, 1974).

Romilly, Giles, *The Privileged Nightmare* (London, 1954).

Roskill, Stephen, *The War at Sea* (London, 1954).

——, *Churchill and the Admirals* (New York, 1978).

Ruge, Friedrich, *Der Seekrieg 1939–45* (Stuttgart, 1962).

Salewski, Michael, *Die deutsche Seekriegsleitung 1935–1945* (Frankfurt, 1970–75).

Salmon, Patrick, *Scandinavia and the Great Powers 1890–1940* (Newcastle, 1997).

Schroeder, Christa, *He Was My Chief: The Memoirs of Hitler's Secretary* (Barnsley, 2009).

Schwarz, Walter A., *Generalmajor a. D. Alois Windisch: Ein Soldatenleben* (Vienna, 1996).

Self, Robert, *Neville Chamberlain: A Biography* (London, 2006).

Seraphim, Hans-Günther, *Das politische Tagebuch Alfred Rosenbergs* (Gottingen, 1956).

Shakespeare, Geoffrey, *Let Candles Be Brought In* (London, 1949).

Shirer, William, *The Rise and Fall of the Third Reich* (London, 1960).

——, *The Collapse of the Third Republic* (New York, 1969).

——, *The Nightmare Years 1939–1940* (New York, 1984).

——, *This is Berlin* (New York, 1999).

——, *Berlin Diary* (Baltimore, 2002).

Showell, Jak P. Mallmann (ed.), *Führer Conferences on Naval Affairs, 1939–1946* (London, 1999).

Skodvin, Magne (ed.), *Norge i krig* (Oslo, 1984–87).

Spears, Edward, *Assignment to Catastrophe* (London, 1954).

Speer, Albert, *Inside the Third Reich* (London, 1975).

Springenschmid, Karl, *Die Männer von Narvik* (Graz, 1982).

Steen, Erik Anker, *Norges sjøkrig 1940–1945*. Vol. IV (Oslo, 1954).

Stevens, R.H. (ed.), *The Falkenhorst Trial* (London, 1949).

Tooze, Adam, *The Wages of Destruction: The Making & Breaking of the Nazi Economy* (London, 2007).

Trotter, William, *A Frozen Hell* (New York, 1991).

Ueberschär, Gerd, *Hitlers militärische Elite* (Darmstadt, 1998).

Undersøkelseskommisjon av 1945 [Investigative Commission of 1945] (Oslo, 1946).

Vian, Philip, *Action this Day* (London, 1960).

Waage, Johan, *Kampen om Narvik* (Oslo, 1961).

Warlimont, Walter, *Im Hauptquartier der deutschen Wehrmacht 1939–1945* (Bonn, 1964).

Wiart, Carton de, *Happy Odyssey* (London, 1950).

Williams, Alister, *Heart of a Dragon: The VCs of Wales and the Welsh Regiments, 1914–1982* (Wrexham, 2008).

Willoch, Kåre, *Minner og meninger* (Oslo, 1988).

Ziemke, Earl, *The German Northern Theatre of Operations* (Washington, 1959).

Årbok for Hamarøy (The Yearbook of Hamarøy, Hamarøy municipality, 2000).

INDEX OF NAMES